OLIVERSON · JAE R. BALLIF · DICK FELT · JA[Y]   [D]ON

MEL OLSON · LARRY CARR · JAY MILLER · LANCE REYNOLDS ·

[NIC]K EYRE · JIM McMAHON · TOM HOLMOE · GORDON HUDSON ·

[R]I · ROBBIE BOSCO · KURT GOUVEIA · LEON WHITE · CHRIS SMIT[H]

[JOH]N TAIT · ROB MORRIS · CHRIS HOKE · BRANDON DOMAN · RYAN

[C]OATS · JOHN BECK · JONNY HARLINE · AUSTIN COLLIE · DENNIS

[M]IKE" MILLS · GLEN OLIVERSON · JAE R. BALLIF · DICK FELT · JAY W[I]

· VIRGIL CARTER · MEL OLSON · LARRY CARR · JAY MILLER · L[ANCE]

[MA]RC WILSON · NICK EYRE · JIM McMAHON · TOM HOLMOE · GO[RDON]

GLEN KOZLOWSKI · ROBBIE BOSCO · KURT GOUVEIA · LEON W[HITE]

[B]EN CAHOON · JOHN TAIT · ROB MORRIS · CHRIS HOKE · BRAN[DON]

[B]RYAN KEHL · DANIEL COATS · JOHN BECK · JONNY HARLINE · AU[STIN]

[MIL]LET · GAYLAND "IRON MIKE" MILLS · GLEN OLIVERSON · JAE R. B[ALLIF]

[F]ORTE · CURG BELCHER · VIRGIL CARTER · MEL OLSON · LARRY C[ARR]

[TODD] CHRISTENSEN · MARC WILSON · NICK EYRE · JIM McMAHON ·

[UM]A · KYLE MORRELL · GLEN KOZLOWSKI · ROBBIE BOSCO · KURT

[EL]LIS · CHAD LEWIS · BEN CAHOON · JOHN TAIT · ROB MORRIS · C[HRIS]

CURTIS BROWN · BRYAN KEHL · DANIEL COATS · JOHN BECK · J[ONNY]

[KI]MBALL · FLOYD MILLET · GAYLAND "IRON MIKE" MILLS · GLEN O[LIVERSON]

WHAT IT MEANS TO BE A COUGAR

WHAT IT MEANS TO BE A
COUGAR

LaVELL EDWARDS ★ BRONCO MENDENHALL
AND BRIGHAM YOUNG UNIVERSITY'S GREATEST PLAYERS

DUFF TITTLE

TRIUMPH
BOOKS

Library of Congress Cataloging-in-Publication Data

Tittle, D. Duff.
    What it means to be a Cougar: Lavell Edwards, Bronco Mendenhall, and Brigham Young University's greatest players / Duff Tittle.
        p. cm.
    ISBN 978-1-60078-579-5 (alk. paper)
1. Brigham Young University—Football—History. 2. Brigham Young Cougars (Football team)—History. 3. College football players—Utah—History. I. Title.
    GV958.B75T6 2011
    796.332'630979224—dc23

                                                                2011017779

This book is available in quantity at special discounts for your group or organization. For further information, contact:

Triumph Books
542 South Dearborn Street
Suite 750
Chicago, Illinois 60605
(312) 939-3330
Fax (312) 663-3557
www.triumphbooks.com

Printed in U.S.A.
ISBN: 978-1-60078-579-5
Design by Nick Panos
Editorial production and layout by Prologue Publishing Services, LLC
All photos courtesy of Mark Philbrick/BYU unless otherwise specified

CONTENTS

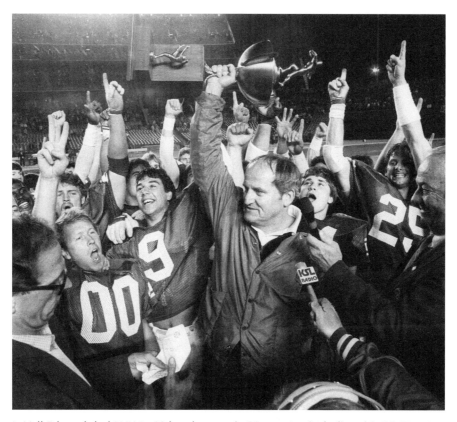

LaVell Edwards led BYU to 22 bowl games in 29 seasons, including this 21–17 victory over Missouri in the 1983 Holiday Bowl.

we had to do was take a knee with six seconds left and run out the clock. But we ended up fumbling the ball, and they threw a touchdown pass on the next play to tie it. Fortunately, they missed the extra point, and the game ended in a tie.

At that point we were 0–3–1. That week a couple of the players came to my office and wanted to have a players-only meeting. I told them that would be fine. I don't know specifically what was said in that meeting, but whatever was said worked. We got on a winning streak and won seven of the final eight games. That was the only time I can ever recall having any doubts about what we were trying to do.

I've often thought about that players' meeting. It probably affected my whole career and really the course of my life. If they had not gotten together and turned the season around, I probably would have been gone. If not that year, sometime soon. It seemed to change everything.

A couple years later, we brought in a guy named Doug Scovil as the offensive coordinator. He had coached Roger Staubach at Navy. I was looking for an offensive coach, and I called Bill Walsh to see if he might have any recommendations. He's the one who told me about Doug.

I invited Doug to Provo and ended up offering him a contract. At the time he said there was no way he could come for the money we offered. Later, Bill and I talked, and I told him what had happened. He said, "Don't give up on him just yet. Let me talk with him." Whatever he told Doug apparently worked, because he decided to come to BYU.

He was the perfect guy for us at that time. We were doing some good things, but he helped us tie everything together into a nice package. We really opened up the offense. We started throwing to the backs and attacking the seams. Doug defined the philosophy of *why* we did certain things. We were radically different from the norm in college football at that time.

I've been fortunate to have some of the best coaches in the game come work in the BYU system. When Doug left, we brought in Ted Tollner. When Ted was hired to be the head coach at USC, we got Mike Holmgren, who later led the Green Bay Packers to a Super Bowl. Eventually guys like Roger French and Norm Chow took over. Each one of them built on and added to the basic concept first designed by Dewey Warren and revised and expanded by Doug.

Another key ingredient in our success over the years has been the string of All-America quarterbacks. They certainly had a variety of contrasting styles, but those who thrived in the BYU system had a great understanding and feel for the game. I think you either have it or you don't. It's not something you can coach. It's a common quality shared by guys like Sheide, Gifford Nielsen, Marc Wilson, Jim McMahon, Steve Young, Robbie Bosco, Ty Detmer, John Walsh, Steve Sarkisian, Kevin Feterik, and Brandon Doman.

When Ty won the Heisman Trophy, it had a lot to do with Gary, Gifford, Marc, Jim, Steve, and Robbie. They helped pave the way and increase the credibility of the program over the years. When Ty had that fantastic season in 1990, he was able to stand on the shoulders of all the great BYU quarterbacks who had come before him.

I get asked all the time about my favorite moments, games, and plays, but there are so many great memories that it's hard to choose. I do know the most relief I ever felt in my coaching career was after the 1980 Holiday Bowl. It was our fifth bowl game and our third straight Holiday Bowl. The whole week leading up to the game, the bowl guys were running around in their red Holiday Bowl jackets telling us we really needed to win for the bowl game to take off. Everyone was telling us this was our year.

The BYU quarterback factory produced some of the greatest signal callers in college football history. Under LaVell Edwards, Cougars quarterbacks won a Heisman Trophy, seven Sammy Baugh Trophies, and four Davey O'Brien Awards.

In a ceremony prior to LaVell Edwards' final home game on November 18, 2000, Gordon B. Hinckley (far right), president of The Church of Jesus Christ of Latter-day Saints, announced that Cougar Stadium would be renamed LaVell Edwards Stadium.

Well, SMU had Eric Dickerson and Craig James. They had a heck of a team—by far the best team we had faced in a bowl game. When McMahon completed the Hail Mary pass to Clay Brown and Kurt Gunther kicked the extra point for the win, I don't think I ever felt any more relief over winning a game than I did over that one.

How we won that game, I'll never know. I don't remember all the details about the decision to punt late in the game. I know Jim came off the field and was mad. He said a few choice words and was telling us that we had quit. We didn't have much time, so we were trying to get him to calm down. The thing that was stunning to me—if I'm honest with myself—is that he was right. Subconsciously, you just think that it's not going to happen—down 20 with about four minutes to play—but Jim was out there trying to win.

So I just figured, *What the heck, we'll go for it*. Jim went out and completed a pass, and we went on down the field and scored. I think there were 18 seconds remaining when we got the ball back after Bill Schoepflin blocked the punt. We ran a couple plays, and there were three seconds left when Jim threw the final pass. When Clay came down with the ball, I just about died. It was amazing. To have it happen the way it did was unbelievable.

Of course one of the more exciting wins was the national championship game in 1984. That night had been so frustrating because we had pretty well dominated the game in the sense of moving the ball, but we had turned it over five or six times. Robbie Bosco got hurt, and it was just not going our way. To come back the way we did and have those two long scoring drives in the fourth quarter, with Robbie hitting Kelly Smith to give us the lead, was a huge relief.

My last game was probably one of the most unreal. By that time, with all the years and all the games, you could probably say it didn't matter a whole lot—and it probably didn't, really—but it did. It was Utah, and it was my last game. To win it the way we did was pretty special. We didn't name Brandon Doman the starting quarterback until the last two games of the year. As I look back, that was probably one of the big mistakes I made by not naming him the starting quarterback before we did. He won both games for us and sent me out a winner. Then, of course, he won the first 12 games the next year. He just had a knack for winning. Brandon was a little unorthodox in throwing the ball, but he would get it there. He was such a great leader— what we call in the coaching profession, a "winner."

From a personal standpoint, when I look back at my coaching career, one of the things I feel the most satisfaction about is we made football a presence at BYU. It had always been a basketball school. When you talk about being a Cougar, and talk about BYU football, there is a certain amount of satisfaction about what we accomplished.

Football to me was always more about personal relationships with players and what they eventually do with their lives. That was paramount to how I approached coaching.

I was an LDS bishop on campus for six years, and that was a special time for me. I really enjoyed working with the students and helping them grow and overcome challenges. I pretty much did the same things as the head football coach. I always had a lot of personal interviews with the players to make sure they were okay. I knew what we were trying to accomplish with football, and I let the coaches do their jobs. I would try to observe the players and talk with them if it seemed like they were struggling.

A lot times what we talked about had nothing to do with football. We would talk about what was going on in their lives. I always had an open door. I rarely ever closed the door to my office. Those private moments with the players were really important to me.

—LaVell Edwards

LaVell Edwards was the head football coach at BYU from 1972 to 2000. His 257 career victories ranks sixth all-time in Division I football history. He led the Cougars to the national championship in 1984 and was named National Coach of the Year in 1979 and 1984. Edwards led BYU to 22 bowl games, including 17 straight from 1978 to 1994. During Edwards' amazing run, his players won a Heisman Trophy, two Outland Trophies, four Davey O'Brien Awards, and seven Sammy Baugh Trophies. He was inducted into the College Football Hall of Fame in 2004. Five of his former players have also been enshrined. Edwards had 137 of his former players selected in the NFL Draft and 57 have played in the Super Bowl. In his final home game on November 18, 2000, Cougar Stadium was renamed LaVell Edwards Stadium in his honor.

FOREWORD

What It Means to Be a Cougar

At about 5:30 AM on December 13, 2004, I walked into my office for the first time as the newly appointed head football coach at BYU. The halls of the football office were dark and quiet. There was nothing on my desk or shelves when I entered the room that morning. It was a surreal experience. I wondered, *What have I done? What do I do now?*

More than a few things raced through my mind as I contemplated the importance of this new position. Feeling a tremendous need for guidance, for direction, and for strength, I immediately knelt and prayed.

Shortly after finishing my prayer, there was a knock on my office door. When I opened the door, there stood LaVell Edwards. His timing could not have been more appropriate. I knew it was not by accident that Coach Edwards was there. His visit could not have been more needed.

We shook hands, I invited him in, and we sat down. He pulled his chair close to mine so our knees were almost touching. He stared into my eyes. Finally, after a brief period of silence that seemed to last forever, he said, "You have a tough job." Those were the first words he said, and I wasn't comforted. Then in a grandfatherly way, he said, "But you have a great job."

At the time, I didn't know what he meant by either statement. Since that time, I have come to realize just how tough, just how important this job really is. At BYU playing and coaching football is so much more than the game itself. There is a legacy here like no other.

While there is certainly a storied football tradition at BYU—the national championship, conference titles, bowl invitations, All-America citations, a Heisman Trophy, a Doak Walker Award, two Outland Trophies, numerous Davey

Shortly after taking over as head coach at BYU in 2004, Bronco Mendenhall established tradition, spirit, and honor as the overriding principles of the football program.

O'Brien and Sammy Baugh Awards, and many other accomplishments—it's the tradition of changing lives that makes BYU such a unique place.

I grew up in Alpine, Utah, about 30 minutes from Provo. Coming out of American Fork High School, all I wanted to do was follow in the footsteps of my dad, Paul, and my older brother Mat, and play football for the Cougars. But I didn't get that opportunity. I went to junior college at Snow College in Ephraim, Utah, and was part of a national championship team before going on to Oregon State. In essence, I was passed over twice by the Cougars. I basically decided to go to Oregon State because BYU was on the Beavers' schedule.

Ironically, even though I wasn't playing for BYU, the experience of playing at BYU did ultimately have an impact in my life. I was starting at safety for Oregon State when we came to Cougar Stadium in 1986. Our defense held BYU to just one touchdown, and we won the game 10–7. I remember lying down at the 50-yard line after the game and just taking it all in. It was gratifying because of the respect I had for the program, for what it represented to me growing up, which was excellence.

Beating BYU that day, I felt like there was justice in the universe. Afterward, I started to come to grips with the fact that I needed more meaning in my life. I had come into Cougar Stadium and helped my team win the very game that had been my motivation for going to Oregon State. I began to ponder, *Now what?*

Looking back, the void left after that moment helped me start to explore what other goals I really wanted in life, what meaning or higher purpose there was to strive for. I returned to BYU some 17 years later when Gary Crowton hired me as BYU's defensive coordinator in 2003. Two years later I was given the opportunity to lead the program as the head coach.

From that first day on the job, Coach Edwards has been absolutely instrumental in helping me as a young, first-time head coach. This university is so unique and so special. It has such a different mission. Who else could provide the appropriate insight other than LaVell?

I value his word, I value his experience, but more than anything, I value his character and the way he ran this program for nearly 30 years. He set a perfect example for me to strive for. I'm not Coach Edwards and I never will be, but I would like to honor his legacy, and I would like to honor the tradition that he established here at BYU.

By embracing the football legacy, we are willing to measure BYU's future against its legendary past. If we can do that, then it will have been a successful journey. We are not there yet, because LaVell's legacy included amazing consistency over time, but I feel that we are on the right path. Over the past six seasons, only 15 teams have won more games than we have at BYU. During

xx

The Cougars opened the 2009 season with a 14–13 win over No. 3 Oklahoma in the first college football game played in the new Dallas Cowboys Stadium in Arlington, Texas.

Bronco Mendenhall leads the team in celebration following a 31–17 victory over
No. 15 TCU in 2006. BYU has been ranked in the top 25 in five of his six seasons.

that stretch, we've been invited to a bowl game each year, winning four of the
last five. That's something that hadn't been done at BYU since the 1980–1984
run. We've also been ranked in the top 25 five of the past six years. We have
demonstrated, and we will continue to demonstrate, that BYU is and should
be considered one of the top programs in the country.

We have great young men in the program, and their success is evident in
many areas of their lives. Six players have been named CoSIDA Academic
All-Americans over the past three seasons. Only one team in the nation has
earned more. These are important benchmarks that link the program to its
past success and prominence. It gives us tremendous momentum to be able
to accomplish our future goals.

The legacy of BYU, however, is much more than football. While some
may believe our football success is related largely to what happens on Saturday, it's the tradition of changing lives through living with honor and being
guided by the Spirit that has created the amazing tradition at BYU.

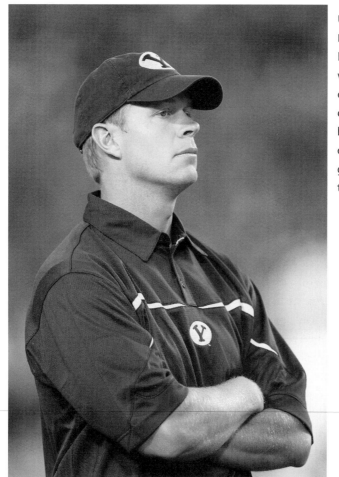

Under Bronco Mendenhall's leadership, BYU has won two outright conference championships and been invited to six consecutive bowl games from 2005 to 2010.

I am honored to serve as the head football coach. I am privileged to be associated with such great young men and to stand with them on the shoulders of the outstanding individuals who preceded them—those who helped create such a lasting and meaningful tradition at BYU.

Upon taking over the program, I felt there were a few principles that needed immediate attention, such as accountability, discipline, and effort. It became clear that for us to be successful in every way, we would need to hold fast to three overriding principles—tradition, spirit, and honor.

I knew the program should reflect the tradition that had been established by past coaches, players, and teams. I realized that, to be fully aligned with the university, we needed to embrace and exemplify the principles of the of the photography in this book, from the 1970s to the present, comes from his career work. A special thanks to Jaren Wilkey, Kylea Knecht, and the rest of the BYU photography staff—Kirsten Burner, Jonathan Hardy, and Alison Fidel—who tackled this project like it was their own.

I also want to express gratitude to my sister-in-law Tanna Tittle. In addition to putting up with my brother Matt for nearly 20 years, she may have literally saved my life on this project. To complete this book I interviewed nearly 60 people in three months. She handled the daunting task of transcribing the majority of those interviews. Talk about an All-America effort.

I owe a heartfelt thanks to my dad, Don, who passed away in 2006, and my dear mom, Elise, for their constant love and encouragement. Dad was an English major who was always correcting my use of the English language. There were many times during the writing of this book that I wished he were here to read the manuscript and offer advice. My parents understood what it means to be a Cougar and instilled it in the hearts of their two sons. I love you.

Finally, a warm *mahalo* to my wife and best friend, Sherry, and our five amazing children—Elisa, Sydney, Brett, Savannah, and McKay. When I agreed to write this book, I knew it would take a lot of support and patience from my family. Thanks for hanging in there with me while the book dragged on. I love you all. Time for a vacation.

INTRODUCTION

For me, being a Cougar began many years before I was born. My dad, Don Tittle, was raised in Columbia, a small coal mining community in central Utah. Elise Durtschi, my mom, was a city girl from Salt Lake City. Somehow Brigham Young University brought them together.

They say the Lord works in mysterious ways and that things happen for a reason. I tend to believe that there is some truth in both statements.

My dad was a very good baseball player. He began playing in the men's coal league at the age of 14. Three years later, the Philadelphia Phillies organization came calling—so did the Cougars. Dad was 17 at the time and couldn't sign a minor league contract without his father's consent. My grandpa was a coal miner who wanted a better life for his youngest son. The agreement was that Dad would go to BYU on a baseball scholarship for a year. After that, he was free to stay in school or pursue a career in professional baseball.

Don Tittle was about to find out what it means to be a Cougar.

Dad arrived at BYU in the fall of 1954. At the end of his freshman year, he was involved in a collision at home plate and blew out his knee. His baseball career was over. One year later, Dad met Mom at a Church activity on campus. She encouraged him to serve an LDS Church mission, which he did from 1957 to 1959. Shortly after returning from the Southern States Mission, they were married in the fall of 1959. The rest, as they say, is history.

I was born to be a Cougar.

My dad began taking me to BYU football games when I was young. He would tell me stories of how the football team struggled through mediocrity during his days as a student. For me it was hard to imagine.

My youth was filled with names like Nielsen, Wilson, McMahon, Brown, Young, Hudson…the list goes on. Eventually I was old enough to go to games with "the boys." We were proud to be part of the knothole gang. We would sit in the end zone bleachers and at halftime play our own version of BYU football on the grass knoll in the north end zone.

During the late 1970s and early 1980s, the BYU aerial attack was reaching its pinnacle. The offense was becoming a juggernaut, and the players were legendary. It was a great time to be a Cougar. Because it was happening just down the road, I didn't realize that LaVell Edwards and his amazing string of All-America quarterbacks were revolutionizing the game of college football. Didn't everyone throw the football 40 times a game? Didn't all the schools pass to set up the run? As a kid, I just assumed everyone had a quarterback who threw for 300 yards a game, and that most running backs and tight ends were really just receivers in disguise. These were the days before ESPN and the cable television explosion. My world was very small, and it revolved around BYU sports.

From the first bowl invitation in 1974 with Gary Sheide to Ty Detmer winning the Heisman Trophy in 1990, I watched as BYU quarterbacks rewrote the NCAA record book.

In an era when college football was dominated by strong running attacks, Air Edwards revolutionized the game with his innovative passing attack. During his 29 years at the helm, BYU quarterbacks completed nearly 7,500 passes for more than 103,000 yards and 789 touchdowns.

LaVell retired in 2000 as the sixth-winningest coach in NCAA history, with 257 victories. Along the way he won a national championship, 19 conference titles, led BYU to 22 bowl games, coached 32 All-Americans, and was named National Coach of the Year twice.

His athletes captured a Heisman Trophy, a Doak Walker Award, a Maxwell Award, two Outland Trophies, four Davey O'Brien Awards, and seven Sammy Baugh Trophies. More important than all the success on the field, LaVell Edwards taught young men character and changed their lives for the better.

As a kid, being a Cougar was about Saturday afternoons in Cougar Stadium. It was about great football and legendary players. Years later—in the late 1980s—I had the opportunity to attend BYU, where I gained additional perspective on what it really means to be a Cougar.

My journey came full circle in 1996, when I had the good fortune to return to BYU as an employee in the athletics department. One of the best things about my job is the occasion to interact over the years with thousands of remarkable student-athletes who have come to Provo in search of their dreams.

Through many years of observation, I've come to understand that being a Cougar is so much more than winning games, matches, meets, or tournaments. It's about developing as an individual—mentally, socially, physically, and spiritually.

Shortly after Bronco Mendenhall became the head football coach at BYU, he established three overriding principles for the program—tradition, spirit, and honor. In doing so, he expressed the core elements of what it means to be a Cougar.

As I interviewed nearly 60 former football players, coaches, and administrators for this book, it became very clear that for them being a Cougar had less to do with what happened on the field and more to do with what happened in their lives as they were influenced by the BYU experience.

Many expressed their love and appreciation for men like George Curtis and Floyd Johnson, who never coached or even played a down of football for BYU. Yet their examples and simple acts of service affected the lives of thousands of BYU athletes and embody the BYU spirit.

The true meaning of being a Cougar is found in the stories of the many individuals who came to BYU as great athletes and left as better people. I hope this book captures their legacy.

The
TWENTIES
through the
FORTIES

EDWIN "EDDIE" KIMBALL

LINEMAN
1922–1925

HEAD COACH
1937–1941 ⋆ 1946–1948

ATHLETICS DIRECTOR
1937–1941 ⋆ 1946–1963

I OWE SO MUCH TO BYU. I got a great education. It's where I met my wife, Althea. It's where I spent the majority of my professional life.

I came to BYU as a student in 1922, but I had intended to go to the University of Utah. My mother drove me from Draper to Utah's campus in a buggy, so I could register for classes. I stood in lines all day and didn't get registered. On the way home that night, I decided I didn't want any more of that.

Bob Howard, who I had played football with at Jordan High School, had come to BYU. The next morning I asked my mom if she would drive me to the train station. She asked me why. I said, "So I can catch the train to Provo. I want to go to BYU." She cried for three or four minutes. Finally I said, "What's the matter? I thought you wanted me to go to BYU."

She said, "I do, that's what I'm crying about. I'm overjoyed you're going to BYU." The next morning I caught the train to Provo and registered at BYU.

I was the oldest boy. We had a farm in Draper growing beets. When I talked with my father about going to school, I didn't ask how much he could help me. I asked if he could spare me on the farm. I'd been working on the

Eddie Kimball (front row, far right), here pictured with the 1922 BYU freshman football team, went on to become the head football coach and later the athletics director at BYU. He was inducted into the BYU Athletic Hall of Fame in 1975.

Photo courtesy of L. Tom Perry Special Collections; BYU Harold B. Lee Library

railroad and had saved enough money for tuition, books, and one month's rent. I also joined the National Guard, and we'd receive $12.50 a month. Room and board was $15, so I had another job to make up the difference.

When I came to BYU, I weighed 133 pounds, but I'd worked on a farm pitching hay, topping beets, and loading wagons. In those days we worked from daylight until dark, so I was in good condition.

Football had been discontinued at BYU in the late 1890s. The year before I arrived, they started a freshman squad and played a small schedule. My first year at BYU, E.L. Roberts was our coach. Roberts received word that spring that we were officially cleared to have football again at BYU. So he went and spent some time, about three weeks, with Knute Rockne at Notre Dame.

BYU started school two weeks before Utah, so I was actually late starting school when I got there. They had already chosen players for the freshman team. They allowed me to participate in the drills, but I didn't practice much. All the equipment was handed out, so I got what was left over, including my cleats, which were about two sizes too big.

My break came in a scrimmage against the varsity. Football was new, and the varsity only had six scheduled games, so they scrimmaged the freshmen on three separate Saturdays. The varsity was killing us, running on the right side. In the second half, Coach Roberts told me, "Get in there and stop them."

My parents had always taught me to be prepared for the chance when it comes. We did a lot better in the second half, and after the game Coach Roberts told me I had earned a spot on the freshman team. I played end on that team, which meant I had to block the tackle. There were some big men I had to block, but I didn't care about that. It was a matter of speed and quickness, and I was strong for my size.

We didn't have much of a schedule that first year, but we beat Utah, Utah State, and Brigham Young College, so we were champions of the freshman league. During the summer of 1923, I got a job working in the Tintic Standard Mine in Dividend, Utah, to save money for college. Two weeks before the season, I quit so I could get in top physical condition for football. I weighed about 158 pounds that fall. Before the first game, they announced the starters. Coach Alvin Twitchell announced all the other positions before finally getting to the ends. Then he announced I would start at right end. I'm not sure my feet even touched the ground from the dressing room all the way to Timp Park, where we played our games.

I learned a lot about football from Coach Twitchell, who was the varsity coach from 1922 to 1924. I started at right guard my sophomore, junior, and senior years. I dislocated my elbow at home against Colorado College in the second game of my senior season. It was the first time I had been substituted for during my college career. Prior to my senior year in 1925, I was elected captain of the team. It was one of the biggest surprises of my life and certainly an honor.

Shortly after the 1925 season, I made an appointment with R.L. Ashby and asked his permission to marry his daughter, Althea. I met her at a Christmas program at College Hall on campus in 1923. She was doing a Christmas reading. After the program was over, I went over and introduced myself. We soon became good friends, and by the end of the year we were going steady. I owe a lot to BYU, including my wife.

I graduated from BYU in the spring of 1926. That fall I signed a contract to go to Fillmore, Utah, and coach at Millard County High School. It was the beginning of my coaching career.

When I returned to BYU in 1935, there were just two coaches—Ott Romney and Fred Buck Dixon. President Franklin Harris couldn't see how we could afford another full-time coach, but somehow he made it work. The school was still very small. I coached freshman football and basketball my first year. The next year Ott moved me up to varsity line coach.

I took over as head football coach in 1937. I coached football for eight years. We didn't have much money back in those days. When I started, my salary was $2,000. When I took over as head football coach, they moved my salary up a little. It remained the same until I went in the Navy during World War II.

I loved to coach, I just loved it. As a coach, you teach kids and see them progress along. Each of the jobs I had at BYU I dearly loved, but if I had to pick just one, I'd rather coach football than be the athletics director. In football you're working with the athletes. As the AD, the coaches are between you and the athletes.

I was an LDS bishop on campus for five and a half years. As a bishop, you get to work with the students all the time—helping them to improve, strengthen their testimonies, things like that.

There was a professor on campus named Harold R. Clark. He had an impact on my life in many ways. He always had a good word for me. All the years I coached at BYU, there was never a game that we lost that I didn't get a nice note or letter from him saying something like, "With the material you have to work with and the limited facilities, Eddie, you're doing a great job." He would see kids on campus that he thought looked down and go over to them and chat. He would tell them, "Don't get discouraged. Hang in there. You'll leave BYU a better man." He was always positive. That's what I loved about BYU, men like that.

5

Sometimes referred to as "Mr. BYU," Eddie Kimball was involved with BYU athletics for nearly 50 years. He played lineman on the football team from 1922 to 1925. In 1935 Kimball returned to BYU as a coach. He took over as head football coach for eight seasons starting in 1937 and also served as athletics director for 23 years. In 1977 Kimball was part of the inaugural class to be inducted into the BYU Athletic Hall of Fame. He passed away on December 26, 1990, at age 87.

Taken from an Edwin R. Kimball interview by Tom Cheney, March 22, 1979; HBLL Special Collections Manuscript; L. Tom Perry Special Collections; University Archives. Also, historical documents on file in the BYU Athletic Department Archives.

FLOYD MILLET

FULLBACK   HEAD COACH

1931–1933   1942

ATHLETICS DIRECTOR

1942–1945 ★ 1964–1970

I WENT TO MESA HIGH SCHOOL in Arizona. I made the varsity basketball team as a junior, although I didn't play very much. My senior year we had a great team. We won the Valley Championship and got second in the state of Arizona. Golden Romney, who was a great former center at BYU, was the basketball coach at Gila Junior College in Thatcher, Arizona. He invited me to come to school with a couple of my friends. At that time, Gila was a private institution run by the LDS Church.

We had a pretty good basketball team the two years I was there. I also played football for the first time and ran track. After two years at Gila, Golden wrote Ott Romney, who was the athletics director at BYU and also coached football, basketball, and track. He told him a little about me and asked Ott if he could help me find a job. In those days there was no such thing as athletic grants-in-aid or scholarships; it was a matter of finding a job to survive.

The BYU athletics department leased a service station for the purpose of supplying jobs to a few athletes, and I was fortunate enough to be selected.

Eddie Kimball and Floyd Millet (right) review plans for a new athletic facility. In 1942, Millet led BYU to its first football victory over rival University of Utah. He was inducted into the BYU Athletic Hall of Fame in 1976. *Photo courtesy of L. Tom Perry Special Collections; BYU Harold B. Lee Library*

Later, I got another job washing towels in the school laundry for the physical education department. I was paid 25¢ an hour, the going rate at the time.

I landed in Provo for the first time in the summer of 1931. It was during the Depression. Ott had a place for me to stay in a little boarding house run by Elwood and Ruth Romney. Elwood was a great basketball player and a junior at BYU when I arrived.

I was fortunate to arrive at the right time because I had the opportunity to play football that first year on the freshman team. Junior college transfers and freshmen were not eligible to play varsity back in those days. The freshman team needed a halfback, and Ott put me in. I played halfback the first year and was named captain of the team.

I played varsity fullback the next two years. I got an additional year of eligibility that had been arranged some way, which helped me because I had the opportunity to do some graduate work.

Our football stadium was located where the Richards Building is now. We had no practice field, so we worked out at the stadium every day. Just west of the stadium was a large apple orchard owned by the university. In the fall we ate lots of apples during and after practice.

In those days Utah was the perennial football power in the intermountain area. In 1932 we thought we had a pretty good team, and we did. We ran the T formation. I think we might have been the only team in the United States using it, but it was a lot of fun. When you didn't have 60 to 70 men on a football squad, you had to play both ways. The T formation made for an interesting game and gave us a lot of opportunities to do things that we couldn't with a regular single wing, which most everyone was using at the time.

We had a fellow by the name of Frank LaComb, who was a very good quarterback and a good passer. Grant Hutchinson was the state sprint champion from Carbon High School, and Pete Wilson was a great hurdler as well as a great halfback and punter. We won all of our games except one. You guessed it; we lost to Utah 29–0.

During my three years at BYU, I participated in all three major sports. I earned eight varsity letters: two in football, three in basketball, and three in track. I was named all-conference in football once and basketball twice. Ott Romney coached all three sports I played. I learned a lot about coaching from him. He had a profound influence on my life and was the determining factor in my going into the coaching profession.

GAYLAND
"IRON MIKE" MILLS
END
1939–1942 ★ 1946

I GRADUATED IN 1939 FROM Pocatello High School in Idaho. I lettered in football, basketball, track, and was the Southeastern Idaho heavyweight wrestling champion for two years. I played first-team varsity football my junior and senior years. We had an all-state backfield my senior year composed of Bob Liday, Herman Longhurst, Bob Orr, and myself. I also went out for track, basketball, wrestling, and boxing.

Throughout my senior year, I was approached by coaches from different colleges. I was offered a football scholarship from the University of Idaho, Washington State, Utah, and Brigham Young University.

My first intention was to attend the University of Idaho, as I thought I wanted to study forestry. I remember taking the train to Moscow, Idaho, arriving on Saturday morning with a large suitcase and 15¢ in my pocket. Coach Banks picked me up at the depot and took me to the university to stay in the dorms for the weekend. He arranged a job for me with the Potlach Lumber Company. Sunday evening I hitched a ride with some loggers some 80 miles to the logging camp. We arrived late that evening, and there was no one there to assign me a bunkhouse. So I slept on some hay in a big barn. I hardly slept all night with the horses snorting and stomping their hoofs.

"Iron Mike" Mills (center) was a preseason All-American for the Cougars in 1942. Mills played both offensive and defensive end and was named all-conference three times. He was inducted into the BYU Athletic Hall of Fame in 2005. *Photo courtesy of Charlene Mills Ashworth*

Working for the logging company was very dangerous. Some men were seriously hurt by falling trees or accidents with axes and chains. One fellow was killed that summer. By the end of the summer, I was in the best physical condition of my life. It really helped develop leg, arm, and hand muscles. There were many ballplayers in camp, and on the weekend we would play a lot of football. We had players from Idaho, Washington, Montana, California, and Wisconsin.

Toward the end of the summer of 1939, I received a letter from Eddie Kimball, head coach and athletics director at BYU. He wanted me to come to school on an athletic scholarship along with Herman Longhurst and Bob Orr. I thought it would be great to be back with some of my old high school chums, so I headed for Provo, Utah.

Coach Kimball really thought he had something by getting three all-state players from the same school. We were fixed up with a scholarship—tuition, room and board, books, and $30 a month. We stayed at Allen Hall—a boys' dormitory—the first year. Bob, Herman, and I were assigned to the same room. We had a great time taking turns working in the kitchen, the dining hall, and the laundry room.

Preseason practices were held twice a day, and we had a training table so we would have a proper diet. During our first scrimmage, they had the freshman team against the varsity. Freshman coach Wayne Soffe had me playing end. I was supposed to block defensive tackle Garth Chamberlain. Garth weighed 230 pounds and had a mean, sometimes unorthodox style of carrying out his assignment. As the ball was snapped, I charged across the line of scrimmage to block Garth. He smacked me across the head with a doubled-up fist that made me see stars momentarily.

As I trudged back to the huddle, one of the coaches said, "Are you going to stand for that, Mills? Give him some of the same." So the quarterback called the same play. When the ball was snapped, I faked Garth with my head, and when he swung at me, I caught him with an uppercut that sent him reeling. He got to his feet, and we got in a few licks before the team members separated us.

The coach said, "Okay, I like the fighting spirit, but no fist-fighting between the players." So after practice, Garth and I were to meet in the men's gymnasium and put on the boxing gloves. He and I fought for 30 minutes. We finally got so tired of pounding each other that we fell into a clinch laughing. From then on we were best friends throughout life.

I played end on both offense and defense at BYU and made the first-team squad after the second game of my sophomore year. Because I played first team on offense and defense my junior and senior years, they gave me the nickname "Iron Mike."

My sophomore year I accepted an invitation to the school Preference Ball from the girl that I would eventually marry for life and eternity. I dated Margaret Vance many times that year. Neither of us had much spending money in those days, so we would go to the show or I would play the piano for her at Pops Ice Cream Parlor. Toward the end of that year, we decided to get married. We were married by Bishop Willard Sowards in Provo, Utah, on May 29, 1941. Bob Orr and his wife, Twila, were the witnesses. We borrowed Rodney Kimball's Model A Ford to drive around town for a while that evening.

A couple of days later, school was out, and Margaret went home to Tempe, Arizona, for the summer. I went to Pocatello to work for the city. I used my first paycheck to buy Margaret a wedding ring, which I promptly mailed to her.

That fall we returned to BYU for my junior year. Margaret worked as a secretary typist for Dixon Real Estate, while I attended school. I recall the Sunday that Pearl Harbor was attacked by Japan—December 7, 1941. Margaret and I were walking around town when we heard the news. President Roosevelt announced we were at a state of war with Japan and Germany. Everyone was really concerned.

At the end of that school year, I went to work for Utah Pomeroy Construction Company on the survey crew at the construction site for the beginning of the Geneva Steel Plant in Orem, Utah—one of the many steel plants being built throughout the country for the war effort.

On September 1, 1942, we were blessed with a beautiful baby girl we named Sherry Ann. She was born at the Utah Valley Hospital. I was the proudest daddy around. Prior to my senior season in 1942, *Football Illustrated* printed its annual All-American Preview. The All-America candidates were nominated by coaches, officials, and sportswriters from coast to coast. There were only two players chosen from the Mountain States Conference, Woody Peterson of Utah and myself.

That fall we beat the University of Utah in football for the first time. I'll always have fond memories of being on the first team to beat Utah. Prior to that, BYU had lost every game since 1922, except for three ties. In 1941 we played Utah to a 6–6 tie. I made the only touchdown in that game. If we had kicked the extra point, we would have won that game, too.

After winning the game in 1942, we came out of the locker room and into the stadium. I'd never seen so much fighting in the stands between the Utah fans and the BYU fans. The BYU fans wanted to take down the goal posts, and there was fighting all over the field. There was an army reserve unit on the field, and they were trying to control the fighting. I remember one of them hollering, "Now don't hit anyone while they are down!" The BYU fans finally got to the goal posts and tore them down.

Due to the war effort and troop movements on the railroad, BYU had its last two games canceled in the 1942 season, therefore eliminating any post-season recognition. I signed up in the Army Reserves in October 1942 and was called up for active duty in April 1943, just two months before I was supposed to graduate.

and there was quite a bit of time left for Utah to score. But we stopped them. I didn't carry the ball—I was a blocker; but I made some tackles.

When the gun went off to end the game, all hell broke loose—up in the stands and down on the field. It was up at Utah. The student body came down on the field. I'm telling you it was a great celebration. The patrons went over and pulled down the goal posts—north and south. Then they took them to Provo and sawed them into small four-inch squares. The next Monday school was canceled, and they had a big assembly. They gave all the football players a piece of the goal posts. Some of the student body got some, too.

I look back on that game and think of that time and time again. BYU had never beaten Utah before that time. I'm not sure how many years the football program had been going before I arrived, but that was the first time we beat Utah.

I joined the Marine Corps Reserve program during that time, so I only played two years before the war. I stayed in school until I was called up and eventually went in the Navy. I was trained in handling antiaircraft weapons. Most of my teammates joined the war effort. In fact, there was no football program at BYU after 1942 until the war ended.

After the war, Eddie came back and installed the T formation. I played halfback in the T formation for two years. I carried the ball quite a bit. I was also one of the place-kickers for PATs and kickoffs.

I became acquainted with my wife, Francine, after the war. After we got married, we lived in Wymount Village on campus. They brought in some war barracks to BYU and made them into apartments for the married couples. That's where we lived.

I remember President Heber J. Grant came to BYU to a religious assembly. I remember the message that he gave really impressed me. He encouraged us to stay true to the faith, study hard, and work hard to complete our education. BYU made me realize the importance of obtaining an education and preparing myself with that education for my life's work. I always wanted to coach, so I took classes in the education and PE program. I guess that's what I remember most—that BYU helped prepare me to enter my profession. I graduated from BYU and then got a job coaching in Preston, Idaho, as an assistant to Joe Johnson. Eddie gave me a printout of all the plays we used at BYU, and I used them for the first two or three years I coached. I had some good years at Preston.

Being a Cougar means a great deal to me. I obtained a college education and played football, which I enjoyed so much. Then, after the war, I got to play baseball, too. I think the most important thing I could say about being a Cougar was that it provided me with an opportunity to do what I thought I could do when I was a kid, and what I hoped I could do growing up. The scholarship I had at BYU gave me the way to get into my life's profession.

There is definitely a sense of pride saying I played football at BYU. The university has a good reputation. It's a Church school. When I got there as a freshman, it didn't take me very long to become a Cougar. After the war, Francine and I were there together, and BYU provided us with the opportunity to do a lot of things in our lives.

Glen Oliverson played three season of varsity football at BYU in 1942, 1946, and 1947. Oliverson is one of the last surviving members of the 1942 football team that defeated the University of Utah for the first time in school history. He served in the Navy during World War II and later returned home to play two more seasons at BYU.

The

FIFTIES

JAE R. BALLIF
LINEBACKER/FULLBACK
1950–1952

M
Y FATHER, Ariel Ballif, joined the BYU faculty in 1938. We lived in a duplex that was located where the west annex of the Smith Fieldhouse is today. The football practice field was just to the northeast of our home.

At the time, Eddie Kimball was the head football coach. I'd go to practice and listen in while he talked to his players. I was enthralled with BYU football even as a boy. I grew up with the hope and anticipation of playing for the university someday.

Chick Atkinson was named the new head coach my last year of high school, although there were other coaches I knew on the staff, like Owen Dixon and Bob Bunker. Wayne Soffe was the freshman coach at the time. Owen had been my high school football coach, so I knew him well.

I went to Brigham Young High School in Provo, where I played all the sports. I was part of a state championship basketball team with my friend, Harold Christensen. We were both recruited by BYU. At the time we both thought we would probably play basketball, but I was also interested in playing football.

Stan Watts was the coach who contacted me from BYU. In those days, the faculty was quite small, and things were done very informally. I knew most of the coaches because of their association with my parents, so I knew Coach Watts, and he knew of my interest in BYU.

Jae Ballif (7), pictured with teammates Lowell Madsen (76) and Gary Paxman (22), played three seasons of Cougars football and was all-conference in 1951 and 1952.

Photo courtesy of L. Tom Perry Special Collections; BYU Harold B. Lee Library

Harold Christensen's father and my father were both on the athletics committee at the university, so there was never really any question where we were going to school. Harold, of course, became a star basketball player at BYU. I played football as a freshman and then decided not to pursue basketball.

It wasn't like it is today where there is a protracted effort to win someone to your team. That didn't go on. I had a few contacts, but not much. My uncle was on the faculty at the University of Utah. He and my dad had an ongoing, friendly but intense rivalry over athletics at the two universities. My dad had played football at BYU in the 1920s. He transferred down from

Rick's College and played center on the team back when they played on the gravel field where the Joseph Smith Building now stands.

I came to BYU in 1949 and played on the freshman team. In those days, we often went both ways, so I played linebacker and fullback and also did a lot of the kicking. However my primary position at BYU was linebacker. Like many of the players today, the fellows I played with had hopes and dreams of doing well and representing the university and the Church in a favorable fashion. We had high hopes and expectations. The coaches struggled with limited facilities and budgets, but we didn't worry too much about that. We just played the best we could.

My sophomore year I started to play quite a bit of defense on the varsity. The University of Utah came to Provo that year, and we played them really well. For those days it was a high-scoring game—a really exciting game. I thought we were going to have a major victory, but it didn't quite happen. We ended in a 28–28 tie.

We had some success in those days. It's been a long time and people probably don't remember that now, but there actually were some successes amid some of the discouragements. We had some good games and some good seasons. Playing football at BYU was something that was very important to me and my teammates. There was great camaraderie in those days.

Rex Berry was an older player whom I played with early in my career. He was a remarkable player who went on to play for the San Francisco 49ers. He was so unassuming and thoughtful to those of us younger players wanting to make the team and succeed. He was quiet and unassuming, yet a remarkable athlete.

There was less financial focus on things when I played. In the off-season I had to have a job to earn my scholarship. Eddie Kimball came to me once and said, "You're the ticket manager for the athletics program." He handed me a box of tickets, stubs, and letters. I had to run the ticket office for the basketball season. If I didn't sell all the tickets by the night of the game, then I'd run downtown and stand inside the pharmacy and try to sell the rest. We played football during the season, but we also had to earn our scholarship with real work in the off-season.

My senior year in 1952, Paul Mendenhall was on the team. Of course, he is the father of Bronco Mendenhall. Dick Felt and Marion Probert were about the same age. They were younger than I and were very fine players who made a contribution to the team early.

I made all-conference at linebacker as a junior and senior. We had a couple of other players during that time who were also all-conference. Ray Oliverson was a lanky, hard-running, raw-boned halfback who was a very good football player. Lowell Madsen was another great player of my era. Lowell was from Orem and went to the same high school as LaVell Edwards. He and I were very close friends. Lowell was a big fellow, especially in those days. He wouldn't be considered very big now, especially for an offensive tackle, but neither would I for a linebacker. Yet, in those days, I was one of the larger players, especially in high school. I'd be dwarfed by the linebackers of today.

When I played at BYU, we did most of our travel by train and bus. When we traveled to Wyoming, we'd take an overnight train. When we got there, they would unhook the passenger car and leave it in the railyard. We'd wake up in the morning and be freezing. Then we would take a bus to the stadium for the game.

I remember on one road trip to New Mexico we took a bus. I was sitting toward the back, studying calculus on the way down. I got motion sickness and had to stand up in the doorway the rest of the way. When we traveled, it usually was a long, difficult trip. On those trips you had to put your own equipment bag together. We would go to the locker room and fill our bag with all the pads and equipment we'd need and get on the bus or the train.

We did actually fly to Hawaii during my sophomore year in 1950. Our plane got grounded, so we had to stay in Hawaii a few extra days until they could fix the plane and get it ready to fly again.

The campus was much smaller during those days. After World War II, it started to grow quite a bit. New faculty members were coming to the university, and more and more students were arriving from out of state. I remember we had dances in the old Joseph Smith Building. One time Elder Spencer W. Kimball came and spoke to the students about dressing modestly. Things were fairly calm and tame back in those days. Provo was still very small, and the student body wasn't nearly as big as it is now.

After graduation, I had several letters of inquiry to play professional football, but I was in the National Guard Artillery Unit and was committed to serve, so I didn't give the NFL much thought.

They called our unit to active duty and sent the battalions to Korea. Because I was in the group headquarters, I stayed on active duty at Camp Williams in Utah. Eventually, they sent me back to school. I finished my ROTC studies and got a commission in the Air Force. I was on active duty for about three and a half years. I spent a year at UCLA in meteorology school, and then we were sent to Japan for nearly three years where I was a meteorologist in the Air Force. I returned to BYU as a professor of physics in 1962. I later served as assistant department chair, dean, vice president, and university provost.

As a player, I was very proud to be part of the football program. I appreciated the opportunity to be involved in the program and represent the university. I always felt, and still feel deeply, that it's an honor to represent the university in any way. There is a huge responsibility to do well in all that we do, including football—to be an honorable representative of the Church. To me, it's so much more than just being a university that has a good football program. It's about having good people who are successful but also represent the Church well—because in my mind you can't separate the two.

Football is a decidedly team-oriented sport. You can't succeed independently in football unless you are part of a cooperative group that has a common focus and desire. Unless you have people who sacrifice for the good of the unit, you won't go far. An individual might make a fine play here and there, but to go far you have to have cooperation toward a common goal.

Football is also a sport that teaches you that you have to persevere during difficult times if you're going to be successful. As with anything, there are positives and negatives in sports. Those who learn how to play as a team will often take those same lessons and apply them in life. These are some of the fine lessons I learned playing football at BYU.

Jae Ballif played three seasons of varsity football at BYU from 1950 to 1952. He was a first-team all-conference linebacker as a junior and senior. He returned to BYU as a professor in 1962 and later served as department chair, vice president, and university provost.

DICK FELT

RUNNING BACK

1951–1954

COACH

1967–1994

I GREW UP IN LEHI, UTAH, and played at Lehi High School. I had an outstanding year my senior year, and we lost in the state semifinals. I made all-state and played in the Utah Shrine All-Star Game. Chick Atkinson was the head football coach at BYU. He talked with me after that game. They took me down to Sutton's Cafe in Provo and bought me a hamburger. That was my recruiting visit. I thought, *Boy, this is great!* They offered me a full scholarship. Similar to what they do now with tuition, books, room, and board.

I came to BYU in 1951. I didn't do much my freshman year. I was just kind of on the team. The second year was when I started to assert myself. I didn't make the first road trip my sophomore year. There were four of us boarding at a home with a family. I went home that night, and the father of the home where I was living said, "I was talking to one of the coaches, and he said you just need to assert yourself more." That hit me big time. It changed my whole outlook.

I went out to practice the next week and really got after it. I was 6′ and weighed 160 pounds. I was running through these big linemen who were

Dick Felt (21), pictured with Marion Probert (81), was a running back for the Cougars from 1952 to 1954. Felt played seven seasons in the American Football League before returning to BYU as an assistant football coach. He was inducted into the BYU Athletic Hall of Fame in 1977. *Photo courtesy of the BYU Athletic Archives*

more than 200 pounds. The next road trip was to San Jose, and I made the travel squad. I didn't play in the first half of that game. I recall they had us down 28–0 at halftime. Then, at the end of the third quarter, Chick put me in on the kickoff return team after San Jose had scored. The ball came to me, and I took off running. I ran it back to about the 50-yard line. When I came off the field, I said to Chick, "Boy, I wanna play!"

He put me in, and I scored four touchdowns in the fourth quarter. I think it's still the most touchdowns in one quarter ever at BYU. After that, I started every game at BYU. I had pretty good statistics, but we didn't win a lot back then. I think we would win three or four games a year, but there were some good players. We just didn't have enough of them. We didn't have any size on the line, and that made it difficult to win.

In those days, we would travel by bus to schools nearby, and by train going to places like Colorado State or Wyoming. I remember we flew one time, I think it was to New Mexico. It was an old Frontier flight. I was in the cockpit just watching, and the pilot said, "Come up here and sit down. Do you want to fly the plane?" He let me fly the plane for a little bit.

In 1953 my junior year, we played the University of Utah in Salt Lake City on Thanksgiving Day on national television. Utah was very good, and they were favored by more than 20 points. I remember we got all worked up to play in that game, and we had a chance to tie the game late. Phil Oyler scored with less than two minutes to play, but we missed the extra point and lost 33–32. I played running back and caught a couple of passes in the red zone that I probably could have scored on.

When I attended BYU, the population of the student body was about 5,000. We played at Y Stadium, where the Richards Building now stands. The dressing room was about the size of a restroom, but we thought it was great. It felt like the big time, coming out of high school.

The atmosphere at BYU was great. Of course, it has grown a lot since then, but the positive influence of the LDS Church and friendliness of the teachers and students have always been great. I developed a lot of good friendships over the years.

I'm not sure I can put into words what it means to be a Cougar. It was just a great experience—a moving experience. BYU gave me an opportunity to grow and develop and gain confidence in life.

I went on a mission after I completed my football eligibility, so I was down the road in age a little bit. I served in the Eastern States Mission from 1955 to 1957. The mission took in quite a bit in Pennsylvania, New Jersey, and a little bit of New York. My experiences at BYU eventually gave me the desire to serve. The Church really had an important impact on my life then and still does today. The spiritual atmosphere at BYU had an effect on all of us. I have strong feelings about the university.

After completing my mission, I came back to BYU to finish my last two quarters for graduation. During that time period, I met my wife-to-be.

I'd been in the ROTC program in college and had an Air Force assignment to complete. The Korean War was going on, and I believe someone was looking after me, because I was stationed at Bolling Air Force Base in Washington, D.C. I was assigned to the security squadron at Arlington Cemetery.

We would work in the mornings and then during the season we'd practice with the Bolling Air Force football team in the afternoon. I played for two seasons. We played other military bases and even some colleges. In 1959 I was named the outstanding football player in the Air Force and was selected as an All-Star for the All-Service Team.

When I got out of the military, the American Football League was just organizing. I was taken by the New York Titans, who are now the New York Jets. Slingin' Sammy Baugh was our coach. We didn't have playbooks. He would just coach on the field. He was legendary. There were times he would jump into our seven-on-seven drills and play quarterback.

I played seven seasons in the AFL as a cornerback—two in New York and five for the Boston Patriots, now the New England Patriots. I was named an All-Pro twice, in 1961 and 1962. I also played in the 1963 AFL championship game, but we got beat by the Chargers.

When I retired from pro ball after the 1966 season, I returned to BYU and got a job on Tommy Hudspeth's coaching staff. They were adding to the staff, and the timing was perfect for me. I worked as a defensive coach with LaVell Edwards. When he became the head coach, he said, "Dick, I think I'd like to keep you on my staff."

I know it's very unusual, especially in today's world, but the only place I ever coached was BYU. I was there for 27 seasons. A lot of guys want to move on or become a head coach somewhere else. I think I stayed because of my feelings for BYU and the success we had with LaVell. BYU is a special place.

My lasting memory of LaVell was his special ability to deal with the players. He had amazing patience in dealing with individuals. Look at all the players who came through and had their lives changed for the better. He also had an amazing ability to find great coaches. Look at the number of coaches who came to BYU and where they are now.

I have a lot of fond memories of my years at BYU. The miracle comeback victory to beat Southern Methodist in the 1980 Holiday Bowl is certainly one. It's hard for me to choose just one, because there were a number of other plays that would fit into that kind of a category.

Kyle Morrell's goal-line play at Hawaii is another one. If he didn't make that play and Hawaii had scored, we might not have won that game. There would not have been a national championship.

I think you could try to recreate that play Kyle made 100 times in practice and not pull it off the way it happened. You would never make it. You would be offside or late getting there, or get blocked, or miss the tackle as you're doing a somersault in midair. It was unbelievable. I think it might be the greatest defensive play in the history of the school, maybe in college football.

> Dick Felt played three seasons as a varsity running back at BYU from 1952 to 1954. He led the Cougars in scoring in 1952 and 1953. Felt also led the team in punting in 1953 and rushing in 1954. The New York Titans selected him in the 1960 AFL Draft. Felt played seven seasons in the American Football League for New York and the Boston Patriots. After retiring from professional football in 1966, Felt returned to BYU, where he was an assistant coach for 27 seasons, retiring in 1994. He was inducted into the BYU Athletic Hall of Fame in 1977.

JAY WEENIG

GUARD

1953–1956

I GREW UP IN OGDEN, UTAH. I started playing football in junior high. In those days, junior high went through 10th grade, so I had just two years at the high school. In high school I was an all-state tackle in football as well as all-state in basketball and track.

I had a lot of college offers to play football. Utah was really recruiting me hard. They came to watch my high school practices and games. They offered a lot, including tuition for other members of my family. Chick Atkinson was the head coach at BYU at the time. I had an uncle named Don Buswell who had gone to Brigham Young. He was a dentist, and I was interested in going to dental school, so I kind of followed his career path. My uncle worked really hard to get me to BYU.

At that time the freshmen were not allowed to play varsity, so I played on the freshman team my first year. That would have been 1953. My first room-mate was from Burley, Idaho. We lived in some old World War II barracks on campus. It certainly wasn't plush, but at least it was a place to stay. Later, I got an apartment off campus with some other athletes. That probably wasn't the best idea because studying wasn't the highest priority for them. I majored in zoology and minored in chemistry.

I was also a pretty good basketball player, but Stan Watts was the coach at the time, and he believed you couldn't play both sports. So we organized a freshman basketball team that was mostly made up of football players. We

Jay Weenig was an offensive and defensive guard for the Cougars from 1953 to 1956. As a senior, he was named first-team all-conference. *Photo courtesy of the Weenig family*

picked up a few good basketball players like Bob Ipsen, who went on to play at Utah State. We called ourselves the Eight Balls. We were pretty good. We scrimmaged the freshman team a lot and beat them pretty badly.

I eventually played three years of varsity football and was named all-conference three times. That was back in the old Skyline Conference. I still hold the record for the longest field goal, 53 yards, in Skyline Conference history. Of course, a few years after I graduated, BYU left the conference to join the WAC [Western Athletic Conference].

I played guard on offense and defense at BYU, but defense was my specialty. I was a selection for All-America as a sophomore and received All-America honors from several publications my senior year—most were honorable mention. My last two years I played all but a few minutes on both offense and defense. I was also a kicker. I learned how to kick from Chris Apostol, who owned a business in Ogden and coached at BYU in the 1960s.

There were a lot of great memories at BYU—probably too many to tell. The one football game I remember, which kind of sticks in my craw, was my last home game versus Wyoming in 1956. They were favored by several touchdowns and had a kid by the name of Jim Crawford who was an All-American. He may have led the nation in rushing. He'd had a good year running the ball, but we held him down. I tackled him behind the line of scrimmage several times in that game. We held Wyoming to a touchdown and had a chance to win. Late in the game we scored to make it 7–6, but I missed the extra point. Later we had a chance to kick a field goal to win it, but the coach was so mad at me that he wouldn't let me try the field goal. The guy he put in to kick the field goal didn't make it, so we lost the game 7–6.

One of my memorable moments of playing at BYU happened on a road trip to the University of Montana. In those days we traveled a lot by train. We pulled into Bozeman, dropped off two rail cars, and woke up. From there we caught a bus to take us to Missoula. Well, the bus took off without me— I guess they didn't count noses. I ended up having to hitchhike to Missoula. In those days we traveled in ties and sports coats, and that's all I had with me. All my other stuff was on the bus.

My first ride was in the back of an old truck with a big dog. It was so cold. They dropped me off in Anaconda, which is out in the middle of nowhere. I thought I'd had it. There was no traffic out there. It was October, and I was just about freezing to death. Finally, I was picked up by a carload of girls who took me into Missoula. That was quite an experience.

When I attended school at BYU, the campus was pretty small. The stadium was located on the west side of campus, north of the Smith Fieldhouse. The seating was on the side of the hill. There was a dressing room on the west side of the field. On the other side of the dressing rooms was a large practice field. With temporary bleachers added on the west side, the stadium would seat maybe 12,000 to 13,000 people—not a lot compared to today. We had a couple of our games nationally televised while I was there. We had a few good players back in those days, but our teams were not very strong.

I participated in a lot of musical events on campus, as well. I'm an operatic tenor, so I had the lead in a couple of operas. I also sang in a male choir and a couple of mixed quartets.

After graduating from BYU, I went to the Detroit Lions for a year. I was hoping to save enough money to go to dental school, but I had my ROTC commitment, so I entered the Air Force in February 1958 and went through pilot training. I later earned five advanced degrees, including a dental and periodontal degree at Loyola University in Chicago.

I was a fighter pilot for 20 years in the Air Force. I flew 304 missions in Vietnam and Cambodia, where I flew A-37 and F-100 airplanes. I had some pretty successful missions.

It was a great thing for me to be a Cougar. I got a balanced education at BYU, and the Church's role in the school was an important part of that. It's amazing, wherever you go in the world, you'll find the influence of the LDS Church. I really appreciated the standards at BYU. They are the standards that have carried me throughout my life.

I'm proud to say that I played football at BYU back in the day. Most of my friends know that I played at BYU and it's my alma mater. I still follow the BYU program and watch the games. We are always talking about the BYU games, and of course my friends give me grief when we lose.

BYU taught me to do the best you can with what you have. I learned to have confidence in myself and work hard. I also learned you can accomplish anything you want if you work hard and set goals.

35

Jay Weenig played guard on offense and defense at BYU, earning first-team all-conference honors in 1956. He also received several All-America citations and holds the Skyline Conference field goal record of 53 yards. Weenig was selected in the 18th round of the 1957 NFL Draft by the Detroit Lions.

WELDON JACKSON

FULLBACK

1956–1958

I GREW UP IN A SMALL TOWN called Fredonia, Arizona, just south of the border from Kanab, Utah. I remember listening to the 1951 basketball team on the radio when I was young. That was the year BYU won the NIT championship. I knew all the players by heart, and I dreamed of one day playing basketball at BYU.

My dad worked in road construction, so my sophomore year in high school we ended up moving to Mesa, Arizona. One day, I noticed an advertisement for high school football tryouts. My mom took me down to the local sporting goods store and bought me some football cleats.

I had never really played football before. They assigned me to a team called the rainbow team. They called us that because we all had different colors and styles of uniforms. It was primarily a sophomore team. I eventually made the J-V team, where I played tailback and defensive back. I played mostly defense at that time. We had good coaches and some real good football players. In three seasons we only lost one game each year. As a senior, I rushed for over 1,300 yards and had a really good season.

One day a bunch of BYU coaches came to our high school to talk to me and a couple other guys. I think it was Chick Atkinson, Owen Dixon, and Rex Berry, who wasn't a coach but was a former BYU player who played for the San Francisco 49ers. I don't remember a lot of what was said, but shortly

Weldon Jackson was the starting fullback for the Cougars for three seasons. As a senior in 1958 he led the Skyline Conference in rushing and was named first-team all-conference. *Photo courtesy of the BYU Athletic Archives*

thereafter I got a letter in the mail stating, "We are pleased to offer you a full-ride scholarship to play football at BYU."

At the time I was considering Arizona, New Mexico State, and Utah State, but when I got that letter, I decided that I would go to BYU. I liked the coaches at BYU, and that's really what made the difference.

After my freshman year of football in the fall of 1955, I ran track in the spring. I was a long jumper. I won a couple of meets during the year, including the Skyline Conference Championship. That meet was held in Denver, and the weather was terrible. It was raining like crazy, but I managed to jump 22'8½" to win the conference title. So that summer I was invited by Clarence Robison to travel with the track team to Europe for six weeks. We had something like 13 track meets in England, Germany, Norway, Ireland, and Finland. It was a great experience.

In the spring of 1956 we got a new head football coach at BYU. His name was Hal Kopp. I got back from Europe just in time to jump into fall practice for football. We were a pretty average football team my sophomore year, but my junior and senior years we had opportunities to win the conference championship. Unfortunately, we came up short.

Hal brought in a new offensive system. We were running the split-T. We were looking forward to the 1956 season. I was starting at right halfback. I played a lot, but we didn't win much. Midway through the year, we tried to throw the ball a little more, but nothing seemed to help. That year was kind of a bust.

Everyone likes to think that BYU football started to turn around in 1972, when LaVell Edwards was hired as head coach. I really feel like it started to turn around in 1957 and 1958. We had winning records both years, which was significant because we'd had a lot of losing seasons prior to then.

As a junior in 1957, we ran a wing-T offense. I played some fullback and some running back. Carroll Johnston was our quarterback. I also played defensive back. In those days the NCAA required you to play both ways. If they subbed for you, then you had to sit out the rest of the quarter. We pretty much had two teams, and they would make wholesale substitutions.

That year we played Utah State in Provo and won 14–0. Bob Olson was our center, and somehow he and Bob Winters, the USU quarterback, got into some fisticuffs. It quickly spread to the whole team, and pretty soon people were coming out of the stands, and we had a full-on riot going.

As a senior in 1958, we beat Utah in Salt Lake City 14–7. Unfortunately, I don't remember very much about that game. About five minutes into the game, I took a handoff into the middle of the line and got hit so hard that I got knocked out. I really didn't come to until about halftime. I know we won, but that's about all I remember.

We opened that '58 season against Fresno State. I had a run of 93 yards for a touchdown. That run remained a BYU record for more than 40 years until Reynaldo Brathwaite broke it against San Diego State with a 95-yard run in 2003. They invited me to a home game later that year, and Reynaldo gave me a game ball from the SDSU game. That was very nice.

I ended up leading the conference in rushing with 698 yards my senior year and was named first-team all-conference as a fullback. Going into the last game against Wyoming, we were actually leading the country in rushing as a team. We felt that was pretty significant for BYU. I was the fullback, and Nyle McFarlane was the halfback. Nyle went on to play for the Oakland Raiders.

We would only play just over half the game because of the way they did substitutions in those days. Unfortunately, Wyoming really did a number on us defensively, and I think Oklahoma finished ahead of us.

Coach Kopp contacted me after my senior season and asked if I wanted to play in the 1958 Copper Bowl in Tempe, Arizona. So that's how I finished my BYU football career, by playing in that all-star game. I played for the West team, and we ended up winning the game. I played primarily on defense. I remember we each made $100 for expenses, which really came in handy at Christmastime.

I have some great memories of playing football at BYU. The Utah State game my senior year was memorable. We got down 6–0 early, but then I scored a touchdown. In the second half I had a 79-yard run that set up a touchdown to win the game. Steve Young's dad, LeGrand, actually scored the winning touchdown. We ended up winning 13–6 on the road in Logan.

We had a lot of good players during my days at BYU and also some guys who played right before me whom I really admired, like Phil Oyler, Jim Keitzman, Dick Felt, Marion Probert. One of my teammates was Fred Whittingham, who of course is the father of Kyle. There was also Jay Weenig, Lonnie Dennis, and John Kapele, who were all-conference guys.

BYU provided me with a lot of things in my life. I met my wife at BYU when I was a sophomore. We dated awhile and eventually got married after my junior year. When it really comes down to it, our lives are based on the little choices we make. So my life was changed significantly by the decision to come to BYU. The people at BYU were some of the greatest people to be around.

I was on campus a few years ago for a game and was having lunch in the Cougareat with my son. We were sitting there watching all the students, and I made a comment to him, "How could you not want your children to come to BYU?" The young people at BYU almost have a glow to them. They're so happy, friendly, energetic, and full of life. You just can't beat that. That was the way it was when I was at school at BYU. I've always felt that everybody says hi at the Y.

The education I received at BYU was great and prepared me well for my career. I got a math degree from BYU, which is as good as any degree you'll find anywhere in the country.

I'm not a real noisy fan, but I still follow the program and am proud to be a BYU Cougar. I attend some of the spring and fall practices. Since Coach Mendenhall took over the program, it's been nice to be invited back to attend some of the reunions and gatherings. He has made the former players feel welcome. I appreciate the job he is doing.

Weldon Jackson was a starting fullback for BYU for three seasons from 1956 to 1958. He led BYU in rushing and total offense as a junior and senior. In 1958 Jackson led the Skyline Conference in rushing and was named first-team all-conference. He also led the nation in rushing average at 6.9 yards per carry and finished seventh nationally in total rushing yards. He helped the West squad to a victory in the 1958 Copper Bowl all-star game.

West Texas State without face masks and got beat 55–8. It was unbelievable. Of course, when we got back, Floyd had to turn around and put all the face masks back on our helmets the day after we got home. I'm sure he was burning the midnight oil to get that job done. I'll tell you what—we never took off the face masks again after that.

In 1962 Hal hired LaVell Edwards to join his staff. LaVell likes to tell the story that the only reason BYU hired him was because he was the only Mormon in the state of Utah who knew how to run the single wing. There might be some truth to that, but in any case, that's how I was reunited with LaVell.

My senior year we opened at Pacific, and we didn't sync right that first game. Then we went to Arizona and should have won that game, but we lost 27–21. We had the ball on their 2-yard line, and we ran our best play where I went off-tackle on the right. I just didn't get in the end zone. It ended up costing us the conference championship. We finished second behind New Mexico.

I have a lot of fond memories of playing football with that group of guys. We only had one returned missionary and two married guys on that team, so it was an entirely different demographic than BYU has today. The prevailing thought among coaches back then was that returned missionaries don't make good football players. They're not tough enough.

That carried on until LaVell took over and said, "Hey, we've got to maximize the talent we've got with these returned missionaries." I believe one of the reasons he turned the program around is he started to recruit returned missionaries and encouraged young men to serve.

I get asked occasionally about the game I had against George Washington my senior year. It was raining as I recall. We didn't have a problem moving the ball, but we just couldn't get in the end zone. I'll always remember a block that Lloyd Smith made in that game. I had broken through the line, and Lloyd came from his left end spot and laid out the defensive back. It was just a perfect block. I cut behind Lloyd and ran it for a 75-yard touchdown. The crazy thing about that game is I rushed for 272 yards, and we still got beat 13–12. It was terrible. During my career at the Y, I set 25 school and conference records, and everything but that great rushing day has been broken. That single-game rushing record has stood for nearly 50 years, which I find amazing.

I started to lead the nation in total yardage at about that time of the season. A sportswriter from the *Deseret News* covering BYU wrote in an article,

45

"He runs like a phantom." From then on the nickname just stuck. I became Eldon "the Phantom" Fortie.

At the end of the '62 season, I got a phone call to let me know I had been named an All-American. I couldn't believe it. Then, sure enough, one of the All-America teams was announced. Then other teams started coming out, and I was on those, too. To be the first Cougar to be named first-team All-America is something that I've always treasured. At halftime of a basketball game, the university retired my jersey. President Wilkinson was there and actually presented it to me in a glass case. It was fun—a great memory.

To me, as I look back, it's the friendships that were formed and the people I met that are the most important things. There were a lot of great people at BYU. When I was playing high school football, you had Glen Tuckett at West, LaVell at Granite, and Talley Stevens at East. They were coaching against each other, and eventually all three ended up at the Y as coaches. Glen was one of those exceptional, extraordinary people who you run across every now and again in your lifetime. He had a tremendous influence on me and countless other athletes at BYU.

I'm not there locally now, but I still follow the program from a distance. Certainly, there's a sense of pride that I played a small role in building the football program early on. There has to be, because the program has done so well over the years. I love the tradition. Anything that involves the Y, I'm excited about.

There's just something about being from the Y that brings everybody together. Anybody who's from BYU has a unique commonality. We have a togetherness that is quite special. Wherever we've moved, there's been friendship and commonality because of the Y.

Eldon "the Phantom" Fortie started three seasons at tailback for BYU from 1960 to 1962. As a senior he led the Western Athletic Conference in rushing, total offense, and scoring, on his way to being named WAC Offensive Player of the Year. In 1962 Fortie became the first Cougar to be named a first-team All-American. Later that year, the university retired his No. 40 jersey—the first jersey ever retired at BYU. In 1963 Fortie played a year of professional football for the Edmonton Eskimos of the Canadian Football League. He was inducted into the BYU Athletic Hall of Fame in 1977.

CURG BELCHER

DEFENSIVE BACK

1963–1966

I PROBABLY HAD ONE of the most unique recruiting stories ever at BYU. I grew up in Vernal, Utah, and was being recruited by all the in-state schools to play football. At the time the program at Utah impressed me, and I thought, *I could picture myself at Utah.*

One day a coach called our house, and I thought it was Ray Nagel, the coach at Utah, but it was actually Coach Hal Mitchell from BYU. For some reason, I had the coaches totally confused. I had pretty much made up my mind to go to Utah, so I said, "Yes, I've decided to go there, Coach." He said, "Great, we'll be out to your house in a couple hours."

I honestly thought the Utah coaches were on their way to Vernal. When they arrived, I opened the door, and there were Coach Mitchell and one of the other coaches from BYU standing there with a BYU hat and T-shirt for me. I think I just about fainted. All the color must have drained out of my face.

I think Coach Mitchell could probably tell I was shocked. I didn't know what to do, so I turned and looked at my folks. My dad invited them in. We had a kitchen off the living room, and my dad told the coaches he needed to have a word with me.

We went into the kitchen, and my dad said, "I've never interfered, but those men came clear out here thinking that you were going to BYU. I think that's where you should go." My folks were always very supportive, so I said, "All right."

Defensive back Curg Belcher (46) with coach Tommy Hudspeth and two of the other stars from the 1965 WAC championship football team—defensive end Glenn Gardner (74) and quarterback Virgil Carter (14).

I think there must have been some type of divine intervention because that's really where I needed to go. It was one of the greatest blessings of my life to go to the Y. That freshman class of 1963 may have been the best recruiting class that BYU had up to that time. There was John and Steve Ogden, Kent Oborn, Virgil Carter, Mel Olson, Moses Kim, and a lot of kids from the Islands. We had some terrific talent.

When I got to BYU, I was just a kid from a small school. As a freshman I played wingback and defensive back. The freshman team played four games that year and went undefeated. My sophomore year I started off playing both ways and then got hurt. When I came back, they put me on the defensive side of the ball. That's primarily where I stayed. I was a very aggressive football player and I loved to hit. I'd rather make a tackle than a touchdown. Playing defense was just a better fit for me.

We played at the old Y stadium, which at the time seated about 10,000 people. To me it was enormous. It was a lot of fun. LaVell Edwards was the defensive coordinator, Chris Apostle was my position coach, and Tommy Hudspeth was the head coach. They were great coaches.

The mid-1960s were a great time to be at BYU. The basketball team was very good, and I became friends with guys like Jeff Congdon and Dick Nemelka. We all lived together in John Hall at Helaman Halls. A bunch of the guys on the football team—Glenn Gardner, Virgil, Steve, Kent, and I—played intramural basketball together for two or three years. We called ourselves the "Blue Darters," which was Virg's nickname. It was a lot of fun. Virgil was a California boy with a lot of confidence. He was a natural leader—very talented. When you played with Virg, it didn't take very long to realize there was something special about him. He was a very smart player.

Probably my favorite memory is when we went down to New Mexico in 1965 and won the first conference championship in school history. It was absolutely fantastic. There were a lot of great football players on that team.

It was also the day the airplane that was carrying a lot of our fans to the game went down. That was pretty devastating. We didn't even know that the plane had crashed until halftime. We were getting ready to go back out on the field, and they stopped us and said, "We'd like to have a moment of silence." I was in the locker room getting taped in another room, so I didn't know what had happened. I had to ask someone, "What's going on?" I was told, "There's been a terrible accident, and a lot of BYU supporters lost their

49

lives." It was very sad. My folks almost flew on that plane. They essentially were going to fly down but decided instead to drive down with some friends.

After my senior year, Virgil and I were invited to play in the Senior Bowl. We were the first guys to represent BYU in that game. I also played in the College All-Star game in Chicago.

My wife Sheila and I got married after my senior year on the money we made from the Senior Bowl. We met at BYU. I had seen her around campus, but I was somewhat shy and didn't date a lot. We had to have a date in order to attend our year-end football banquet. A good friend of mine, John Greene, who played baseball and football, found her name and number. John actually called her on the phone and pretended to be me and asked her if she wanted to go to the football banquet. We laughed about that story for years. So that's how I met my wife. We went to the football banquet together. She was a California girl who swore she'd never marry a Utah hick. She's as big a BYU fan as I am. There have been several times when I thought maybe the Lord intervened with my going to BYU. I will always feel that way.

Coach Edwards was actually our campus bishop. He flew down to Los Angeles and went through the temple with us. That was a great experience for us. LaVell was like a dad away from home to all of us. He was an assistant coach during my time at BYU, but I always knew he was destined for greatness. We had a really close relationship. I knew he cared about me, and it wasn't phony.

After my senior year, I was drafted in the third round of the 1967 NFL Draft by the Washington Redskins. Virgil went a couple rounds later to the Chicago Bears. At that time I was also drafted into the military. I signed with the Redskins and went back to Washington. They tried to get me out of the military draft, but I had a real strong belief that I needed to go serve my country. I served in the Army during the Vietnam War.

When I got out, I had been overseas and had a little girl who was five months old. It was the first I had seen her. I went back to the Redskins because I though I was still good enough to play, but I just wasn't right mentally. Coach Hudspeth called me and said, "Hey, I need some help. I want you to come back to BYU, be an assistant coach with the freshmen team, and finish your education." I always wanted to be a coach, so I went back to BYU and coached the freshmen in 1969. I finished my education at BYU in 1970.

A lot of people think that BYU football started in the 1980s with Coach Edwards, but I believe it started earlier. There were great athletes at BYU in the 1960s, guys like Eldon Fortie and Virgil Carter. I'm telling you, Virg started the quarterback factory. We won the first conference championship in 1965, and my senior year in 1966 we went 8–2. About 10 years ago, BYU brought us all back and gave us championship rings for winning the first conference championship. It was a special moment for all of us.

I bleed BYU blue, I always will. I don't care if we win or lose, I will always love BYU because of the value system. You just can't go on that campus and not be impressed with the school. It means everything in the world for me to say I was Cougar. Honestly, I think that's the difference between BYU fans and alumni of other schools. Once you're a BYU fan, you're always a BYU fan. Anywhere you go in the United States, you'll find BYU alumni. We are all very proud of the tradition at the Y and what the school represents. I just think it's the greatest university in the world.

Curg Belcher lettered three times at BYU as a defensive back from 1964 to 1966. In 1966 he was named first-team All–Western Athletic Conference. Following his senior season, Belcher played in the Senior Bowl and also the College All-Star Game in Chicago. He was drafted by the Washington Redskins in the third round of the 1967 NFL Draft. At that time Belcher was the highest Cougar ever taken in the NFL Draft.

51

VIRGIL CARTER

QUARTERBACK

1963–1966

As a kid from the third through sixth grade, my dad was in the ROTC program at BYU. After my senior year in high school in 1963, he was retiring from the Air Force, and his plan was to go back to the Provo area and take more classes at BYU. He was working on his master's degree, as I recall. So they were headed to Provo, which meant that, if I could get a scholarship, I could live at home, and it might be a pretty good deal to go to school at BYU. As a kid I grew up watching Terry Tebbs play BYU basketball and sneaking into the knothole gang for football games. I was familiar with the university and the town, so that was a comforting decision for me.

I had two other opportunities for college. I passed on a scholarship to go to Stanford. At the time, I had no clue that Stanford was a pretty good academic school, and I didn't spend any time looking. As I look back, that would have been a great education. The second one was the Air Force Academy, but I thought, *Do I really want to go four years to a military academy and then spend the rest of my life saluting?*

I'm not sure that I was very high on BYU's list, but LaVell Edwards was recruiting me. We ran a T-belly offense in high school, which is an option off-tackle. As it turned out, that's really what we ran at BYU for the years that Tommy Hudspeth was there. At the time, BYU had Hal Mitchell, who ran a single-wing offense. So LaVell's job, in his opinion, was to tell me that I could be a tailback and talk me into going to BYU. We still laugh about it to this day. He was a pretty good salesman, because I sure wasn't a tailback.

Because I had good grades, LaVell was pretty wise and knew he could save the athletics department a full scholarship by getting me an academic scholarship and then subsidize it to make a full ride. That way, if I didn't turn out to be a tailback, it didn't really hurt the athletics department that much.

After about a month of trying to be a tailback, I went to LaVell and explained to him that this wasn't my cup of tea, and, "By the way, remember I'm on an academic scholarship, so instead of going to the football field and getting the crap kicked out of me, I think I'll just go to the library and maintain my scholarship for academics, and you guys can have a nice day."

I remember at the time he said, "You know what, I can't tell you what's coming, Virg, but just bite your lip, be patient, hang in there a couple of more weeks, and I think you'll be happy you did." Of course, LaVell wouldn't have betrayed a secret of the athletics department or the football team, but he was giving me a hint that change was coming. I thought, *Okay, I'll give it two more weeks*. At the end of those two weeks, it turned out that Hal Mitchell changed to a T formation. I was on the freshman team at the time, but I was the only guy on scholarship who knew how to take a snap from center. So during the week I would go practice with the varsity—even though we couldn't play varsity at the time—to work on the T formation. I helped them figure out how they were going to prepare for the last couple of losses for the year—and they did get powdered terribly.

I went to Sacramento to visit friends during Christmas, and I remember somebody called me and said, "Hey, they just hired a new head coach at BYU." It was a guy named Tommy Hudspeth. I didn't know anything about Tommy. Somebody said he was coaching up in Canada where they only have three downs, so they were running a wide-open offense. I thought, *You know, that's interesting.*

When I went back to BYU and we started spring practice for the 1964 season, our team was very limited in who could take a snap from center. In fact, it was basically me. Because of that, I took every snap for the next three years, and because Tommy was only used to having three downs, he obviously wanted to throw on most of them. As a result, it was an opportunity for me to throw a lot of passes. He ran the outside belly series, which was right up my alley, so being able to have that experience for three years gave me a lot of recognition.

Nicknamed "the Blue Darter," Virgil Carter led BYU to its first conference title in 1965. The following year, he led the nation in total offense and TD passes and was the first Cougar to be named Academic All-America. He was inducted into the BYU Athletic Hall of Fame in 1977. *Photo courtesy of the BYU Athletic Archives*

Our freshman class had some pretty good players. I think we were unbeaten as freshmen—four games—not a big deal, but at least we had a little momentum rolling. It was kind of one of those unique classes that comes in where there are a lot of good players, and they all stay healthy and have a good attitude. But we were still young and immature. We were 18- and 19-year-old kids. Tommy brought in a bunch of marines who had played football—I think there were six or seven of them. A couple of them had kids. They had four years of maturity beyond high school that none of us had. So it was a good mix, having them come in and provide stability and maturity to go with the enthusiasm of the freshman team that had ambitions of greatness.

A few of those guys were crucial in the passing game—Phil Odle, Casey Boyette, Perry Rodrique. But it was more than just Phil's ability to catch passes. He was a leader. People looked up to him. He was mature. You respected him, so you didn't want to disappoint him. You worked a little harder to get him the ball rather than having him come back and say, "Why did you miss me again?"

I have fond memories of playing at BYU, but of course nobody's alive to remember that time anymore. Without a doubt my favorite is when we won the conference championship at New Mexico in 1965 for the first time in school history. That was coupled with the plane crash of some of our best fans who were on their way down to the game that morning. It put a damper over that game, but it brought the team together, rallying for a cause beyond our own. As a result, we accomplished something that had never been accomplished in about 50 years, because BYU had never won a conference title. That was a big one.

Then on a personal level, I think of the UTEP (then Texas Western) game my senior year. It was Tommy Hudspeth against his old nemesis, Bobby Dobbs. Billy Stevens was their quarterback, and we were both high in total offense in the nation. We beat them 53–33, and I had 599 yards of total offense for the game. I didn't play half of the fourth quarter because Tommy didn't want to run up the score on his old buddy from Tulsa. That was personally a high-water mark.

That 1966 team was very good. It might have been a better team than '65. We had an off night against Arizona State and ended the season with two losses. The 1965 team kind of came through the back door, but you have to give it credit because it was a team that didn't quit. Even when it looked like there wasn't much of a chance, we kept fighting and just wouldn't give up.

For a long time, Utah loved the rivalry with BYU because we never beat them. The fact that we were able to beat them in 1965 for the first time in a long time sort of started it toward even being called a rivalry. We had a lot of catching up to do, but I think we won a couple in a row after that. Then, of course, LaVell took over and beat them like a stepchild for a lot of years. But previously it wasn't much of a rivalry. It was more of a massacre. The win in 1965 was a big deal.

I take a lot of pride in the fact that BYU gave me the opportunity and I took advantage of it, but one injury could have changed that. Looking back it was nice to be a part of the program when we were starting to experience success, but life moves on. That was one of the reasons I put an emphasis on getting an education. I knew, even if I played in the NFL, it wouldn't be forever, and it probably wouldn't be very long. I'd have to make a living at something else, which meant I needed to use my brain.

Academics were an important part of my life on campus. I was basically an athlete who spent a lot of time in the classroom. I was very serious about school. I don't know why I was so motivated, but it just meant a lot to me to graduate from the university. Most of my time was spent in the library, working on assignments and getting schoolwork done. The rest of my time was spent down in the old Smith Fieldhouse in the west annex working out in the off-season—throwing passes into the net or finding a spot to work out between seasons. It was certainly rudimentary compared to what they have now. Of course, that is true with any program that has grown and become successful. It was not a very glamorous existence but one that just happened to be my motivation.

I played in the stadium that was located near the Smith Fieldhouse. It had stands on one side and nothing across the field, so during freshman football the wind would blow from the west with nothing to protect us. The university did a lot for the football program back then. My sophomore year we opened the season at the new stadium, where it stands today. It just had the two sides back then, but it was a big improvement.

My idea of football life at BYU is nothing like what the quarterbacks have today, where the game film is delivered instantaneously through closed circuit. They don't have to get their hands blackened from threading game film or bringing their own masking tape to fix the film when it breaks. It's a different world, but it doesn't mean we didn't enjoy what we did. We played hard and trained hard.

A few years back, I attended a reunion for the championship year of 1965. After having lunch, we were all sitting around and telling stories, and I was thinking to myself, *You know what? I really missed a lot!* I didn't remember any of the funny stories the guys were telling. The truth is, I was such a serious football player at the time that nobody included me in the horseplay. I was out to lunch. I was in Tommy's office studying game plans, or I was in looking at film, or in the library while the rest of the players, Curg Belcher, Kent Oborn, John and Steve Ogden, were out looking for ways have a good time or get into trouble.

I learned a lot at BYU. The education was paramount, and although I've worked mostly for myself through the years, the discipline of having a formal education—being able to write memos, communicate with people, jog out points for or against a decision, and take some analytical direction—has been absolutely critical in my professional life.

The discipline of having to be committed and spending time on practice and study, and trying to perform and improve—those are all things that easily translated into the normal world of business and life. Those are lessons that once you learn them, even though it might be in athletics, you can apply them all through your life. BYU helped me lay a foundation to be disciplined, competitive, set goals, and work to accomplish those things.

57

Virgil Carter started three years at quarterback for the Cougars. In 1965 he led BYU to its first conference title in school history. The following year as a senior, Carter led the nation in total offense and touchdown passes. He finished 11th in the Heisman Trophy voting and became the first Cougar to be named Academic All-America. Carter was drafted in the sixth round of the 1967 NFL Draft by the Chicago Bears. He played seven seasons in the NFL for the Bears, Cincinnati Bengals, and San Diego Chargers.

MEL OLSON

LINEBACKER/CENTER

1963–1966 ★ 1969

COACH

1970–1989

MY DECISION TO COME to BYU worked out really well. I went on the mission and then I came back and ended up making all-conference and being one of the captains. I got my degree, which was really, really important. When I finished my career, I went from being a player to a coach. Because I had been there for five years, I was pretty close to getting my master's degree. We used to get the summers off, so it just took me a few years to finish up my master's. Eventually, I kept plugging away and got a doctorate.

LaVell Edwards recruited me out of high school. He came up to Star Valley, Wyoming, and offered me a scholarship, and I came to BYU to play for him. The other reason I came to BYU was because of the opportunity to go on an LDS mission. The other schools that I was being recruited by—Utah, Wyoming, and Colorado—did not understand the concept, so I chose BYU. It certainly wasn't for the football prowess, because BYU wasn't very good during that period of time.

I played fullback and defensive tackle in high school. The rules in college during that period of time were you could only substitute two players at a

Mel Olson was a captain of the 1969 football team and the last Cougar to be named all-conference on both offense and defense. Olson began his BYU career as a linebacker before switching to center following a knee injury. *Photo courtesy of the Olson family*

time until you got your whole defense on the field, so I played running back on offense and linebacker on defense.

I came to BYU in 1963. We had a real good group of freshmen, and we basically made the commitment that we were going to stay with the new coach, Tommy Hudspeth, and bring winning football to BYU. Back in those days, freshmen were not allowed to play varsity football.

We got it going my sophomore year, but we didn't have enough depth. At that time I was playing linebacker, and I was doing really well. I ended up being named second-team All–Western Athletic Conference. That season, 1964, we also opened up the new stadium where it is today. It seated about 33,500. In my opinion, that's where it all started. That was the first step to building the football program at BYU.

The old stadium seated about 10,000, and everybody thought, *How are we going to fill that new stadium?* Tommy was a great public relations guy. He got the enthusiasm going. People got really excited, and we ended up selling out the stadium. Then the next year when we won the conference championship, it started to roll. Basically, the whole attitude toward football switched and got people on board. The administration was behind us, and we had good coaches.

Before the next season, coach Chris Apostol went and recruited a bunch of marines. They had won a military championship. He said, "Anybody who is interested in a scholarship at BYU see me after the game." We had 16 of them who signed. He brought them in to supplement our freshman nucleus. Then, of course, Tommy put together a good team, and we won the first conference championship in school history.

I was really looking forward to my junior season, but during spring football I got clipped and just totally wiped out my knee. So I actually missed the 1965 season, the year we won the first conference championship in football. After I came back from knee surgery, they switched me to offensive line.

I started at center my junior year, and we were 8–2. Virgil Carter had a great year. The 1966 team was probably better than 1965, but Wyoming was really good during that time, too. So, even though we went 8–2, we finished second in the WAC behind Wyoming. The program was starting to turn around. We had three winning seasons in a row, which was pretty good for that time.

That was the time that I was going to go on my Church mission. Kent Oborn and several of us were all going on missions. So I went to tell Coach

Hudspeth that I was planning on leaving. He was very angry and basically said, "You're not going to have your scholarship when you come back." I said, "Well, I'm going to go on a mission; that's the reason I came to BYU."

Tommy was a convert to the LDS faith and very active in the Church, but when individuals wanted to go on a Church mission as opposed to a "football mission," that was really hard for him to understand. At that time he just couldn't quite grasp the mission process of the Church.

I went to talk to LaVell. He was an LDS bishop on campus, and I figured he would understand. LaVell said an interesting thing to me. He said, "In my opinion, if a kid can play football before he goes into the mission field, he can play when he comes back. If he can't play before he goes, he's not going to get any better out serving." He told me, "Hey, just stay in contact. When you come back, we'll get you a scholarship."

There where a couple of guys who played during my era who were returned missionaries, but not very many. Not very many had served a mission in the middle of their eligibility. That was kind of a breakthrough.

When I came back from my mission, Marc Lyons was the quarterback. It was 1969. We were pretty good and went 6–4. I was named a co-captain and ended up making first-team All-WAC at center. The following summer Coach Apostol left, and Tommy asked me to join his staff. I took over coaching the freshman program.

In 1972 Coach Hudspeth was let go, and LaVell Edwards took over. I moved up to working with the offensive line. It was a great period of time to be at BYU. When LaVell took over the program, he decided he wasn't going to fight the missionary issue. He was going to embrace the kids who wanted to go on missions. It ended up being one of his strengths. Coach Lance Reynolds, who was in the program at that time, was probably the next era who went on a mission and came back to be a very good player for us. He was all-conference and went on to play in the pros.

In 1984, when we won the national championship, *Sports Illustrated* ran an article with a photo where all the kids who had been on a mission were in blue, and the kids who had not were in black and white. Two-thirds of the kids on that national championship team were returned missionaries.

LaVell surrounded himself with good coaches. Then he let them do their work and got out of the way. He always had great offensive and defensive coordinators, but his genius was he let them do their job. LaVell is who LaVell is. I was on his staff for 20 years, and, of course, he recruited me, so I also played for him. We're talking more than 25 years he never changed—always consistent. He's just a great person. He was and is a legend. LaVell is a competitor. He loves to win. Ask anyone who has coached or played for him. But he also has this way of keeping things in perspective.

During the 1980s we beat Hawaii over there on a regular basis. Some of the games were close, but we always seemed to win. In 1990 Ty Detmer won the Heisman, and everybody thought that we were going to roll, but Hawaii was ready for us, and we got smoked. I remember LaVell came in the locker room after the game and said, "We've come here for years, and we've had a lot of success, but the roof fell in today. So we're just going to regroup, we're going to move on, and we're going to keep winning championships."

Obviously, BYU has done a lot for my life. I've associated with great people and great players who have the same ideals and standards. So many have gone on to be great citizens and great individuals. It has to make you a little bit better as a person. W's and L's are important, but in the long run the Church and the people are really what it's all about.

During my time being associated with the BYU football program, we went from the bottom of the league to dominating the conference for a long period of time and eventually winning the national championship. We don't apologize. We didn't send the trophy back. It's still here. We have it. It's something I'm proud of because we earned it. Those individuals who were a part of it understand the sacrifices.

Anybody who has played here or has been involved understands because you deal with the physical, the spiritual, and obviously the academic. If you do that, you're going to be a Cougar. You're going to bleed blue forever. It gets ingrained into who you are and what you do.

Mel Olson has been a Cougar for nearly 50 years. He came to Provo in 1963 on a football scholarship and later captained the 1969 team. Olson was the last Cougar to be named all-conference on both offense and defense. In 1970 he joined the coaching staff, where he remained until 1989. From 1990 to 1996 Olson worked in the athletics academic office before becoming a professor in exercise sciences. He has his bachelor's, master's, and doctorate degrees from BYU.

JAY MILLER

RECEIVER

1972–1974 ★ 1976

I GREW UP IN SAN JOSE, California. Back in the late 1960s BYU didn't have much of a reputation for football. Although I was LDS, BYU was not really on my radar. It's funny how fate works—some might call it divine intervention. I was headed to the University of California–Berkley. I hadn't signed yet, but recruiting is a lot about relationships, and I really liked my recruiter at Cal. His name was Jim Criner. One day I got a call from Jim. He said, "Jay, I've got news for you. I'm not going to be coaching at Cal. I've decided to take a position as linebackers coach at BYU, and I want you to come with me. I want you to at least go on a visit."

So I ended up going for a visit. I walked on campus and immediately fell in love with the place. It's just a beautiful place, even back then. Jim ended up helping recruit guys like Gary Sheide, Tim Mahoney, and quite a few other players who, in my opinion, were instrumental in turning around BYU football. Gary ended up being a tremendous quarterback. Tim Mahoney was a great fullback, and the program just started to get better.

In the early 1970s they had a California High School all-star game that was Northern California against Southern California. The Northern all-stars practiced at USC. LaVell came to the practices and watched. He really didn't talk to me much, other than to come over and say hi and, "Good luck in the game."

My freshman year in 1972 was the first time freshmen were eligible to play varsity. It was also LaVell's first year as head coach. Part of the draw for me at BYU was they said I would get to play as a freshman. Of course, they were true to their word, although most of the time it was just special teams. I have no regrets. Playing at BYU was a great, great experience.

We had a really good team my freshman year. Pete Van Valkenburg led the nation in rushing that year. We played at Long Beach State in the fourth game of the year, and I got permission to stay in California and hang out with my friends that weekend in San Diego. When I got back to Provo, I went into LaVell's office and said, "I'm just not happy here. I'm homesick. I want to transfer to San Diego State and be closer to home."

He settled me down and said, "Look, Jay, I really want you to stay. You're going to be our first consensus All-American before you leave here." He said, "You've got the future ahead of you. BYU is a great school, and we need you." Then he said, "Do this for me. Finish out the semester. If you still want to leave, I will personally call the coach at San Diego State, and we will get you a scholarship there."

As I was getting ready to leave, he said, "By the way, why don't you come up to my house on Monday night and watch *Monday Night Football* with me and my kids." I said, "Okay." So I went up to his house, and his boys were young, maybe eight and 10, and they instantly made me feel like family. LaVell isn't one of the greatest coaches of all time by not being a smart man. He knew I was missing my family, so he made me feel like part of his family.

I would go up there pretty much every Monday night, play games with Jimmy, watch *Monday Night Football*, and then go home. Eventually, I got over my homesickness and decided to stay. That's one of my favorite recollections of LaVell. It changed everything for me. I was only 17 years old, but I was able to grow up a little bit in that short amount of time.

About four games into the 1973 season, we played Iowa State. I caught 12 balls in that game and, if I'm not mistaken, became the nation's leading pass receiver. We should have won that game. On the last drive I scored a touchdown that got called back on a holding call, and then we missed a field goal to win the game as time was running out.

A couple games later we played New Mexico at home, and it snowed the night before. I was wondering what kind of condition the field was going to be in, but when they took the tarp off, the footing wasn't too bad. I remember there was snow stacked up at the back of the end zones. Everything just came together that day—it seems like yesterday. Gary was totally on, and we were connecting. We won by a landslide, 56–21. It wasn't close. I was having

On November 3, 1973, Jay Miller (88) caught 22 passes for 263 yards against the University of New Mexico and was carried off the field by his teammates. Nearly 40 years later, both are still BYU records.

fun catching the ball, which I loved to do, and it just turned out that it added up to a lot of catches.

I had about 10 catches at halftime, and it was still a game. I think when I got to about 17, the team was aware I was closing in on the NCAA record. Our offensive coordinator, Dewey Warren—they called him "the Swamp Rat"—said, "Let's get Jay that record! What is the record?" Someone said, "I think it's 20." So I got to 20. Then Dewey said, "Are you sure?" No one was sure. So a couple more quick outs later, I had 22 catches. A few years ago when the record was broken, some friends of mine told me, "That's not right. At the end of the game they just kept throwing him the ball to beat your record!" But that's what they did to me, too, so that's just part of the deal. Because of injuries I was never able to play in the NFL, so it's been nice to have that BYU record as an accomplishment.

The other game that I remember most was against Arizona State. They were an unbelievable team with Danny White at quarterback. I think they ended up in the top 10 in the nation that year. When we went down there to play in their stadium, the first thing I remember is that it was a dirt field painted green. It was the regional game of the week on television. Even though we'd get revenge the next year and win the conference for the first time, we were totally outmanned that day. I'm telling you, it was like men among boys. I remember I got to line up against Mike Haynes, who is in the NFL Hall of Fame now. It was a great experience for me to line up against that caliber of a player and hold my own. If I remember right, I think I caught 14 balls and had a touchdown.

I think those are a couple of my favorite playing memories at BYU because, as you know, my career was pretty short-lived. I played that year as an 18-year-old sophomore and then tore my knee up the next year. I came back and made the team my senior year, but I didn't play. After two operations, I just didn't have it anymore. So those memories of 1973, which was really my only real playing year, will stick with me forever.

On game days, I remember getting butterflies after the pregame meal. Believe it or not, some guys would actually get physically ill before games. I never did that, but a lot of them did because the nerves would be there. Larry Carr, who was an all-conference linebacker, would get physically sick before every game, he was so keyed up. I was just anxious to get out on the field and play. I couldn't wait to get out there. The fans were always great, although we didn't have the fan base they have now, as LaVell was just starting out and we were building the program. When you're a kid that age, you just don't understand how fleeting those moments are. You think you're going to play forever. It's there, and then before you know it, you're done with college. Sometimes I wish I could tell the current players, "Hey, this is the time of your life. Go out and have fun. Play your heart out. Appreciate every second on that field, because you're not going to have many more opportunities to do that."

After college I went into coaching for a couple of years and then got out for personal and family reasons. I always admired LaVell and have tried to be like him in my profession. One thing I learned from LaVell was to always be totally honest. Be honest with yourself. In sales it can be easy to leave out truths, but he was always up-front and honest, and he expected the same from his players. I also learned to have integrity. I've tried to incorporate those things in my own professional career.

Fred Whittingham, Kyle's dad, was someone else I always admired. Fred had a big impact on me because his work ethic was incredible. He put in the time. He was also direct and honest with everyone. Everybody on the team totally respected him.

I was lucky to be a part of a key group of guys who helped get the program going. Guys like Keith Rivera, Paul Linford, Gary Sheide—they were critical in making it happen. It was the beginning of LaVell's dynasty. There's a lot of pride involved in being a former player. Whenever I watch BYU play, I remember what it feels like, what they're going through, what it's like to step on that field, the cheers, the people coming to watch you play as a team—those are things you never forget. It's not just about football, either. I'm the biggest Jimmer Fredette fan in the country. I like to watch him play. I love anything BYU.

In 1973 Jay Miller led the nation in receiving with 100 receptions for 1,181 yards and eight touchdowns. He was named first-team All-WAC and first-team All-America. He still holds the BYU record for most receptions (22) and receiving yards (263) in a game, which he set against the University of New Mexico on November 3, 1973.

LANCE REYNOLDS

OFFENSIVE LINE

1972–1973 ★ 1976–1977

COACH

1983–Present

I WAS IN NINTH GRADE when I started playing tackle football. I was a pretty big kid at that age, so I played on the offensive and defensive lines. I had no idea what I was doing. I remember we were a few practices into the season, and they said, "Okay, Reynolds, go to left tackle," and I stood there because I didn't know where left tackle was. I had no idea what a center, guard, or tackle was. I was clueless.

I went to Granite High School. It was a huge high school when I went there. I played quite a bit of running back and offensive line, as well as nose tackle on defense. A lot of guys from Granite went to BYU—Golden Richards, Doug Richards, Paul Linford, and the other Linford brothers.

In those days, you would sign a conference letter of intent, and then a few weeks later you would sign a national letter of intent. Being from Salt Lake City, I actually went to a lot of Utah football games as a kid. My dad got tickets through work. I thought I might go to Utah, but then LaVell Edwards started recruiting me, and that influenced me. I ended up signing a conference letter with BYU, which meant I couldn't go to any other WAC school.

Then Cal got heavily involved in recruiting me and did a really nice job. I actually signed a national letter of intent to go to Cal. My mom had signed it, too. It was sitting on the desk in our house when my dad got home from his Church meetings. When he saw it, he said, "Oh, you can't do that."

I don't know this for sure, but I think my dad went in and called LaVell because Coach Edwards called me about 15 minutes later. He said, "Hey, don't do anything right now. Wait until I come up to see you tomorrow. We'll go out to dinner and talk."

So LaVell came up to the house and hung out with the family. I don't think he was going to leave until I decided I was going to BYU. When he finally got ready to go, I said, "Hey, what about dinner?" So we went outside and jumped in his Volkswagen. He drove us to the McDonalds by the Cottonwood Mall and said, "Order whatever you want."

I'd been to Cal, and they had fed me prime rib and drove me around in a Porsche, and here I am in LaVell's Volkswagen, headed to McDonald's. "Order whatever you want," he said. I still give him grief about that.

I finally decided to go to BYU for two reasons. I felt confidence in LaVell, I could trust him. The other guys recruiting me were flashy recruiters—gold chain kind of guys. I just felt a trust with LaVell. The other reason was the chance to play closer to home.

75

When I arrived at BYU in 1972, it was the first year that freshmen could play varsity. Usually freshmen would play JV and then redshirt the second year. During two-a-days I got a note on my door that I was supposed to go to varsity practice the next day. I was nervous. I showed up to practice the following day, and I ended up being heavily involved with the varsity team as a freshman.

I was actually recruited to play nose guard, but then they moved me to the offensive line, and I was traveling and playing. I was excited about it. I played as a freshman and the next year as a sophomore. All the time I was trying to decide if I should serve a mission. At that point very few scholarship guys went on missions, so the choice was sort of hanging over my head. It was a big decision for me.

It wasn't easy in those days. There were people saying, "You ought to just serve your mission by playing football and being a good example." Other people were saying, "You ought to go. It's the right thing to do." I think the influences of being at BYU, along with equipment manager Floyd Johnson, my home bishop, and my family, helped me make the decision to go.

Lance Reynolds played four seasons at offensive tackle for the Cougars. He has been an integral part of the BYU coaching staff since 1983.

Shortly after I left on a Church mission, there were six or seven guys out in my class who decided to serve. It really turned the whole attitude around about serving a mission. I don't know if it was the kind of kids we were recruiting or LaVell's acceptance of the missionary program. It was proba- bly some of both. I think LaVell had to make the decision he was going to support it, which hadn't been done before. I don't think it's a hard decision today. Things have really evolved. Now we have more than half our team, around 70-something players, who are returned missionaries.

I served my mission in Seattle, Washington. I was working in north Seattle just a few blocks from where Marc Wilson lived. He was still in high school. We would play basketball against each other on P-days, the missionary preparation day we had each week. I told him about my experiences at BYU, and we became close friends. I was really glad when he chose to attend BYU.

When I came off my mission, he was already in school. It was nice to be able to play offensive line for him. Obviously, he had a great career at BYU. That was a really unique deal being in Seattle while he was trying to make the decision where to go to college. We had a great relationship then and still do now.

When I came home it was tough on me the first spring back. I got home just before spring football and jumped right into camp. My body just wasn't ready. I'd never had trouble before, but it was tough physically and mentally. There were days when it snowed and we didn't practice. I was so thankful just to have a day to recover.

Back in those days people would say, "If you go on a mission, you won't be as tough when you get back," or, "You'll lose your killer instinct." I think all of us who returned and played right away eliminated the perceptions that you couldn't serve a mission and be a successful football player when you returned.

When I went into the mission field, the program was starting to have success. We were winning games, but it was a battle. Two years later, when I returned, I could see a huge difference. Philosophically and schematically, the program was a mile ahead in just two years. LaVell had made a complete commitment to the pass, and they had worked out a lot of the schemes and details of pass protection.

It wasn't the same feel, or the same look, or the same skill level. There were better athletes and more depth. Everything had dramatically improved between 1974 and early 1976.

My last two years were so much fun. Before my mission we were working so hard and earning every inch. Then, when I returned, we were throwing the ball around and had better athletes, and all of a sudden everything got easier. We were still working as hard, but we were much more productive.

BYU was one of the first teams to really commit to throwing the football. Defensively, that was an issue for some of the teams we played, just trying to figure out how to defend us. We went 9–2 in the regular season in 1976 and 1977 and won back-to-back conference championships. Those years really put BYU on the map and started a string of 10 straight conference titles. It also proved that guys could go on a church mission, come home, and be successful football players. My guess is we had maybe 10 to 12 guys on those teams who had served. At that point people thought it couldn't be done.

There have definitely been some memorable moments during my time at BYU. I remember going into the locker room after the Holiday Bowl victory in 1984. We still weren't sure if we would be named national champions, but guys were celebrating, spraying soda pop around and pouring it on each other's heads.

Because I knew the history of the program and what had transpired before to get to that point, I thought about all the people who had sacrificed and worked so hard, who had given the program their all for years just to get us to that point—former coaches, administrators, players. We stood on the shoulders of all the great players and teams that established the tradition that enabled us to get to that point.

To those of us who have been Cougars, the school and the football program digs deep into our hearts and has a special place there. BYU is part of who I am. I played here, I've been a coach here for a long time, and recently I've been able to watch my boys play here. That's a sweet deal. Actually, *sweet* doesn't even describe it. It's been an absolutely euphoric ride for my family and me. BYU is part of our family. We bleed blue.

What makes BYU great isn't the fantastic facilities or the great football or the outstanding education or even the spiritual development. Sure, all of that is important, and we have that here. To me, the real difference is the type of people who are at BYU—players, coaches, administrators, and teachers. It's about the opportunity to be around great people—guys like Floyd Johnson. I can't say enough admirable things about Brother J. He left a legacy. We are surrounded by great people at BYU.

To me, being a Cougar means we should conduct our lives in a first-class manner. This should be a different place, because we follow the example of the Savior. We should act differently. We should try to be a little better every day. It doesn't mean we are going to be perfect, or that things aren't going to go wrong. We are human beings, and people are going to make mistakes.

That's life. But I love that I'm around people who are trying to do what's right and trying to be good—people like the Floyd Johnsons of the world.

Win or lose, I would rather be here at BYU than anywhere else. I love to be around our players. They are the right kind of guys. They work hard and try to do what's right. Just look at the 2010 season. We were in a difficult situation, facing an uphill battle. A lot of teams would have folded, quit. What's special about being a Cougar? Our players tightened their chinstraps and kept going. It wasn't pretty at times, but they found a way out of it. They found a way to finish strong and win.

BYU is a special place with great tradition and great people. There is no place like BYU.

Lance Reynolds played four seasons as an offensive tackle at BYU from 1972 to 1973 and 1976 to 1977. As a senior, he was named first-team All-WAC and Academic All-Conference. Reynolds also received All-America honorable mention in 1977. The Pittsburgh Steelers selected him in the ninth round of the 1978 NFL Draft. Reynolds has been on the BYU coaching staff since 1983.

GARY SHEIDE

QUARTERBACK

1973–1974

I DIDN'T KNOW ANYTHING about BYU when they started recruiting me out of high school in Antioch, California. I was not a member of the LDS Church. Coach Edwards came to my high school and told me they were really interested in signing me. I said, "What school are you from, Coach?" He said, "I'm from Brigham Young University."

I told him, "I'll be honest with you, Coach. I've never heard of that university. I don't want to waste your time, because I don't have an interest in going there." I thanked him for coming to see me, and I thought that was probably it. BYU would contact me every now and then and say, "We're still interested."

At the time I was being recruited to play football by at least one school in every major conference in the country. I had a couple of good basketball and baseball offers, as well. I pretty much had my choice of what sport I wanted to play in college. I really wanted to play baseball. That was my first love. I had a chance to sign a minor league contract and maybe start in Class A, but my coach, Babe Atkinson, suggested that I go to a junior college and improve my draft stock.

So that's what I decided to do. I turned down a bunch of Division I scholarships to attend Diablo Junior College. The goal was to improve my baseball skills and hopefully my stock for the draft. I enrolled at Diablo Junior College in the fall of 1971. I was not planning to play football, but two weeks

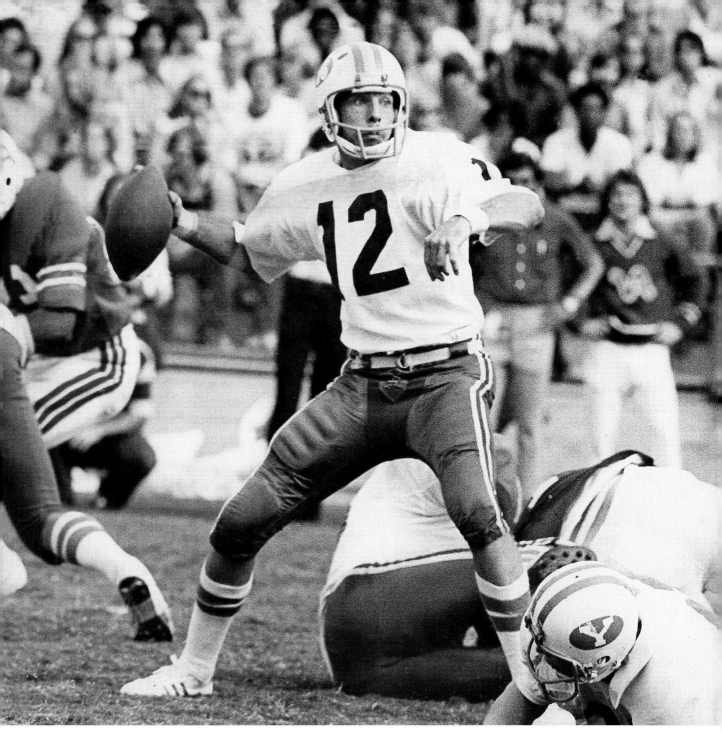

As a senior in 1974, Gary Sheide led BYU to a WAC Championship and its first bowl appearance in school history. He also won the Sammy Baugh Trophy as the nation's top passer.

before the season started, both of the quarterbacks got hurt. One of the coaches at Diablo was a former coach at my high school. He came to me and said, "We need you to come play quarterback. You can still play baseball next semester, but come play for us in the fall."

I told him I didn't think so, but I would think about it. The next day he brought the whole team over to my house. There were like 60 to 70 guys at my house asking me to come play. I knew they really wanted me, so I told them I would consider it if they would agree to certain things. First, I told him we had to throw the ball at least 50 percent of the time. He said, "We're a throwing team. That's what we do." Then I told him I'd work on the sprints with the quarterbacks in practice, but I didn't want to run the mile runs. He said, "Fine, you can work on your drops and footwork during that time."

Finally, I said, "In practice when we're running drills, I don't want to get hit. It doesn't make sense to take a chance on getting hurt in drills." He said, "Agreed. You'll wear a red jersey, and you won't get hit." So I agreed to play.

We started out hot and were undefeated after three or four games. We were the No. 1–ranked junior college in the nation. Then in the next game I ended up breaking the navicular bone in my right wrist. The bone takes six months to heal in a cast. So I missed the rest of the football season and also my freshman year of baseball.

The next fall I decided to play football again. We got off to another great start, and then I got hurt again. This time I broke the radius bone in my right wrist. Once again I was done for the season. At the time, a lot of schools were still recruiting me. One of them was BYU. Right after I got hurt, I received a call from LaVell Edwards wanting to know if he could come see me.

I said, "Sure." So LaVell made a visit to my house. My mom just fell in love with Coach Edwards. He was just the nicest guy—very polite. He did a good job pitching BYU. After he left, my mom said, "Gary, I really like that man. There's something about him. I think you need to go check out the school."

I ended up taking a recruiting trip just a couple of days later. It was during the football season, so I was able to attend a game. They brought me down on the sideline, and I got to watch the game and meet some of the people. It was an atmosphere that I had never really been around before. Everybody was so nice. The girls were absolutely beautiful and well dressed. Then there were the mountains and the fishing.

I just couldn't believe it. It was a great trip. I also liked the competition that I saw and thought to myself, *I could really do well at a college like this.*

When I got home, I told my mom, "That's the neatest school I've ever seen. I think I want to go there." She said, "I really liked that Coach Edwards. I hope you do." My mom had a great influence in my life. So that's how I ended up coming to BYU.

When I was on my recruiting trip, Coach Edwards told me he believed that BYU would need to throw the football on a consistent basis to be competitive. He said he was looking for the right quarterback to run the offense he had in mind. I told him, "Coach, I want to believe you, but you have the leading rusher in the nation right now in Pete Van Valkenburg. You're really planning to throw the football?"

He said, "Gary, I guarantee you we are going to throw the football." Well, that was good enough for me. If LaVell said we were going to throw the ball, then so be it. I just really liked Coach Edwards. It was obvious he was a guy you could trust.

I came to BYU in 1973. LaVell also brought in a new quarterbacks coach named Dewey Warren from Tennessee. He had a very creative offensive mind and a grasp of throwing the football. They called him "the Swamp Rat." He used to tell me in his southern drawl, "Hot dog, Sheide, step and throw. Just step and throw!" I had a strong arm, but my footwork wasn't very good, so he would always be telling me, "Step and throw." I heard him say "step and throw" thousands of times.

We would talk all the time about schemes and how we were going to take advantage of defenses. Dewey really knew the passing game. Our plan was pretty simple. We took advantage of every situation the defense gave us. No one knew how to stop our passing attack.

We would run guys in motion to give us a pre-snap look of the coverage. We'd run two running backs into pass routes, or run them on delays and crossing patterns. We used all kinds of outs and flares and sprint-outs. It was not uncommon for our running backs to be our leading receivers. Some of the stuff BYU runs today, we were doing 35 years ago.

Right before the start of the 1973 season, I got injured. I could hardly walk. I missed the first game of the year. By the second game against Oregon State, it was starting to feel better. I got in during the second half of that game, and my first college pass was a 68-yard touchdown to Sam Lobue.

BYU was a unique place. It was such a different atmosphere than I had ever been around. I had a lot of offers to attend other schools. There is no question in my mind that I was meant to come to BYU. Football brought me to BYU and changed my life for the better. My brother Greg ended up coming out to Utah, and we both ended up joining the Church at the same time.

BYU is also where I met my wife. So the university not only changed my life from a religious standpoint but also from a family standpoint. I found the best girl in the world, and we've been extremely happy for a long time.

I was also fortunate to play for LaVell Edwards. He was honest and fair. He became a real father figure to me and a lot of players through the years. A few years ago we had an event with LaVell in California. Each guy who got up to speak talked about LaVell being a father figure. At the end, LaVell got up and said, "You know, that's nice of you guys to refer to me as a father figure, but I sure hope you treated your real fathers better than you treated me." How funny is that? That is so LaVell. He was so witty and just a good people person.

When I came to BYU, LaVell had just taken over the football program and was starting to change the attitude. BYU didn't have a long tradition of winning back then. We began throwing the ball a lot and started to win. He was an innovator. People were getting excited about football at BYU. It's fun to look back and say, "Hey, I was a part of it." We started a tradition that has grown to be something special.

I remember the game against Colorado State my senior year. We led 33–27 with only six seconds left in the game. They had no timeouts. All we had to do was snap the ball and the game was over. When the ball got snapped, it never touched my hands, so I went down on the ground looking for it and couldn't find it. CSU ended up recovering the ball. They had time for one play, and a guy named Willie Miller ran a post-corner for a touchdown.

Their crowd and team went crazy. They came onto the field and ended up getting an excessive celebration penalty that moved them back for the extra point. Fortunately, their kicker missed the PAT, and the game ended in a 33–33 tie. We were 0–3–1 on the season.

I think it was Monday after our team meeting, all the coaches left and the players stayed. The captains got up and spoke. I think Larry Carr and maybe Brad Oates got up, and some of the other leaders on the team. We basically said, "This is not acceptable. We're not playing up to our abilities." Everyone committed to give his best effort.

We had only played one conference game, and we all committed in that meeting to play together as a team and try to win a championship for the seniors. After that, we became a team. The whole team demeanor changed. We were rooting for each other on the sideline.

My favorite memory that year was beating Arizona State. Once we beat them, we knew we had a great opportunity to win the conference title. A couple games before that, we had defeated Arizona. It was probably my best moment as a Cougar. They were favored to beat us, and we came out and just dominated them. I had five touchdown passes and was named ABC Player of the Week. The best part was we had defeated a nationally ranked team. Beating Arizona and Arizona State were certainly two of the highlights of my career.

I'm proud of the quarterback tradition at BYU. It's a great legacy. A lot is expected of the guy who steps into those shoes. It's a fraternity like no other in the country. Winning the Sammy Baugh Trophy after my senior year was a real honor for me. I went to Ohio for the ceremony. We had no idea who would win until about 15 minutes before the announcement. One of the staff came up to me and told me I had won. He said, "Congratulations on what you accomplished this year."

I had separated my shoulder in the bowl game, and my arm was still in a sling. I hadn't really planned an acceptance speech, so when I got up to the podium, I didn't know what to say. I said, "Boy, this must have been a tough year for quarterbacks if the winner had to come up here and accept the award in a sling."

It was a great honor. At the time, it was the top college quarterback award, presented to the passer of the year. Several other BYU guys have won the award since, and I think it's a reflection on the program and the standard of quarterback excellence.

Gary Sheide played two seasons at quarterback for BYU in 1973 and 1974 after transferring from Diablo Junior College. As a senior, he led the Cougars to a WAC championship and their first bowl appearance in school history. Sheide won the 1974 Sammy Baugh Trophy as the nation's top passer. He was also named WAC Offensive Player of the Year and UPI Most Valuable Player for the WAC. Sheide was selected in the third round of the 1975 NFL Draft by the Cincinnati Bengals.

GIFFORD NIELSEN

Quarterback

1973–1977

I ACTUALLY CAME TO BYU as a basketball player and a football player, so I went from playing freshman football to playing varsity basketball. I got quite a few minutes of playing time my freshman year. Then right after basketball, I jumped into spring football. It was a challenging situation.

The following year was that magical 1974 season where Gary Sheide and Jay Miller were playing so well. I redshirted that year and was the scout team quarterback. I can remember practicing against that great defensive line of Paul Linford, Wayne Baker, Stan Varner, and Keith Rivera. Larry Carr was the middle linebacker. That team really started to show that BYU had the potential to have an excellent football program. Of course, that team went on to play in BYU's first bowl game in the 1974 Fiesta Bowl.

When football was over that season, I jumped right back into basketball. In fact, while I was playing basketball, the football team went to the bowl game. After my sophomore basketball season, they made a coaching change, and BYU hired Frank Arnold. Frank and LaVell got together and determined—I think Frank was pushing it—that I needed to decide if I was a football player or a basketball player. At that time, with Sheide graduating, LaVell told me, "Hey, we need a quarterback. Come play football."

So I put a lot of thought, effort, and prayer into that decision. I knew I could play college basketball; I wasn't sure I could play college football. In the end, I said to myself, *I'm going to go play football for LaVell Edwards*. It was an unusual decision because basketball was always my first love.

The next year I was competing for the starting quarterback position with Mark Giles, who ran the option very well—he was a tough, tough player, and Jeff Duva, who was a talented quarterback out of California. During fall camp I just didn't play very well. Consequently, I was the backup quarterback when we started the season.

The third game of the season, we were playing at Arizona State. They had a great football team. We were struggling offensively, so LaVell put me in. I think I completed 4 of 11 passes and eventually got knocked out of the game. When we went to practice on Monday, I had actually been moved down to the third-string quarterback position. I was just devastated. A lot of my friends said, "Hey, listen, go back and play basketball. Forget football. You're not very good."

I can remember a conversation I had with my dad. He told me, "Be the first one out to practice and be the last one off the field. Just keep working."

I wondered if I'd ever get a chance to play again. Then, the following week, we played New Mexico at Cougar Stadium. We were losing by a couple of touchdowns late in the third quarter, and LaVell looked at me and said, "Let's see what you can do." It was my first time to play in front of the home fans. I was from Provo High School, right across the street from BYU. I was the hometown kid. It was a magical night. It was one of those experiences that you dream about—as close to a football fairy tale as you could possibly imagine.

I didn't have a lot of confidence, but I hit the first pass over the middle to Jeff Nilsson. The second play I ended up running around the right side for six yards. The third play they came after me, and I flipped a little screen pass to Dave Lowry, and he ran for a 37-yard touchdown. The place started to wake up. The stadium started to get excited, and our defense went out there and held them.

We got the ball back and started marching down the field. At about the 30-yard line, our tailback, Jeff Blanc, came in the huddle and said, "Look, if you'll roll out and then throw back, I'm all by myself." So the play came in, and I remember saying, "What the heck!" I changed the play, rolled out to my left, and then turned around and looked back to my right and there was Blanc all alone going down the sideline. I threw one of the easiest touchdown passes I've ever thrown. All of a sudden, we were right back in the game.

Nicknamed the "Mormon Rifle," Gifford Nielsen was a first-team All-America quarterback for BYU in 1976. He went on to win the prestigious NCAA Top 5 Award as a senior and later became the first Cougar to be inducted into the College Football Hall of Fame in 1994.

Our defense held again, we marched down the field, and Dave Taylor kicked a field goal to win the game.

It was an amazing comeback. It was just magical. The place was going crazy. I was not as excited as I was actually marveling in the process. I knew that for some reason I needed to go through what I went through in order to do what I did. I knew I had made the right decision to play football.

Sunday night I rode with LaVell to Salt Lake to be on his coach's show. On the ride up he told me, "You know, most of the coaches don't think we should start you next week against Air Force." But he said, "I'm going to start you, anyway. Just keep playing within yourself." Right there was the beginning of a relationship of trust and mutual respect between LaVell and me. The following Saturday we beat Air Force 28–14 in our homecoming game, and we were off and running. That's how my career began at BYU.

LaVell made the decision we were going to do something different. We were going to change the face of college football. We were going to be committed to throwing the ball at BYU. It was the brilliance of LaVell. Nobody in college football was really committed to the pass. LaVell was. He saw Virgil Carter win with it while he was an assistant coach. Then, Sheide got a connection going with Jay Miller—who was just an outstanding receiver—and that was it. We started to throw the ball all over the place.

In 1976 it really got cranked up when Doug Scovil came to BYU. Doug had coached Roger Staubach when he won the Heisman Trophy at Navy. Scovil was an offensive genius. LaVell somehow convinced him to come to BYU. I'll never forget the first time I met Doug. He looked at me and said, "You must be the great Giffer." I said, "The great Giffer?" He said, "I am here to light up the scoreboard. Let's go!" That was my first introduction to Doug Scovil.

So we got started, and he worked with me, and he worked with me, and he worked with me. He would always tell me, "You know what? They've got 11 guys over on the other side of the ball, and whatever they do, they're wrong."

That's how he approached it: "Whatever they do, they are wrong." The only way we were going to lose is if we were not disciplined in our reads, or got overpowered by some big-time program. So just as Doug predicted, we started to light up the scoreboard. It was a process, but we had fun and did some miraculous things.

When Doug arrived at BYU, he didn't know a whole lot about the LDS Church. He had a hard time trying to get a grasp of everything, but you could tell that he loved what he was doing. We spent a lot of time together, and he asked me all kinds of questions about the Church and about what we believed. During one of those conversations, I ended up telling him about food storage.

I remember his first year—my junior year—the very first day of practice he was talking to the quarterbacks and wide receivers. "Okay, boys," he said,

89

"we are going to start putting in the offense." So he goes to the chalkboard, and starts writing. "We're going to put in the entire offense in two weeks, and it's just going to be repetition, repetition, repetition. We are just going to get good at it. It's a lot like food storage."

We said, "What? Food Storage?" He said, "Just hang with me. We're going to put our year's supply of offense up here." He wrote offense in the left hand corner of the chalkboard. "Here's our year's supply," he said, and then he started to put play after play on the board. Then he told us, "During the season, we're just going to use a little of our food storage each week. So, as we put together these game plans, we'll just pick a little something out of our food storage and only use that." We all just cracked up. He was funny like that. Doug was going to figure a way to get into our world, and that's how he did it.

Without question, LaVell Edwards changed the course of college football. He had Sheide and then he brought in Doug, who coached Marc Wilson and me. Doug left for a year, but LaVell hired him back, and he coached Jim McMahon. When Doug left for good, I thought, *Oh, no. It's over*. But then LaVell had Steve Young. Then Robbie Bosco, who won a national championship. When Robbie left, I thought, *Oh no*. Then he had Ty, who won the Heisman Trophy. Every time I thought, *Well, we're in trouble now*, it just got better.

As I look back, the most important things I learned at BYU were trust and responsibility. I learned to trust myself, trust the system, trust my teammates, trust the university, and trust everything that was going on around me. That principle was continually taught by LaVell in the way he trusted me. That was LaVell Edwards. He came in and trusted his instincts, trusted the system, trusted his coaches, and trusted his players. That's what I was taught at BYU. Everything about that just encompasses and encapsulates the entire experience at BYU.

Then there's responsibility. At BYU you're responsible in all parts of your life. Not just on the football field and not just in the classroom, but with everything you do. You are taught to take care of your responsibilities, and as your responsibilities increase, you adapt. You just learn that. What could be better as you leave campus life and go into the world?

It means the world to me to be a BYU Cougar. I spent the first 22 years of my life within a five-mile radius of that football stadium. To watch the

my career at BYU progressed, I started to run the ball a little bit more, and when they realized I could catch the ball, the position really evolved to where I was a pass catcher. In fact, I think in my junior year I actually led the conference in receptions, which seems strange for a fullback. Then the next year I averaged, I think, close to 12 yards a catch on 50 catches.

During that period of time, BYU had some outstanding offensive coordinators. Doug Scovil in particular was just a whiz in terms of maximizing what he had to work with. Certainly guys like Gifford Nielsen and Marc Wilson were the beneficiaries of his expertise. I remember practices where he would say, "You know, about two o'clock this morning I was sitting there with my pencil and pad…" Back then, people weren't doing the 24/7 football thing, but Doug really lived, ate, and breathed football. He wasn't one of those guys who was passive about it. He saw the big picture. He maximized what he had to work with.

Even though he was a tough guy and not altogether friendly to be around, he understood offensive football, and he understood what he had to work with, so he never made the players adapt to a system. He adapted the system to what he had to work with. In the case of Gifford Nielsen, here was a guy who was a drop-back passer, very accurate. Then Marc Wilson came in when Nielsen hurt his knee, and suddenly we're rolling out and doing some things differently in the middle of the season because Doug was able to adjust and adapt to what he had to work with. I have nothing but respect and good things to say about Doug Scovil.

I'm really proud of the fact that our group came to BYU in 1974, and by the time we left in 1977, football was a big deal in Provo. The crowds were coming, offensive records were being broken. I like to think that my group, John VanDerWouden, Roger Gourley, Mekeli Ieremia, Keith Uperesa, and a number of other great players, helped make football relevant in Provo. Better recruiting, better facilities, expansion of the stadium, all of those things that now say Brigham Young football—they didn't exist when we started, so I think that we have reason to be proud that we contributed to the program the way we did.

As much as I enjoyed my experience as a player at BYU, I actually enjoyed being a student more. Not only did BYU educate me in terms of life, but the professors I encountered were people of integrity and dignity who wanted to do the right thing for the students. My older brother was a tremendous influence, as well. He got back from his mission in Brazil, and we lived together. He was a brilliant student. He didn't allow me to fall into the "living with three football players in the apartment" kind of thing. I was very fortunate to be part of an institution like BYU and associate with people of the highest caliber.

I also learned fairly well to be a spear-carrier, that it wasn't always about the star. That was something I learned at BYU. The quarterback was always featured when I was at BYU. I realize that there were an awful lot of people behind the scenes who were working hard, who were playing some tremendous football, but who won't get the same amount of credit. Harold B. Lee, the former prophet, made famous this statement: "There's no limit to the amount of work we can do if no one cares who gets the credit." I was around a lot of people at BYU who genuinely lived that maxim.

I owe a debt to the university and the community. My wife and our four sons also attended BYU. The university created a work ethic for me. I have always tried to operate by the belief that men are made or broken in their idle hours. I was encouraged to do things on my own and to be a self-starter. I think that's a big, big deal. Whether it is studying in class or working out, it's what you do on your own that's going to set you apart. You have the group dynamic, and that's a good thing, but it's the preparation on your own, when nobody is watching, that's going to set you apart.

Todd Christensen led BYU in receiving for three straight years, from 1975 to 1977. As a senior in 1977 he was named first-team All-WAC fullback and also honorable mention All-America by the Associated Press. Christensen was selected in the second round of the 1978 NFL Draft by the Dallas Cowboys. He played 10 seasons in the NFL with the New York Giants and the Oakland/Los Angeles Raiders. Christensen won two Super Bowls with the Raiders and was selected to play in the Pro Bowl five times. He was inducted into the BYU Athletic Hall of Fame in 1992.

MARC WILSON

QUARTERBACK

1975–1979

I ACTUALLY CAME TO BYU to play both football and baseball. At least that was the plan. I was a much better baseball player in high school. I loved to hit, run the bases, and throw. I really liked everything about baseball. In high school my main position was pitcher, so the coach used me in the outfield the other games to rest and protect my arm.

When I started to get recruited for college, some teams really wanted me as a baseball player. But I was getting a lot of attention from recruiters to play football, as well. Some of the baseball coaches wanted me so badly that they put pressure on the football coach to recruit me. It became humorous. Eventually, it came down to BYU and the University of Oregon.

I grew up in the LDS Church, but I didn't know anything about BYU. We were a semi-active family, and I really didn't learn anything about BYU until my junior year in high school. It sounds funny, but it's the truth.

There were two missionaries serving in our ward in the Seattle area, and we would get together with them on their P-day and play basketball at the church. One of those missionaries was Lance Reynolds. He, of course, was a football player from BYU. It's not like he was trying to recruit me—we just became good friends, and he would talk about BYU. I had received some recruiting letters from BYU, but I hadn't paid much attention to them. After meeting Lance, I started to pay more attention.

Gary Sheide was the BYU quarterback at the time, and he was so great. I loved what BYU was doing with the passing game. There were a lot of option and wishbone teams at that time, and I clearly was not one of those guys. The thought of throwing 30 to 35 times a game was appealing to me. Eventually, Dave Kragthorpe and LaVell Edwards came to Washington to meet my family. I liked Dave, and of course I loved LaVell, but I really think it was probably Lance Reynolds who was most instrumental in my coming to BYU.

My first year at BYU, I played on the freshman team and dressed for one varsity game. I had a lot to learn about playing quarterback. I had never really learned the position in high school. At BYU there were a lot of guys who played the quarterback position well. So I loved going to practice. I loved going to meetings and watching film. I loved seeing how we planned to take advantage of certain defenses. I loved the mental aspect of the game. It was all brand-new and fresh. It was so exciting.

Doug Scovil, our offensive coordinator, was the orchestrator of all that. I can't say enough about Doug Scovil. He was without doubt the greatest coach I ever had in any sport at any level.

In the spring of 1976 I played on the junior varsity baseball team as a freshman. That fall, as a sophomore, I redshirted in football. The understanding was that as soon as January rolled around, I would join the baseball team for the 1977 season. I was the prep team quarterback that fall, and even though we were running the other team's offense, we gave our defense everything they wanted. There were many days where we got the best of our starting defense because we approached every practice like it was Saturday. What it did was galvanize our group of guys. That became important later on as we progressed to the varsity level.

At Christmastime I talked to my dad and determined that I wanted to concentrate on football, so I didn't play baseball anymore at BYU. During the summer of 1977 I worked out really hard. My goal was to make the varsity team. We had a wide receiver named Kent Tingey who lived near my home in Seattle. We got together almost every night, and I would throw to him. That fall I was the backup quarterback behind Gifford Nelson. Watching him play was just amazing. He was a wizard. He knew the offense so well, and we were scoring a ton of points. I was having a lot of fun playing the fourth quarters because we were so far ahead.

Then we went to Oregon State in the fourth game of the year, and Gifford got hurt. He was gone for the year. At the time he was leading the nation

As a senior in 1979, Marc Wilson was a consensus All-America quarterback and a recipient of the NCAA Top 5 Award. He went on to play 10 seasons in the NFL and won two Super Bowls with the Raiders. Wilson was inducted into the College Football Hall of Fame in 1996.

in passing and total offense. I think he was the leading candidate for the Heisman Trophy. What a devastating loss. I think most people would think that I would be excited for the opportunity to play. In fact, it was just the opposite. I was scared to death. I'm telling you there were a lot of nights that week I spent lying in bed wondering if I could do it. We had a great team and a great season going, and I was worried I was going to let everybody down.

Doug Scovil called me into his office on Tuesday that week. He put the playbook in front of me and said, "Marc, Gifford was a great quarterback, and I think you're going to be a great quarterback. In all truthfulness, you're not Gifford—but Gifford's not you, either. I want you to go through this playbook and put sticky tabs on every play that you like and feel good about running."

So that's what I did.

The next day I took the playbook back to Doug; he looked through it and said, "What's the deal with all the rollout plays?" I told him I grew up playing football in the street with the neighborhood kids and my brothers. We played two-hand touch. As the quarterback, you had to run around. After the defense counted, "One alligator, two alligator," it was a free-for-all. That's how I learned how to play. I told him, "I'm much more comfortable throwing the football on the run."

As it turned out, the next game was against Colorado State. They had two defensive ends that ended up being No. 1 draft picks in the NFL. Scovil put in a few rollout plays that we had never shown before and that no one would ever expect from a 6'5" quarterback. It worked perfectly. It's what led to those seven touchdown passes that day. It caught CSU completely by surprise and, in retrospect, was the greatest game plan ever devised because no one would have ever expected us to do that.

As I got more comfortable in the pocket, you hardly saw those rollout plays anymore. It took me a while to get there, but I eventually became very comfortable with the whole system. When we executed correctly, no defense could stop us. We just had too many options.

The thing that made Doug Scovil so great was that he was able to put Gifford into situations that let him do what he was good at. Then he had to make the change to my style mid-season, and he was able to do that. Doug did the same thing with Jim McMahon, who was a great quarterback, but we had totally different styles. There are very few guys who have a fertile enough mind to do that or who are willing to adapt because of their ego. Doug was totally different. He never let his ego get in the way. What an incredible thing that is.

One of my favorite moments at BYU occurred when I was a sophomore against the University of Utah. We broke the NCAA single-game passing record with 571 yards. That was a great moment. Then really my whole senior year in 1979 was just one great moment. It's unfortunate we lost the bowl game. I would take that '79 team and play any team in the country from any era. It was such a great team.

I had a lot great moments with LaVell, but my favorite memory doesn't have anything to do with football. Colleen, my wife, was a convert to the

Church. I actually baptized her before we got married. She comes from a big family that was not too excited about her joining the Church.

When it came time to plan our wedding, we decided to get married civilly so all her family could be there and participate. It was a very important decision for us. After we were married for a year, we went to the Salt Lake Temple to be sealed. In the sealing room that day were LaVell and Patti Edwards and a lot of guys on the football team. That's my favorite memory of LaVell. To me, that's BYU. At what other university in the world would that happen? That was LaVell and Patti. That's just how they were.

For me, "What does it mean to be a Cougar?" is too broad a question. I love athletics at BYU. I love the football program. I love when we win, but truthfully it's not the most important thing in the world. I would never want to sacrifice the integrity or reputation of the school for the success of the football program. In that respect, I love what LaVell did, and I love what Bronco Mendenhall is doing. I'm so impressed with him. I also love the guys I played with. I think about them all the time. I think that's part of what it means to be a Cougar. To recognize the guys who suffered and sweated through all the difficult times together and came out the other end having success.

I learned a lot at BYU. One thing I learned, not just by playing football at BYU but by going to school there, is that hard work matters. There are really no shortcuts. LaVell and Doug Scovil taught us that well. We practiced so that we were prepared for anything that might be thrown at us in the game. Consequently, we were successful.

One of the roles of the quarterback is to motivate guys. Everyone leads in his own way. I'm not an in-your-face kind of a guy. I never have been. My attitude is, "Do your job, be an example, and others will follow." In that process I learned that everybody is motivated differently. I've never forgotten that. I kind of approach it that way in everything I do. "How can I best help this particular person?"

Another lesson I learned was it takes everyone working together to be successful. In football the big guys up front matter the most. It doesn't matter how talented the quarterback and receivers are, or how flashy the running backs are. The truth is, if they don't have time to do their jobs, it's not going to matter.

The big linemen do their jobs without fanfare, without much notoriety. They are the backbone of what happens in football. They set the foundation for everything that happens. I played with some great linemen. Without them, we would have never achieved the success we did. In every organization you have people like that, who do things without fanfare and really set the foundation for what happens.

Last, but not least, I learned that chemistry matters. In my experience you cannot win or become the team that you have the potential to be without chemistry, without camaraderie, without a feeling of togetherness on the team.

The genius of LaVell Edwards was he realized that BYU could not win unless we outscored the opponent. We were not going to run everyone over. They were likely going to be bigger than us and probably faster. So he figured out how to score a lot of points.

In those days no one knew how to throw the football very well. What Virgil Carter did at BYU in the 1960s was very unique, because nobody really understood the passing game. That was the genius of LaVell. He was able to get quality coaches to come to Provo, Utah, and develop a passing attack. He let them do their jobs, and for the most part he stayed out of their way.

As great as the quarterbacks have been at BYU, you can pretty much match up all the quarterbacks with a great offensive coordinator. There's something to that. We've had a list of "who's who" All-America quarterbacks at BYU—some of the greatest in NCAA history. But we've also had some of the greatest coordinators ever who developed those guys.

LaVell did it all behind closed doors. He coached the coaches. The coaches all knew what they were doing. When it was time to practice, there wasn't wasted time. Everyone was fully prepared and knew their role. All the work had been done beforehand. When it was time to play the game, it was the same thing. That was LaVell.

Marc Wilson played four seasons at BYU, from 1975 to 1979. He started two and half seasons at quarterback and led the Cougars to three straight conference titles. As a senior in 1979, Wilson was named consensus All-America, was the recipient of the NCAA Top 5 Award, and finished third in the Heisman voting. He finished his BYU career with a 22–4 record as a starter. Wilson was drafted by the Oakland Raiders in the first round (15th overall) of the 1980 NFL Draft. In 10 seasons in the league, he won two Super Bowls with the Raiders. Wilson was inducted into the College Football Hall of Fame in 1996.

The

EIGHTIES

NICK EYRE

OFFENSIVE TACKLE

1977–1980

I T'S AMAZING WHAT YOU can remember 30 years later. A lot of people talk about the 1980 Holiday Bowl. It was an incredible comeback, but we made a lot of mistakes against a very good team. We were lucky. The last few minutes of that game were kind of a blur. They really were.

When the punting unit came on the field, [quarterback] Jim McMahon basically said, "We're not leaving." We all looked at LaVell, thinking, *Okay, what's going to happen now?* McMahon was using some pretty good words. I remember LaVell just kind of said, "Go with it."

You've got to hand it to LaVell for trusting Jim. If we had punted, the game would have been over right there. All of a sudden we were running a play and picked up a first down. Everything just sort of fell into place after that. I see Craig James on TV now, and all I can remember is that guy running down the sideline all game long.

After the game I remember sitting on my helmet on the sideline, and President Holland came walking up to me, all excited. I was about ready to cry because it finally hit me that my BYU career was over. It was probably the greatest time of my life, and it went by too fast. We were all excited about the game, and then all of a sudden the reality sank in that it's over, and I was thinking, *What am I going to do now?*

I grew up in Las Vegas and began playing tackle football in the eighth grade. I was a fairly good athlete as a ninth grader, so they had me playing linebacker and some tight end on the high school team. I played in a few varsity games that year. By the next season I had grown enough that I started varsity as an offensive tackle and a defensive end. My high school coach idolized Frank Kush at Arizona State. I remember playing in a basketball game and looking over to see Coach Kush sitting with my parents in the stands. When my coach saw Frank, he got all excited and started acting like a little kid. He told me, "You've got the greatest football coach in the world sitting in the stands watching you play!" I remembering thinking, *What if don't end up going to ASU?*

A lot of Pac-8 schools were recruiting me to play defensive end, and other schools wanted me on offense. One of my biggest concerns was I didn't want to sit around until I was a senior to play. I'd ask some of the bigger schools about their depth chart. Some were eight deep at different positions. I thought, *Nah, I want to play.*

On signing day I told my mom and dad, "I think I'm going to Arizona State." My mom started crying, and my dad was so mad he called me a name that I can't repeat. So I called Norm Chow, who was in Las Vegas, and said, "Well, I guess you'd better come get your papers." He came over, and I signed with BYU. I had a lot of family in southern Utah, and that's where my parents wanted me to go. Thank goodness for my parents. It was the greatest decision I ever made—or they made. They had good sense. I didn't at the time.

When LaVell came and visited at our house, he walked in and sat down in our big recliner chair. I was thinking, *He's going to give us some big sales speech.* Next thing I knew, he was undoing his tie and reclining back in the chair—just chatting away with my mom and dad.

I thought, *There's something funny about this.* But LaVell Edwards is LaVell Edwards. Then they were eating ice cream, and I thought, *When's he going to start talking to me?* He just kept on talking to my mom and dad, which is pretty smart. That's the first time I met LaVell Edwards.

My freshman year was 1977. I played behind Kelly Harris, but I traveled and played a lot. LaVell told me it would take a little time because we threw the ball a lot. He said, "You're an athlete. You're going to pick it up fast." Gifford Nielsen was the starting quarterback until he got hurt at Oregon State. That was a shame because he was one of the leading candidates for the Heisman Trophy.

During my time at BYU I blocked for Gifford, Marc Wilson, and Jim McMahon. You've got a wide variety of styles right there. Marc and Gifford

Nick Eyre played four seasons for the Cougars, from 1977 to 1980. As a senior he finished third in the voting for the Outland Trophy and was a consensus All-American. He was inducted into the BYU Athletic Hall of Fame in 1990.

were obviously straight drop-back passers. They were tall and could throw over the line. You just had to provide a pocket for them. I remember Marc throwing seven touchdown passes against Colorado State. He was tall, a big 6′5″ guy who could stand back there and really throw it.

Now Jim, he might be in the pocket or he might not. You never knew. He usually made offensive linemen look really good. As an offensive line, we hated giving up sacks. We just hated it. We had a goal not to give up any. We took a lot of pride in that. Jim would make you look good because he could escape, a lot like Steve Young. Jim wasn't going to take a sack. He would improvise and do whatever he had to do to get rid of it.

Doug Scovil was our offensive coordinator. We had a couple of plays, like a quick screen, where he would let the tackle pull. I was fast enough to pull it off, and he started calling me "the Bear." The nickname just stuck. It was funny. Doug had this ability to adjust to the different types of personalities and styles on the team. He knew what Marc and Gifford could do. He knew Jim's ability to improvise and used it to our advantage.

I think that's part of the genius of LaVell Edwards. He let his people coach. Jim was a tremendous competitor. He was going to find a way to win. Sometimes he would throw a tirade, and LaVell would have to settle him down a little bit. That's also where LaVell's genius was. He knew how to handle the individual players, and he would let his coaches coach.

People have misconceptions about Jim. A lot of the flamboyant stuff was just to grab attention. When we were hanging out in our apartment, he was just a normal guy. He was a happy-go-lucky kind of guy, but, boy, was he a competitor. He had a tremendous will to win. He would do whatever it took. He was an incredible athlete.

When Jim was on his game, it was uncanny. I remember one time we were talking, and he said, "When I'm on my game things just slow down. It's like everything is in slow motion. I can see all my reads and go through my progressions." For some reason the game just came so naturally to Jim.

As a junior and senior, things started to slow down for me, too. I remember trying to have perfect games. If I got my job done, I'd try to go get someone else's guy. I'd try to have a second knockdown. They would grade the offensive linemen after every game, and my goal was to have perfect games.

I started to get some attention my junior year in 1979. We played Texas A&M the first game of the season. They had a kid named Jacob Green they were touting for the Outland Trophy. We shut him down pretty good and ended up beating them 18–17. Danny Frazier, one of our linebackers, broke his neck in that game. That was one of the first times I saw anybody get seriously hurt playing football. It was scary. It made you kind of think about what was really important.

One game that stands out was at San Diego State later that season. We led 35–7 at halftime, and the coaches took the starters out. It was kind of fun that we had played so well that they could let other guys play in the second half.

I remember Norm Chow talking to me before my senior year in 1980. He told me that I would be getting a lot of attention and I needed to keep everything in perspective. I said, "What is there to keep in perspective?" He said, "Well, a lot of things are going to happen for you this year." I said, "Norm, it really doesn't mean that much." I know that sounds kind of funny, but to me I just liked playing football at BYU. We won a lot of games—a lot of big games. That's really what I liked. I liked scoring a lot of points. That was exciting. The rest of the attention really didn't mean that much.

At the end of my senior year, I was hanging out at my apartment and got a call from Norm. He said, "Hey, you've been named All-America." There have been a lot of great players come through BYU, and I think I was really lucky to play when I did. A lot of it is just timing, I think. We had some great teams, and we helped lay the foundation for the national championship team a few years later.

I loved it at BYU. I remember after my first year I couldn't wait to head back home. By the end of my career, I loved it there. I got to know a lot of people with whom we still keep in contact today. My wife is from the Bay Area, and I'm from Vegas, but we chose to stay in the Provo area. I like the lifestyle here. This is where I wanted to live. This is where I wanted to raise my family.

I learned a lot of important life lessons at BYU, and I think a lot of it had to do with LaVell Edwards. He had a very big impact on my life. I look at the way I run my business today, and I have to stop and laugh sometimes. I feel like I'm LaVell Edwards.

He showed me that you have to let people have ownership in what they do. You can't do everything yourself. I learned if you work hard, you're going to be successful. It doesn't mean you've got to work 24 hours a day, but you work hard when you're there. You give your word, and your word's good. Keep it real simple. Sometimes I think we make life way too complicated.

Nick "the Bear" Eyre was a four-year letterman and three-year starter for BYU, from 1977 to 1980. As a senior, he was named a consensus All-American and finished third in the Outland Trophy voting. Eyre was a two-time first-team All-WAC offensive tackle. He helped lead BYU to four WAC titles and three Holiday Bowl appearances. Eyre was selected in the fourth round of the 1981 NFL Draft by the Houston Oilers. He played four seasons of professional football for the Oilers and the Arizona Wranglers of the USFL. He was inducted into the BYU Athletic Hall of Fame in 1990.

JIM McMAHON

QUARTERBACK

1977–1981

Smu had a great football team in 1980. They certainly had the best team money could buy. They had all the horses. I think about eight or nine guys went on to have successful careers in the NFL. But we had a lot of guys who could really play, too. I was never afraid to play anyone. I didn't care who they were. As long we did what we were supposed to do, we were going to win.

The Holiday Bowl would not have come down to a miracle finish if I hadn't played so poorly in the first half. I think I may have put a little too much pressure on myself to win a bowl game. We hadn't won one yet. The thing that really electrified me and got the team going was Vai Sikahema's punt return for a touchdown late in the second quarter. That gave us some life. I'll tell you, we were having a great season, and I certainly didn't want to go out like that. I always believed that if I had the ball in my hands at the end of the game, we would find a way to win. So we were down three scores with less than four minutes to go. It was fourth down, and they sent in our punting unit.

I basically refused to come off the field. I told the offensive unit to huddle up, and a couple guys said, "Mac, here comes the punting team." I just felt as long as we had the ball, there was still a chance to win. There was a lot of confusion, and we had to call a timeout. I came off the field, and I wasn't

Jim McMahon rewrote the NCAA record book—setting 70 records—while playing quarterback at BYU from 1977 to 1980. He was named first-team All-America as a junior and senior. McMahon went on to play 15 seasons in the NFL and led the Chicago Bears to a Super Bowl title in 1985.

very happy. I told them they were giving up. Finally, I think they realized, "What have we got to lose?"

I went back in and called a play. It was a multiple-option play at the line of scrimmage. We just took what the defense gave us. For some reason no one covered Clay Brown. Well, that's like shooting fish in a barrel. It was an easy completion, and we converted the fourth down. After that, we went down and scored. Everyone talks about those last three or four scoring drives, but people forget we had to come up with a couple big defensive stops late in that game. We hadn't stopped them all night. But when the defense had to get a stop, they did.

On the final play of the game, everyone knew what was coming. We called it the "Save the Game" play. We practiced it maybe once a week or once a month. Everyone knew the concept, but we never had to use it during the season. I just told everyone in the huddle, "Look, hold them off a little longer and give the guys a chance to get in the end zone. We've come way too far to lose now. Someone catch the ball, and let's win this damn thing."

The way it turned out was unbelievable. The ball never touched a single SMU guy. I've seen the replay from multiple angles. It came straight out of the air and right into Clay's hands. Not a single SMU guy touched it. It was unbelievable. It certainly is up there on my list of great football memories. Anytime you can come back from a deficit like that and win a ballgame is something special. We had a lot of great players on that team, not only on offense but on the defensive side of the ball, as well.

Coming out of high school in Roy, Utah, I really wanted to go to UNLV, but my dad said, "No, you're not going to go there. The school's not big enough." Eventually, I chose BYU so my folks could see me play in college, and also because BYU was one of the few schools that told me I could also play baseball. That's really all I ever wanted to do, play baseball. BYU told me I'd have a chance to play. What they didn't tell me was that I couldn't get out of spring football practice.

I played in about 10 baseball games my freshman year. I'd play in a doubleheader and then have to run down the hill and change uniforms for football practice. Throwing a ball from the outfield is a lot different than throwing a football. After a while doing both at the same time was hard on my arm. I really wanted to play baseball, but eventually I had to make a decision. Since football was how I got my scholarship, I decided to stick with that.

Garth Hall was the BYU coach who recruited me. He was at my house on signing day along with coaches from three other schools because I still hadn't made up my mind. We sat around talking for a while, and finally someone asked me where I was planning to go. I said, "Well I guess I'll go to BYU." So the other coaches left in a huff, and that was it.

I was a Cougar.

LaVell was really creating something unique at BYU. His offensive style was way ahead of the rest of the country. BYU was about the only team in the country throwing the football. The rest of the teams were run, run, run. They were running offenses like the wishbone and the veer.

BYU offered an exciting brand of football. As a player, it was a great system to play in. It was a heck of a program all the way around. The BYU offense was a lot more exciting than any other offense I played in during my career, that's for sure. We were throwing the ball all over the place. The defenses at that time had no clue what we were doing. Especially when we played teams out of conference. A lot of those teams didn't respect us, and they couldn't beat us, either. Our game was about precision. Guys knew their job and made adjustments. When everyone did his job, we were impossible to stop.

As a freshman in 1977, I was the varsity punter, so I traveled with the team. I was third on the quarterback depth chart behind Gifford Nielson and Marc Wilson. The toughest part about BYU was waiting to get a chance to play. We had an assembly line of great quarterbacks waiting in the wings. Your competitive nature makes it hard to wait your turn.

People try to compare or rate the quarterbacks from the different eras at BYU, but you can't. We all played on different teams in different time periods. A lot of us had different position coaches when we played, as well, so there were different schemes and personnel. The one commonality is we all had success. That's the key to being a great quarterback at BYU. If you can't play quarterback at BYU, you can't play anywhere because it's a pretty easy system to run if you know what you're doing.

Other than punting, I didn't play much at all my freshman year, and I only played part of the season my sophomore year. Then I got hurt and needed surgery on my knee, so I sat out the 1979 season.

Doug Scovil was the offensive coordinator for most of my career at BYU. He was one of the biggest reasons for my success. Doug would always pull me into his office and have me diagram plays on the chalkboard. We'd discuss defenses and schemes. We'd talk about my thought process. Then we would go out to practice for two hours and go over and over and over it. Pretty soon it was second nature.

By my junior year, it was a cakewalk because I knew so much about the system. It didn't matter what the defense did—we were going to be successful. We would find a way to isolate our best players and just throw the football.

I enjoyed playing football at BYU. Saturdays were always great. The rest of the week may have been a little rough, but Saturdays were always fun. I learned more about football while I was at BYU than I learned anywhere else. I learned a lot about life, as well. There's no doubt I benefited immensely from my time at BYU. If I had to do it over, I'd do it all again. I spent five years at BYU and met a lot of great people.

I was certainly a lot more prepared heading into the NFL than most guys coming out of college. Who knows how my career would have gone if I had not come to BYU? I tell everyone the BYU system is the best offense I ever played in, bar none. If we had all 11 guys on the same page, we couldn't be stopped.

Roger French did a heck of job with the linemen. Football is a team sport, and you can't throw the ball without protection—it's the key. You can't throw the football unless the big boys upfront block for you. It was the first thing that Doug Scovil talked about in our team meeting at the beginning of every year.

Another key to winning football games is trusting your teammates. You just have to know that each guy is going do his job and be where he's supposed to be. That's one of the great things about playing at BYU—everyone was always in the right spot.

I have great respect for LaVell Edwards as a coach and as a person. He was a big part of my life. I always joke with LaVell that I probably spent more time in his office than I did on campus in class. One of the great things about LaVell is he is so even-keeled. He never got too excited or mad.

I travel around quite a bit, and everywhere I go people ask about him. He is an icon. Everyone talks about the BYU program and everything he did for college football. He is so well-loved all over the country. The genius of LaVell Edwards was getting good coaches and letting them coach. Even

grew up and that's what I had been taught. I thought about what to do for at least a week. During that time I didn't tell anybody.

By this time my parents had moved to Colorado, but they still had our house is Salt Lake City. About a week after meeting with LaVell, they came to town, and I went up to spend the weekend with them. I can remember being scared to death to tell my parents about my dilemma. Finally, I got up enough guts and said, "I'm ready to go on a mission when I turn 19 in June, but LaVell just told me that if I choose to stay I'll likely be the starting tight end this fall."

I had no idea what they were going to say. I thought my dad would be mad. The first thing my dad said was, "Well, let's go talk to our stake president." So the next weekend I made the trip to Colorado to meet with my parents' stake president, whom I had never met.

We sat down and told him we needed his counsel. I told him I'd been planning to serve a mission and leave that summer. I also explained my conversation with LaVell and the opportunities ahead at BYU. I further explained I thought I could use my playing days at BYU as a missionary tool—that, if everything went as planned, I could be a positive influence on a lot of people.

Then I said, "What do you think?" I can remember his answer as if it happened yesterday. He looked me straight in the eye, and in a matter-of-fact way said, "Gordon, there's no question what you should do." I thought, *Okay. He's sending me on a mission.* Then he said in these exact words, "You should stay and play football at BYU." That was it. So when I got back to Provo, I went and told LaVell I would be playing football in the fall. My understanding is that Steve Young had a similar experience.

From that day on, when I told LaVell, "Okay, let's do it," Steve and I became speaking partners. I'm not just talking about speaking around the state of Utah; I'm talking about speaking all over the country. They wore us out. By my estimation, in the four years I spent at BYU, I probably attended 500 speaking engagements. It was something we took very seriously. We tried hard to be good examples, to use our station as athletes to influence the youth and be positive examples of the Church and what it stands for. When I stood at a pulpit or a podium and talked to people, it was genuine and from the heart. For the next three years, I literally felt that that was my calling. That was my mission.

Steve became my very best friend and confidant. There wasn't anything we wouldn't do for each other. We spent so much time together as roommates and

125

speaking partners that I could probably write a book filled with the things we accomplished and went through together. When I look back on it now, I'm proud of the fact that we helped put BYU on the map. The late 1970s and early 1980s were a magical time at BYU. There were so many players on those teams who ended up playing in the NFL.

BYU revolutionized college football. Everyone always talks about the West Coast offense and Bill Walsh. Well, BYU did the same thing at the college level with LaVell Edwards, Doug Scovil, and the other guys who followed him. We revolutionized college football. We passed to set up the run. We ran at the opportune times. That was the legacy we left at BYU.

I was fortunate to play with two of the greatest quarterbacks in NCAA history. Jim McMahon was a legend. I was in awe at what he could do and extremely intimidated by his presence. If Jim told me to do something, I didn't even ask questions—I just did it. I knew that if I dropped a ball, which didn't happen very often, I did not want to go back to the huddle.

I played with Steve, Robbie Bosco, and even John Elway in Denver. They were fantastic quarterbacks—some of the greatest to play the game—but I've always said, the best pure drop-back quarterback I ever had the chance to play with was Jim McMahon. He just demanded that type of respect. He was a player. I feel fortunate that I got to play with him for one year. It was a big year for me. It took him a couple of games to gain confidence in me, but once he did, we were unstoppable.

The greatest game I ever played was my sophomore year against Utah in 1981. You talk about being in the zone. I had 13 catches, two touchdowns, and 259 yards. I felt unstoppable. I ran away from people, around people, and when I couldn't do that, I ran over them. It was like a whole game of slow motion football for me. It was Jim's last home game at BYU, and I'll never forget it.

I look back at my time at BYU as an awesome experience. At the time, I think I took it for granted. I caught passes from Jim McMahon and Steve Young. I got to play for the immortal Doug Scovil. I played for Ted Tollner. I played for Mike Holmgren. I played for Norm Chow. I played with Andy Reid. They are legends. They have left their imprint all over the game of football. You start to appreciate those things when you get older.

Obviously, to culminate my career and be elected on the first ballot into the College Football Hall of Fame kind of brought everything full circle. It has changed my life quite a bit. It has made me a much better person, realizing the journey I've taken and knowing there are still many things for me to do.

I don't think I've said enough about LaVell, but he's the greatest man ever. Without him, I wouldn't be here today. When he sat down with you and said, "I've got a piece of advice for you," you would listen. I did. He taught me service to others and how to be a team player and selfless in my actions. His genius was to hire good assistants and leave them alone. He knew what he didn't know, if that makes any sense. He knew that to compete at a national level, he had to throw the ball. So he went and found coaches like Doug Scovil who could help him create this unbelievable offensive machine.

LaVell directed the backroom issues. Who are we going to sign? Where are they going to play? He did that for me. He took a shot at a kid who really had nothing to show as far as credentials and said, "We're going to give you a scholarship. We're going to give you a shot at tight end." He had never even seen me play, but that's LaVell. That's what he did. He's one of a kind.

Maybe the best years of my life were the four I spent at BYU. I'm proud of the things we were able to accomplish on the field and all the time we spent—three to four days a week—speaking at schools, youth meetings, and firesides, sharing the Gospel and promoting the values of the university and the Church. That's what it means to me to be a Cougar. I was very humbled and grateful to be at BYU and be a part of the BYU football legacy.

Gordon Hudson played four years as a tight end at BYU from 1980 to 1983. He was named consensus All-America as a junior in 1982 and as a senior in 1983. Hudson still holds several NCAA records for tight ends, including most career passes caught per game and yards in a single game. He helped BYU win four WAC championships and four Holiday Bowl invitations. In 2009 Hudson was inducted into the College Football Hall of Fame. He was selected in the first round of the 1984 NFL Supplemental Draft. Hudson played two seasons with the Los Angeles Express of the USFL and one with the Seattle Seahawks of the NFL.

STEVE YOUNG

QUARTERBACK

1980–1983

FOOTBALL HAS BEEN an important part of my life for a long time. I started playing quarterback when I was eight years old. I think I wanted to play quarterback because that was the guy who got to call the plays.

I grew up in Greenwich, Connecticut. Other than my siblings, I was the only Mormon in town. My dad's name is Grit. He played football at BYU in the late 1950s. He was the toughest man I knew, and I really looked up to him. In high school I lettered in football, basketball, and baseball. I was a captain of all three teams my senior year. When it came time to decide where to go to college, I chose BYU—not because my dad went there, but largely because I had relatives in the area. I figured it would be a home away from home.

I remember they posted the depth chart about two weeks into summer camp my freshman year in 1980. I was looking down the list, and there was my name—eighth-string quarterback. You couldn't be further from having a chance to see the field.

I remember walking back from practice to my dorm room in Helaman Halls and feeling so dejected. I had never left home before coming to BYU, so I was already homesick. It didn't take much for me to want to go home.

I called my dad and told him I'd had it. I quit. I want to come home. His comment was immediate. He said, "Well, Steve, you can quit, but you can't come home, because I don't live with quitters." Well, I didn't have any other options. I had $20 to my name, and there was nowhere else to go.

As a senior in 1983, Steve Young led the nation in passing and total offense and was named a consensus All-American. He went on to play 15 years in the NFL, winning three Super Bowls and two league MVPs. Young was inducted into the College Football Hall of Fame in 2001 and the Pro Football Hall of Fame in 2009.

It's simple things like that in your life that keep you moving forward in the right direction. My dad didn't allow me to have an excuse or provide me an early exit door to easily bow out. What if he would have reacted differently? What if he had said, "No problem, son. We're sorry things didn't work out.

We understand that you are dejected. Come home, and we'll take care of you." My life would have been so different.

My freshman year was Danny Ainge's senior year at BYU. I couldn't afford tickets to the basketball games, so I went to Floyd Johnson, our equipment manager, and asked him if I could help at the games. He said sure. So I got to sit on the visitors' bench and be the towel boy. That was maybe the best basketball team to ever play at BYU.

I remember being so inspired by how Danny played the game. I wanted so badly to be a part of the great athletic tradition at BYU.

When I got to BYU, I wasn't a very good passer. I ran an option-style offense in high school, so I really didn't know how to throw the football. Fortunately, I had the opportunity to play behind Jim McMahon. He could really throw the ball. I watched him closely and studied his throwing motion. Almost immediately I got better by imitating his throwing style. The better I got, the harder I worked to improve.

It's difficult to follow a legend—and Jim McMahon was a legend—but we had a great relationship. I will always appreciate Jim because he taught me how to play quarterback. I spent the first two years at BYU working and sweating and training just to live up to the standards of the BYU quarterback tradition.

There was Gifford Nielsen, then Marc Wilson. You could just see the tradition was building. Then Jim came along and sent it into the stratosphere. He did things that were unheard-of at the college level, and I witnessed them firsthand.

Backing up Jim was one of the greatest gifts I could have ever been given. I learned there was no room to be complacent. I had to work hard every day to improve, just to get a chance to follow him.

Those first two years at BYU I just wanted to play. Then Jim graduated, and it was my turn. Now the only thing I wanted to do was run away.

Reality hit me pretty hard. I was following Jim McMahon—the greatest college football quarterback in history. The man broke 70 NCAA records. Not like seven, or 14, or even 25—70! I remember when I finally set my first NCAA record, I told everyone, "Hey, I got *one*. Isn't that great?" I got *one*.

At that time, if you were a BYU quarterback, you won the WAC championship. You just did. It was part of the pedigree. Then you better go win the Holiday Bowl. I remember thinking about the 1980 Holiday Bowl against SMU and wondering, *How am I going to top that?*

two parts of the offense were open. I remember thinking at the end of that game, *Okay, here we go!* We were explosive.

At the same time our defense was unreal. How many games that year did our defense save us? It was a complete team effort. Again, we had guys who had been in the program for a while who were excited for the opportunity to prove they could play. You had guys like Mark Allen, Marv Allen, David Neff, Kerry Whittingham, Leon White, Kurt Gouveia, Steve Haymond, and Larry Hamilton. About half of our defense ended up playing in the NFL for a couple years or longer. They were talented and out to make a name for themselves.

I played high school football for Doug Berry at Alta. He was one of those unique high school coaches who realized that just because you were big doesn't mean you're an offensive lineman. I was the second-biggest kid on our team, and I was playing tight end and linebacker. Doug put me in a position to make plays, and at the same time he was always trying to get me to become a better person. He realized that athletics was just a short-lived thing, and there are other things that are more important.

My recruiting process was easy. My final two choices—other than the in-state schools—came down to Stanford and BYU. I was getting ready to make my trip to Stanford, and my father said something that stuck with me. He said, "I don't care where you play, but it sure would be fun to watch you play every weekend." I'm very thankful I made the decision to attend BYU. It was a very interesting five years, but at the same time, I grew up a lot in those years.

I was blessed to play for LaVell Edwards. I learned that there's a lot more to life than just football, and sometimes you learn those lessons the hard way. The first time I met LaVell was on my recruiting trip to BYU. He came over and talked to my father and mother. He knew them not only by their first names, but he knew what they were doing, where they worked. That's the magic of LaVell. He was connected to everybody. LaVell was always about the people, not about winning football games. He won a lot, but he was about people. He tried to put people in positions where they could succeed. Even to this day, as a high school coach, I try to emulate that. I don't know if I'm any good at it or not, but his example is what I try to follow.

BYU is a large school, but it seemed like everybody kind of knew everybody else; or, if you didn't know them directly, you had a friend who knew somebody. There was a real community feel at BYU.

David Mills celebrates after scoring one of his seven touchdowns during the 1984 national championship season. Mills led the Cougars with 60 catches for 1,023 yards and was named first-team All-America.

Running out onto the field at Cougar Stadium was always fun. I remember Mark Allen was quoted in the student newspaper as saying, "The students weren't loud enough." So they kind of took it as a challenge, because the next game they were probably the loudest I've ever heard a BYU crowd. They really got involved in the game. As the season went on, people were painting their faces and doing things that are pretty normal now.

We had a lot of competitive people on that '84 team. I don't think people understand how much we would actually compete back and forth. Glen Kozlowski and I were always competing at something. It didn't matter if it was a card game, neither of us wanted to lose to the other. That carried over onto the football field. One week he would have a great game, the next week I would have a great game. It was all done in fun, but at the same time we were always trying to set the standard a little higher. That's the way the whole team was. As soon as the standard went higher, there was no trash talking or putting someone else down. It was a simple fact of, "Here's the new standard. Are we going to raise it higher or are we going to leave it there?" It seemed like someone was always able to raise it higher.

I don't remember that team ever thinking we couldn't win a game. I also don't ever remember being in the huddle or being on the sideline and thinking, *All right, who's going to make a play?* We had 25 guys who were ready to step up and make a play. Another thing is we never got upset with each other. If you ever got mad, it was at yourself, because you knew personally you could do better.

There were some great tight ends during my time at BYU. When I got to BYU, it was Clay Brown and Rob Anderson. A lot of people won't remember Rob, but he was a tremendous tight end. He just happened to be behind Clay. Then it was Gordon Hudson, Steve Harper, myself, and Trevor Molini. We always had good players at tight end because BYU is such a great place to play tight end.

We were never the greatest blockers in the world, but we had a lot of pride in what we did. We liked being tight ends, and we wanted to be tight ends, so that's why a lot of us chose BYU. There have been a lot of good ones who have gone through BYU—a lot of great players. It's just a fun brotherhood.

There are several plays I remember from the Holiday Bowl game against Michigan in 1984. The game-winning touchdown that Kelly Smith caught was a 69 with an H option, which is basically a weak-side flood. Robbie saw the play break down and started to scramble, then Kelly broke it upfield, and Robbie found him—game-winning touchdown.

There were lots of emotions after we won that game. A lot of celebrating, a lot of relief, and the emotion of, "Okay, it's over." For myself, I was almost sad because I realized that team was never going to play another game together again. In a way, you want to keep playing forever. So there was some sadness in the joy. I guess it was about every emotion you could feel.

One of my favorite stories of that game came from Louis Wong, a tackle on the team. While we were celebrating on the field, raising our fingers in the air and doing all the things you do, Louis took a knee in one of the end zones and just kind of observed the whole thing. He just sat back and watched it. He said he just wanted to sit back and take in everything. Just absorb it rather than be a part of it. It's interesting to listen to him talk about what people were doing, the expressions on their faces—the release of all kinds of emotions.

When you are away from BYU for a while, you forget how important it is to be around other BYU people. I recently went to St. Louis to visit Bryan Kehl, who is playing for the Rams. I coached Bryan at Brighton High School. It was fun to talk with him and have the BYU connection. There is something very unique about the experience of playing at BYU. Nobody really understands or appreciates it like another BYU player. It doesn't matter if they played 10 years before you or 15 years after you. You have an appreciation for each other and what it meant to play at BYU, what it meant to be a Cougar.

You'd think on the college level at a program like BYU it would be all about football, football, football. I don't ever remember a year-end interview with LaVell where we spent more than five minutes talking about football. He wanted to know about you as an individual—your family, your goals, your career aspirations. He had the ability to listen to people and say the right thing at the right time. He had that gift. You can say what you want about coaching and everything else, but he always had the ability to recruit great coaches and great players and to get them to work together.

David Mills was the starting tight end on the 1984 national championship team. He led the Cougars in receiving with 60 catches for 1,023 yards and seven touchdowns. Mills was named first-team All-WAC and first-team All-America. He caught 11 passes for 103 yards in the 1984 Holiday Bowl to help preserve the undefeated season and BYU's No. 1 ranking.

VAI SIKAHEMA

KICK RETURNER/RUNNING BACK
1980–1981 ★ 1984–1985

M**Y FATHER WAS A HIGH SCHOOL** security guard, and my mother worked 12-hour shifts as a seamstress. Together, they never made more than $25,000 a year. I left our home in Mesa, Arizona, with their hopes and prayers that I'd make something of my life. I was very much aware of that and carried with me the burden of their dreams.

Because my dad worked for the public school system, he had to find summer jobs. He and I would canvas wealthy homes in East Mesa and Scottsdale, Arizona, with flyers of our fledgling landscaping business. One day, I vividly remember my father getting berated by a man in the posh suburb of Paradise Valley. For some reason, he wasn't happy with our work. My dad stood there nodding politely and apologizing profusely. Then he reached into his shirt pocket and returned the man's check.

To my amazement, the man kept the check. It couldn't have been more than a hundred dollars, but it was a sizable amount to us. My dad is the toughest man I've ever known, yet as a boy, I was embarrassed for him and wondered why he didn't just punch the guy. But, over the years, as I matured, I realized that my dad was never more dignified and gallant than at that moment.

On our quiet drive home that afternoon, he said to me softly in Tongan, "Alu o ako." Which translated means, "Go to school." He didn't have to elaborate; I knew exactly what he meant and why he was saying it.

Growing up in Mesa, I didn't like BYU. In fact, I hated them. In those days BYU and Arizona State were both in the WAC, so they played each other every year. ASU had a Polynesian All-American named Junior Ah You, who was friends with my parents. Arizona didn't have a pro team in those days, so we were huge ASU fans.

My feelings toward BYU started to change a bit in 1977 when the Cougars came to Tempe to play ASU. Earlier that season, Gifford Nielsen had suffered a season-ending knee injury at Oregon State. He traveled with the team to Tempe and stayed an extra day to do a stake priesthood fireside that Sunday night. I had just started playing high school football, and my father asked me if I wanted to go see him speak. My dad thought it was amazing that an All-America quarterback was speaking at our church. The things Giff said that night were quite impactful to me as a 15-year-old kid. In fact, to this day I still remember the stories he told that night. His message moved me. I went home and thought long and hard about the things he said.

It was the turning point for me. It changed my mind about BYU.

When it came time to make a decision where to play college football, my father was pushing for ASU. He felt it was the better route to the NFL, and it would give my parents more opportunities to see me play. I took recruiting trips to Arizona, ASU, UCLA, BYU, Colorado, and Hawaii. I committed verbally to ASU, but midway through my senior year they fired legendary coach Frank Kush. That led me to change my mind and decide to go to BYU.

When LaVell Edwards came to my high school for his recruiting visit, my dad was also there at work. After LaVell made his scholarship offer official, my dad reached across the desk to accept on my behalf with a handshake, then a hug, and said in his broken English, "Goach, my zon weel be All-American."

LaVell just smiled. I was mortified.

As a kid, I sometimes struggled with the English language and my self-esteem, but I was always confident in my athletic ability. Part of that had to do with the grueling training my father put me through as a boy in his quest to make me a professional boxer. It required hours of work and training on footwork, doing thousands of push-ups and sit-ups, and running five miles a day. The routine was so regimented that it fostered in me a single-minded focus—at least, athletically.

I was a classic counter-puncher, so making people miss was my forte. I was taught to bob and weave, turn the shoulder slightly to avoid the jab, then dip

During his four years at BYU, Vai Sikahema set numerous BYU punt and kickoff return records. His 153 career punt returns is still an NCAA record. Sikahema played eight seasons in the NFL and was inducted into the BYU Athletic Hall of Fame in 2002.

141

inside to pull the trigger with the left hook. The skill set required for being a counter-punch boxer was nearly identical to being a punt returner. You've got to be fearless in the face of oncoming traffic, have tremendous focus, and then bob and weave to make defenders miss.

Near the end of my freshman year at BYU, the team's punt returner and starting halfback, Homer Jones, pulled his hamstring. Because there are so many decisions that punt returners have to make instantaneously—Is it catchable? Do I fair catch? Do I let it bounce into the end zone? Do I have room to make a play?—it's typically not a job given to a college freshman.

The most important characteristic in a good punt returner is sound judg-ment, so it was rather fortuitous when LaVell handed me the job of return-ing punts and kicks just before the 1980 Holiday Bowl. From the opening kickoff of the Holiday Bowl, it seemed as if we were running on sand and SMU was on a Tartan track. By late in the second quarter, we were trailing 29–7. We somehow held their vaunted "Pony Express" offense for one series and forced them to punt just before halftime.

I retreated 45 yards or so to give myself plenty of room, anticipating a booming punt. Instead, the punter shanked it short and to my right. It only carried about 30 yards, so I had to come a long way to get to it. When the ball hit the ground, it took an unusually high bounce. A couple of the SMU defenders overran the ball and a couple others turned their back to me and let up while trying to locate it. In an instant, I thought if I could catch the ball off the bounce in full stride I might just catch them off guard. So I caught the ball on the run as the SMU defenders were all standing flat-footed. Eighty-three yards later, I was dancing in the end zone, even though we were still trailing badly, 29–13.

The miraculous conclusion to the end of the game is well chronicled, but I feel my contribution was just as important as Jim McMahon's and Clay Brown's, just not as memorable—which is the way it should be.

I was fortunate to play in a great time period at BYU. I played in a lot of memorable games—some of the great football moments in school history. One of my favorite games was in 1985. We played Air Force at Cougar Sta-dium. The Academy was ranked No. 4 in the nation, and I think we were ranked No. 11. Robbie Bosco was wearing Kozlowski's No. 7 jersey in honor of Glen, who had injured his knee and was out for the season. Robbie threw a couple of interceptions in the first half. I remember Glen coming in at half-time and telling Robbie to take off his jersey because he was embarrassed that he was throwing interceptions wearing his number. That's such a funny memory—Koz trying to lighten the mood in the locker room.

We were down 21–7 at halftime. I returned a punt 72 yards in the third quarter for a touchdown. Later in the fourth quarter, I scored the winning touchdown on a 69-yard pass from Bosco. Our defense held Air Force score-less in the second half. That was one of my favorite moments at Cougar Sta-dium, now LaVell Edwards Stadium.

Even though I went on to play eight seasons in the NFL, there is nothing more exciting than coming out of the locker room and walking down the ramp onto the field at Cougar Stadium. The setting against the Wasatch Mountains is breathtaking—hearing the band play "Rise and Shout," 65,000 people on their feet going crazy, the "B…Y…U…Cougars!" chant circling around the stadium. I've been to stadiums all over the world, and there is nothing like that feeling at BYU. You can't duplicate it. BYU has an amazing fan base. Every place we traveled we had fans.

Being part of the national championship in 1984 was something I'll never forget. We entered the year with no expectations. We had lost 10 guys to the pro draft, including a couple of future hall of famers. We were starting new. Every week we looked to improve. That may have been the best defensive team ever at BYU. I know that's a bold statement, because there have been a lot of great Cougars defenses.

We had a bunch of future NFL guys like Kurt Gouveia, Leon White, and Kyle Morrell. For my money, Kyle was pound-for-pound the greatest safety to ever play at BYU. The defense was filled with great athletes who just made plays. They were tough.

I can't begin to describe how ultra-competitive the atmosphere was at practice. As an offense, we were facing one of the best defenses in the country every day. Sometimes the games seemed easy after going to practice all week. It was a dog-eat-dog environment that required your best. That's one of the reasons why those teams in the early '80s were so good. I mean, I played eight seasons in the NFL, and I couldn't even get on the field as a starter at BYU—we had that much talent.

Think about that. I was a backup running back at BYU, and yet I later played in two Pro Bowls in the NFL. Gouveia played 13 years in the league—won a couple Super Bowls—and yet he was a backup at BYU for two years behind Todd Shell, who was a first-round draft pick. It was the same thing with Leon White. Many of those guys would have been four-year starters at just about any other school in the country. That's how good we were.

As I look back at my time at BYU, I realize that being a Cougar is an important part of my identity. It certainly shaped my life. I'm proud to say I played at BYU. It's something I cherish. To me, and a host of other players who wore the uniform, that Y on the helmet means something. It's an iconic symbol. It stands for something great. I hope the way I live my life represents the school well and what it stands for.

I loved my time at BYU. I miss the simplicity of life there. There are so many people at BYU who had a huge impact on my life, but none more than

143

our equipment manager Floyd Johnson. Brother J was one of the first people I met when I arrived at BYU because I had to report to him to get my equipment.

When you would interact with Floyd, he would ask you things about your personal life. He would learn about your family and your upbringing. In those conversations, I learned that Floyd was someone I could trust and confide in. In retrospect, I think he found ways to intentionally keep me in his office longer than necessary because he wanted to have an excuse for us to talk.

Brother J was a great listener who gave great counsel. I knew he cared about me. He helped me understand the importance of serving a mission. He was one of the main reasons I chose to serve. I had a lot of questions, and he was someone I could seek out for answers. Floyd Johnson to me is BYU. When I think of BYU, I think of the hundreds of men and women like Brother J. My life was forever changed because I made the decision to be a Cougar.

LaVell Edwards was another guy who really cared about you as an individual, not just as a football player. He let his coaches do the coaching, and he worried about the players. LaVell was a visionary. He had a real sense for people. He was concerned about what was going on in your life. In my mind, his greatest success was he developed leaders out of young men. I'm grateful I had the chance to play for him.

Vai Sikahema played four years at BYU from 1980 to 1985. He set numerous BYU punt return records and still holds the NCAA record for most punt returns in a career, with 153 for 1,312 yards. Sikahema was drafted in the 10th round of the 1986 NFL Draft by the St. Louis Cardinals, becoming the first Tongan to ever play in the NFL. He played eight seasons in the NFL for the Cardinals, Green Bay Packers, and Philadelphia Eagles. Sikahema was named to the Pro Bowl twice in 1986 and 1987. He was inducted into the BYU Athletic Hall of Fame in 2002.

KYLE MORRELL

DEFENSIVE BACK

1981–1984

W<small>E WERE PLAYING</small> M<small>ICHIGAN</small> for the national championship. It was late in the game, and Marv Allen made an interception. They had this big running back who had just crushed me a couple of times during the game. He was standing there, and when Marv intercepted the ball, I thought, *I'm going to get him no matter what!* When the whistles blew, I had a full head of steam and I didn't stop. I hit him right underneath the chin.

There were about three seconds left in the game. They threw a bunch of flags and kicked me out of the game. When I came off the field, LaVell Edwards scolded me like a little kid. I felt so bad that I had disappointed him. Then, after the game, LaVell came in the locker room and said, "Where's Morrell? Where's Morrell?" Everyone pointed at me over in the corner. He came running over and stuck his face right in my chest, forearm tackled me to the ground, and started kissing me all over the face, telling me how much he loved me and how sorry he was for getting mad at me. It caught me so off guard.

It's a memory I'll never forget.

I played baseball, basketball, football, and ran track in high school. I was all-state in baseball, football, and basketball. I would be at baseball practice while a track meet was going on, and they would say, "Last call for the 100-yard dash!" I would run over to the track, run the race, and then go back to baseball practice.

I started getting recruited my senior year, especially during the state play-offs. Dick Felt and LaVell from BYU came to watch me play. They knew I was a good football player, but they later told me, "Once we saw you play basketball, that's when we could tell you were an athlete." I was 6′2″ and maybe 175 pounds at the time. They knew I would fill out. I ended up getting up to almost 200 pounds while I was at BYU.

I was also getting a look as a pitcher by a couple of pro baseball teams. I threw pretty hard for a 17-year-old kid. I got called by the Philadelphia Phillies and the Cincinnati Reds and was invited to a workout at Hillcrest High School. I got on the mound, and the coach at Hillcrest said, "Kyle, just throw as hard as you can." So that's what I did. I threw about 91–92 mph. I had one of the scouts talk to me about signing. He said, "Look, you don't want to go play football. You'll get beat up."

My dad and I talked about it. He said, "They're probably not going to give you much money. BYU is offering you a free education to play football." So that's what I did. I decided to go to BYU to play football. That was by far one of the best decisions I've made in my life.

I arrived at BYU in the fall of 1981. I was only 17 years old. I was very fortunate to be able to play as a freshman. LaVell told me when he was recruiting me, "Kyle, come to BYU, and I promise you will play as a freshman." He kept his word. I played on special teams and was our nickel back. They would bring me in on passing situations.

If LaVell told you it would happen, it would happen. No question about it. The integrity he had is something that not too many people have anymore, especially in the coaching profession. They'll tell you whatever they think you want to hear. Not LaVell, his word meant everything.

LaVell was like a father figure. He would bring you into his office just to chat. We wouldn't even talk football. He would ask how I was doing in school, how I was doing in my personal life. He would ask if there was anything he could help me with. He is a great man, no question about it.

I remember opening up the expanded stadium in 1982. It was amazing. We came running out, and the place was packed. People were going crazy, and I thought, *Holy smokes, this place is huge!* Then we lost to Air Force, and I remember thinking, *I can't believe we lost our very first game in this beautiful stadium.*

I grew up a lot while I was playing football at BYU. The thing that really helped me the most was being around a bunch of guys who were older, who were more mature, and who had been on LDS missions. I used to sit and listen to them talk. I grew up in the Church, but we weren't active. I enjoyed sitting around and listening to guys talk about the Gospel. It was a unique experience for me. It's hard to explain, but every one of my teammates at BYU gave me some type of inspiration to do better.

Later in life, my wife and I and our kids were all sealed together in the temple. All those times listening to guys talk about the Gospel really affected my life, even though it took maybe 10 years to sink in.

Being a Cougar meant everything to me. It meant a sense of pride and excellence. To go out and do whatever it took to win, to show people that we were the best. I love saying that I played football at BYU. The time I spent there were four of the greatest years of my life.

I would go home to Bountiful a lot of weekends. Some of my Utah friends would give me a hard time about being at BYU, and I'd say, "You have no idea what it's like to be a Cougar. You don't know what it's like to be on that campus." There's a special feeling you get when you're down there. Let me tell you, if I could have the chance to go back and play four more years, I would. It was that fun playing football at BYU.

It was a real thrill for me to play on the national championship team. The thing that made that team unique was there was no division between the offense and the defense. It was a team of guys who were like brothers. We all loved each other. There was never any animosity back and forth.

Yeah, at practice we would fight like cats and dogs, but once practice was over, it was all forgotten. Once we got in that locker room, we were all brothers and best of friends. We were a unique group of kids who came together and pulled off something that may never happen again. We had a lot of great players—guys who weren't maybe the greatest all-around athletes, but who knew how to play as a team. That was the most important thing. We all did our assignments. We did what we were supposed to do, and it worked.

I used to get asked a lot about the goal-line stand at Hawaii. On that play I just had this feeling, *I've got to make something happen no matter what.* I was supposed to be covering the tight end in that situation, but I told Steve Harman, "Steve, you take the tight end. I'm going up and over." He looked at me like, *What are you talking about?* I said, "Just take the tight end!"

I noticed their running backs had scooted up closer to the line of scrimmage, and I thought, *They're going to run another quarterback sneak.* It was all instinct. My memory of the play seems like slow motion. I remember flying

Arguably the greatest defensive play in BYU history, Kyle Morrell leaped over the top of both lines to tackle Rainbow quarterback Raphel Cherry on third-and-goal at the 1-foot line, forcing Hawaii to settle for a field goal. Morrell was named first-team All-America by the Associated Press.

through the air and seeing the whites of Raphel Cherry's eyes. They looked like two saucers, they were so huge. I was fortunate enough to be able to get a hold of him and stop his progression. Then the line surge just collapsed on him. It was an exciting moment. At the time, I didn't think it was that big of a deal. I just thought I made a pretty decent play. When I got home, my parents were still over in Hawaii. They called me and said, "Have you seen that play you made?" I said, "No."

My dad said, "It's all over the news here every night. Wait until you see the film." When I finally saw the play in slow motion, I thought, *Wow. That was pretty cool.* I thought, *It looks like I was jumping off a trampoline or something.* I'm sure I could never jump that high again.

I just believe the 1984 season was meant to be for BYU. LaVell had put in so many years of hard work and dedication. No one ever gave us much respect, even though we had so much success and all those wins for several seasons. I think it was meant to be.

Prior to the season during spring ball, we ended up having a scrimmage in a blizzard. I mean, it snowed about six inches while we were out at practice, but no one was complaining about the cold or anything. Afterward, LaVell brought us all in and said, "I want to tell you guys something. I can tell by the way you worked today that something special is going to happen to this team this year. I don't know what it is, but something special is going to happen." LaVell was right—it did.

Kyle Morrell was a four-year starter for BYU from 1981 to 1984. As a senior, he was named first-team All-America by the Associated Press. Morrell was also honored by the WAC as Defensive Player of the Year, finishing the 1984 season with 70 tackles, three interceptions, and one sack. The Minnesota Vikings took him in the fourth round of the 1985 NFL Draft.

GLEN KOZLOWSKI
WIDE RECEIVER
1981 ★ 1983–1985

I WAS BEING RECRUITED by many of the West Coast schools. It was back in the day when a lot of schools were still cheating. I remember it seemed like BYU was the only school that didn't offer a little extra something on the side. In the end, BYU basically recruited my mother. When it was all said and done, I ended up going to BYU because that's what my mom wanted.

I was recruited by Norm Chow, Doug Scovil, and eventually LaVell Edwards. At that time, Doug Scovil was the offensive coordinator at BYU, and Ted Tollner was the offensive coordinator at San Diego State, in my hometown.

After my senior year, Doug was named the head football coach at San Diego State, and Ted became the quarterbacks coach at BYU. Being from San Diego, that was a big rivalry. The funny part was, after they switched schools, they both came to me and said forget about everything I told you last year— I want you to join me at my new school. It was very funny.

When it came time to go on recruiting trips, I took the six that you were allowed, plus a few unofficial trips. I went to Texas, UCLA, Arizona, Arizona State, San Diego State, and Colorado—my older brother had played there. I talked with several Midwest schools, but I really wanted to stay out West. When I came on my trip to BYU, I really fell in love with LaVell Edwards. He was just a real honest guy, and I felt like BYU was a good place for me.

I remember when I sat down with him, I said, "Okay, Coach, what's the deal?"

He looked at me, kind of laughed, and said, "Well, here's the deal. You get to work really hard, and we'll allow you to get a free education."

I laughed and said, "Oh, okay. That sounds like a pretty good deal."

He also told me, "I think you've got a lot of talent, but I can't promise you anything more than we'll give you a great opportunity here at BYU." That was it.

I didn't officially commit until signing day. I woke up that morning, and there were a bunch of assistant coaches from other schools waiting outside my house. So I walked outside and said, "Hey, I'm going to BYU, and they all jumped in their cars and took off. I remember LaVell was there because he was also trying to recruit Sean Salisbury. We were in the same graduating class, but he chose USC, and I chose BYU.

I was hoping to graduate early from high school and start at BYU before spring practice. I think I was one credit hour short, but I was such a piece of work in high school that my principal told me, "If you'll go to BYU, we'll count one of your college classes toward high school graduation." I was always getting in trouble, and I think she was looking for a way to get rid of me. So I called Norm Chow, and they cleared it. I enrolled at BYU in January 1981 and went through spring ball. Then they allowed me to go home and graduate with my high school class that summer.

After two weeks of spring ball, I was still the last guy on the depth chart. I was so cocky, I would go into Norm's office and complain. I'd tell him, "What are you doing? I'm better than those guys ahead of me." Norm would look at me and say, "Get out of my office."

By the time the season began, I had earned a starting spot at wide receiver. I had a couple of nice games early, but then I got hurt in the UNLV game in the sixth week of the season. I had a high ankle sprain. Back then they weren't quite sure how to treat it. I had a hard time getting healthy the rest of the season.

Unfortunately, I goofed around a lot that first year. I didn't go to class, and the worst part was I thought that was okay. I was doing things you weren't supposed to at BYU. I wasn't a good example. At the end of the fall semester, BYU asked me to leave.

It was a defining moment for me. I thought to myself, *I'm out of here. I can go anywhere and play football.* I debated the decision all summer. It was a real

Known for his acrobatic catches, Glen Kozlowski was a four-year starter at wide receiver for BYU. He was a co-captain of the 1984 national championship team and received honorable mention All-America honors from AP, UPI, and *Football News*. Kozlowski went on to play six seasons in the NFL for the Chicago Bears.

crossroads for me. I could have transferred to another school. It seemed like every time I was ready to transfer to Miami, or somewhere else, I got a phone call from LaVell Edwards. He just seemed to have a sense when to call. Ultimately, it was LaVell and my future wife, Julie, who convinced me to stay.

I also knew in my heart it was the right thing to do. I knew it was time for me to grow up. Fortunately, I made the right decision for me. I appreciate the fact the BYU didn't give up on me. They were very firm, they said, "Here are the rules, you need to follow them." But at the same time, they were encouraging and honestly wanted me to return and make it right.

When I came back to school, there were several people who had a profound impact on my life. I remember going to meet with the dean of students. He laid down a challenge. He told me he didn't think I could make it at BYU. For me, telling me I couldn't do something was like inviting me to do it. Maybe he knew that, but I took his challenge. To the day I left BYU, I would go back each semester and show him my report card. He actually became a good friend. I now know he did it because he cared, not because he didn't think I could do it. He had a real impact on the person I am today.

As I look back at my college career, my favorite moments were putting on the pads and heading out to practice—just being with my teammates and playing football. For me, BYU was about winning. It wasn't about whether I had a bunch of catches or scored a bunch of touchdowns. During the week at practice, it seemed like the offense and defense were fighting every day, but on Saturdays we were teammates. We went to battle together. That was the thing I remember the most, and the most enjoyable part for me.

Coming into the 1984 season, I was voted a captain. I really wasn't the captain type. Part of the captain's responsibility was to speak to the team before the game. We opened the season at Pittsburgh, and we knew we had an opportunity to do something special. They were ranked third in the country and had a bunch of All-Americans. We were playing in the first live national broadcast on ESPN.

After we beat Pitt, the captains started talking about going undefeated. We got together as a team the night before the Baylor game—no coaches, just us players. The captains spoke. We talked about the opportunities ahead of us. Then someone suggested we have a prayer. It was just a spontaneous thing that brought us all together. We put our arms around each other and said a team prayer. We had a lot of different faiths on the team, and I'm pretty sure Louis Wong, who was not a member at the time, gave the first prayer. Looking back it was just a surreal moment. From that moment on we were bound together. Each week on Friday night, we would meet as players and do the same thing.

BYU is a really special place. Every time you put the uniform on, you represent a lot more than just yourself and your teammates. You represent the school and ultimately the LDS Church. There was a lot of responsibility that went with that. I'll always be proud to be a Cougar. You represent the university and a lifestyle. Attending BYU is something I will always be proud of.

After we beat Michigan in the Holiday Bowl to finish the season undefeated, we were all in the locker room celebrating. LaVell walked in, shuffled everybody out, and closed the door. He had us all take a knee, and he said a real humble prayer. I'll never forget how grateful he was and the humility he showed at that moment. It was incredible. This was the pinnacle of his coaching career. From a coaching perspective, you can't have a bigger moment than that. We had just won the national championship, but it clearly wasn't about him. It was about expressing gratitude for his players and the blessing that we enjoyed as a team.

For a kid like me, who was so cocky, it was a great lesson. There will never be a moment so great that you can't get on your knees and express gratitude. I will always remember that.

I've always wanted my sons to go to school at BYU because I know how it changes your life. I really didn't care if they played football or not. In 2006 Tyler came to BYU and walked on. It took him two years to earn a scholarship. When I first saw him run out on the field, it was a proud moment. It wasn't about whether he would be a star player. That didn't matter to me. I was grateful he got to experience what I got to experience at BYU. He had an opportunity to be a Cougar and represent a school that I love.

Glen Kozlowski was a four-year starter at BYU at wide receiver. He was a co-captain of the 1984 national championship team and was named first-team All-WAC. He also received All-America honorable mention from AP, UPI, and *Football News*. The Chicago Bears took Kozlowski in the 11th round of the 1986 NFL Draft. He played six seasons in the NFL, all with the Bears.

ROBBIE BOSCO

QUARTERBACK

1981–1985

I GREW UP IN ROSEVILLE, California, and playing sports was my life. Obviously, we didn't have computers, video games, and all the things the kids have today. It was all about being outside and finding a bunch of neighborhood kids to play whatever sport was in season.

Football was actually my least favorite sport as a kid, mostly because I loved basketball. Most kids in our neighborhood played basketball or baseball. When I was old enough to play Pop Warner football, I really didn't want to. I didn't think I was tough enough to play tackle football.

When I got to the ninth grade, I decided to try football. After a couple weeks of summer practice, I was really struggling to understand the plays and didn't like the physical nature of the game, so I quit.

I really appreciated my dad because he didn't put any pressure on me. He didn't say, "You need to go play; you're not a quitter." He just let me do my own thing. My brother was a senior and the starting varsity quarterback. He was great. He came to me and said, "Look, Robbie, it's not that hard to learn the plays. Let me help you."

Because of their influence and patience, I finally decided, *Hey, I'll go give it another try*. That's how close I came to not playing football.

When I got to high school, we were running the wishbone. My coach knew I could throw the ball, so we switched to a passing offense. As a junior,

I led Northern California in passing and was named first-team All–Northern Cal. It was weird because football all of a sudden became my sport.

I started getting letters from universities and was being recruited by several teams in the Pac-10. At that time, not many schools were throwing the football. I knew I wanted to go someplace where I could throw the ball a lot. Cal and San Diego State were recruiting me hard. Doug Scovil, the former offensive coordinator at BYU, had just been named the head coach at SDSU. He told me he had coached the great BYU quarterbacks and he could do the same thing for me. I also started to get interest from BYU.

I remember watching BYU play San Diego State on national television in 1979. Marc Wilson threw three touchdowns on his first three passes of the game. The following year, Jim McMahon was literally rewriting the NCAA record book. I became mesmerized by BYU and its passing attack.

I didn't take a lot of trips during the recruiting process. I knew going to college and just being away from my family was going to be hard for me. My parents were originally from Utah, and by the time I was a senior, my sister and my brother were both going to school in Provo. That played a big role in my decision to attend BYU.

After taking visits to Cal and SDSU, I knew I wanted to go to BYU. I wanted to be a part of that great quarterback tradition. The problem was BYU was also recruiting Sean Salisbury. What I was in Northern California, Sean was in Southern Cal. I decided to wait on my decision until I saw what he decided to do. If Salisbury chose USC, I was going to BYU. But if he chose BYU, I was back to square one. I really didn't have a backup plan.

Tom Ramage was recruiting me for BYU. He went to high school with my mom, so he knew our family. On signing day, I remember sitting in math class watching him pace back and forth outside the room. It was so funny. Eventually, there was a knock on the window, and he was waving for me to come outside. When I got outside, he said, "We just got word that Salisbury has signed with USC."

So, without knowing, Sean Salisbury made the best decision of my life. That was a great day for me because BYU was the place I really wanted to be. When I first got to BYU, I loved the football part, but I didn't like being two states away from my parents. I hadn't spent a lot of time away from home growing up. It was so hard for me to adjust. After about three days of fall camp, I checked out of the dorms and moved in with my sister. I didn't tell anybody. I don't know if any of the coaches knew what I did. I stayed with

In 1984 Robbie Bosco led BYU to its only undefeated season in school history. He was named All-America, won the Sammy Baugh Trophy, and led the Cougars to a national championship.

my sister during fall camp, then moved into the dorms with Blaine Fowler, who I had become friends with.

I'll never forget running out onto the field at Cougar Stadium for the first time my freshman year. It was before the stadium expansion, but there were still 45,000 people in the stands. I think I had goose bumps the entire first quarter.

I was very fortunate to play behind two of the greatest quarterbacks to ever play NCAA football. As a freshman, I watched how Jim McMahon ran a football team. I watched how he interacted with his teammates. I learned what motivated him—how he acted on the field. I watched him in meetings and saw how he broke down film. He was so smart and had a great football IQ. He could see what defenses were trying to do before they even showed it. I watched him and said to myself, "I've got to learn that. I've got to be like that."

The next year I redshirted. Steve Young was a junior. Then I backed Steve up his senior year. I was a sophomore at that time, and I knew my chance was right around the corner. I would watch him and ask myself, *What do I need to learn from Steve?*

Football-wise it was the same type of stuff, but there were additional things. I was around Steve a lot more than Jim. I saw the interviews he did, the firesides he spoke at, and all the things that go along with being a BYU quarterback. I was a shy, homebody kid from Roseville, California, and I was thinking to myself, *Am I going to have to do this?* That was a hard thing for me.

I remember Steve and Gordon Hudson would pull me aside after practice and do these mock interviews with me. At first I would just bust out laughing and say, "I can't do this. I can't answer these types of questions." They would ask me tough questions, and I would say, "How do I answer that?" Eventually, I got so I felt comfortable with answering questions.

We were so good offensively during Steve's senior year in 1983 that I got to play quite a bit as a mop-up guy. I got to throw the ball some and got a lot of great experience without too much pressure. In the Utah State game Steve got hurt in the first half, and I actually got to play in a game when it mattered. I led our team on a drive and threw my first touchdown pass to Gordon Hudson. I remember the feeling to this day of throwing that touchdown pass and 65,000 people screaming and cheering. As I walked off the field, I thought to myself, *I love this. This is what it's all about.*

My sophomore year, backing up Steve, was like a dream. It was fun. But when it actually happened my junior year, and that quarterback mantel was on my shoulders, things changed dramatically. There was a lot of pressure. BYU teams didn't lose. We won a lot of games. I didn't want to be known as the quarterback who broke the string of consecutive WAC championships. I put a lot of pressure on myself.

To me, the guys who came before me were larger than life. They were legends. They knew how to play the game. They came through in the clutch. It scared me to death. The night before we left to go back to Pittsburgh to open the 1984 season, I lay in my bed and literally cried. I kept thinking, *I don't know if I can do this.* I wondered, *If I don't win games, if we don't win a conference championship, is that what I'll always be known for?*

During fall camp I was fine. I was running the offense, making plays, but that night it hit me, *This is it, we are playing for real now. I'm not going to be playing against my friends Leon White, Kurt Gouveia, and Jim Herrmann. If I throw an interception, we don't just get the ball back to try it again. We're opening up against the No. 3 team in the country. This isn't practice anymore.*

It took me all of one series in the Pittsburgh game for me to tell myself, *I can't do this.* The first pass I threw was incomplete. The second pass went over Mark Bellini's head by about five yards. He didn't even jump it was so far over his head. My next pass hit Adam Haysbert in the back of his shoulder pads, and we had to punt.

I'll never forget coming off the field after that first series. LaVell met me out by the numbers. I was thinking to myself, *Oh, great, I'm done. He's going to yank me.* He looked me in the eyes and said, "Just relax. Were not going to take you out. You're our guy. Just go out there and compete." Fortunately for me, and the team, our defense was amazing. They were unbelievable. They just kept battling and battling and giving the offense chances.

What changed everything for me was that, in the third quarter, Mark Allen intercepted a pass in Pittsburgh territory. We were down around the 10-yard line, and I handed off to Lakei Heimuli. The safety came up to hit him, and Lakei knocked him on his back and went in for a touchdown. For me, there was a sense of relief. I realized, *Maybe I can lead this team and we can score touchdowns.* After that, I settled down a little. Our defense came up with play after play and gave us a chance to pull it out in the last two minutes of the game.

The next week we played Baylor at home. It was a sold-out stadium. The offense clicked. I started to see the field better. I knew where guys should be. The speed of the game was slowing down, and I started to believe that I could

159

do it. More important, as a team, we found our swagger. To me, that game identified us as a team and identified me as a player.

As the 1984 season went on, we continued to build confidence. With four or five games left in the season, I think we all believed we could run the table. The question was would it be enough—could we be No. 1? We knew that being No. 1 would be the one thing that could set us apart from all the great BYU teams before us. We played Utah with two games to go in the season, including the bowl game. We had just come off the field after beating Utah, and we learned the two teams in front of us—Oklahoma and Washington—had just lost. The polls had not come out yet, but the anticipation was, "Could it be? Could we really be No. 1 in the country?" When it happened, we all said, "Wow, what do we do now?"

After we beat Michigan in the Holiday Bowl to finish the season undefeated at 13–0, we all went home for Christmas. There were still a lot of bowl games to be played. I was at home when I got the call we had won the national championship. It was a surreal feeling of, "We did it." We didn't get a chance to celebrate as a team until we all went back to school in January. For me, it was fitting. It was hard for me to leave home and come to BYU, but when we were named No. 1, I was actually at home and got to share it with my family. The story couldn't have had a better ending.

Obviously, one of the great things about BYU was playing for LaVell. I learned a lot from him and Patti. One of the most important things I learned was how to treat people. I would watch LaVell and notice how he reacted to things. I especially noticed how he would handle difficult situations. When things go wrong, some people get mad, become real negative, or refuse to talk. Not LaVell. He never changed. He was always the same. He was always steady. I would watch him and think, *I want to be like that. I want to treat people like that.* I was always amazed at how he was able to remain consistent with people.

I was not a member of the Mormon faith when I came to BYU. I came strictly to play football. My mom was a member of the Church, and my dad was not. I knew a little bit about the Church because of the things my mom taught me. Once I got to BYU, my friends, roommates, and teammates, for the most part, were LDS. So, as I was investigating the church, I was able to go to church with a lot of people I knew. I had a lot of conversations with Blaine and Chris Germann. We talked a lot about the faith. I had always lived the LDS lifestyle, so it wasn't a big adjustment for me when I found the truth and realized this is what I wanted to do.

Part of it was just being at BYU. I watched and observed some of the men I interacted with. I thought a lot about LaVell and Jeffrey Holland, the president of BYU. I saw what type of people they were, the kind of leaders they were. They were amazing men and had a profound impact on my life.

I love BYU for what it stands for. Being able to compete at the highest level of athletics and still remain true to the values the university stands for is what makes it special. There's just no place like it. I've been all over the country, to other schools and campuses. I've also talked with a lot of people who have been to BYU and have a hard time expressing how they feel while they are on campus. BYU is unique that way.

I look at the athletes I played with and especially the athletes at BYU today, and I think they are amazing. I see the type of individuals they are and what they do with their lives, and I'm just amazed. It's what BYU is all about. It's the spirit of the Y. I've been very fortunate to play for the school, coach for the school, and now work in athletics administration. That's why I want my children to attend BYU. I want them to experience what I experienced and have the university affect their lives the way it did mine.

Being a Cougar means a lot of things to me. This is where I met my wife, Karen. This is where we've raised our children. BYU is where my life changed and I found direction. It's helped me grow, not only as a person but also as a husband and a dad. I can't imagine what my life would have been like had I not come to BYU. I love what BYU stands for. I love that when things get rough, we don't back down. We stay true to our beliefs, our faith, and our actions.

Robbie Bosco led BYU to the 1984 national championship and the only undefeated season in school history. In 1984 he won the Sammy Baugh Trophy, was runner-up for the Davey O'Brien Award, and finished third in the voting for the Heisman Trophy. He was named All-America in 1984 and broke 10 NCAA records. Bosco was drafted in the third round of the 1986 NFL Draft by the Green Bay Packers. He was an assistant football coach at BYU from 1989 to 2003, and he currently works in the development office as the director of the Varsity Club. Bosco was inducted into the BYU Athletic Hall of Fame in 1995.

KURT GOUVEIA
LINEBACKER
1982–1985

I PLAYED QUARTERBACK and free safety in high school. As a senior, I was named both the offensive and defensive MVP in Hawaii. I was very proud of that accomplishment. At the time I was getting some Ivy League schools recruiting me to play basketball. I knew my family couldn't afford to send me to school, because they were helping my two older brothers, so I needed a full-ride scholarship.

Norm Chow contacted my family to let us know BYU was interested in me. Then Coach Whittingham came to Hawaii during my senior year and offered me a scholarship. He said they were interested in having me play strong safety. I committed right away. Dick Tomey was the head football coach at Hawaii at that time, and I never heard from UH—no contact, no nothing. I never even went on a visit. So I was very fortunate Brigham Young University came into my life. I came to Provo on a recruiting trip, and Louis Wong was my host. He grew up in the islands, so I knew all about him. Having some familiarity with a local kid from Hawaii gave me even more confidence to accept the scholarship at BYU.

I knew BYU was where I wanted to go, and I knew I could play at the next level. My parents thought it was a great opportunity for me. They knew it was going to be hard—that I would probably be homesick. They also had faith in me and knew that I could manage and do the right thing. I didn't realize at the time how homesick I'd be.

Kurt Gouveia celebrates after a big goal-line stand in Hawaii. He was co-captain of the 1984 national championship team and was later named honorable mention All-America as a senior in 1985. Gouveia went on to play 13 seasons in the NFL, winning two Super Bowls.

A couple of weeks into my freshman year, I was starting to miss home. I was thinking about leaving BYU and just going home, giving up on school. Luckily for me, Louis Wong came to my rescue. He helped me understand that I wasn't a quitter, that I could fight though being homesick and achieve my goals. I owe a lot to Louis for that, no question about it. He also helped me understand how I could help open doors for other Hawaiian kids, to help them achieve their goals. Without Louis coming to my rescue, I wouldn't be who I am today.

There were so many great people at BYU. My freshman roommate was Bob Jensen. He was a great athlete. We did everything together. Another guy who really made a difference in my life was Coach Mel Olson. He and his family took me in and made me feel like family. They were really good, loving people whom I enjoyed. Mel coached the offensive line, and I was obviously a defensive player, so figure that one out. It showed they cared about me as a person. Norm Chow and his family were also very good to me. Being away from home and not having family around, these people became my family. They were instrumental in helping me succeed in life and in college.

When I got to BYU, I was lifting weights, and I got a lot bigger and stronger, so they moved me to linebacker. My sophomore year in 1983 is when I started to play varsity football. Todd Shell was in front of me as a linebacker. He and guys like Steve Young and Gordon Hudson showed me how to be a champion—to have pride in being a Cougar.

When I came to BYU, I really didn't understand why people didn't like us—what they had against the Mormons. I just didn't get it. I saw hardworking, dedicated people who loved their families and loved what they did. They were trying to be the best people they could possibly be, no matter if it was on the football field or off the football field.

That really made a difference in my life. Back home I had an attitude. I didn't know how to carry myself in a social climate. At BYU they taught me how to be successful. I learned to have pride in what I do. Play football with passion, go to school, and try to do things the right way. I learned that from my teammates. I think that's really cool. I was a kid coming out of Hawaii who needed guidance, and I got it from my teammates.

To be a Cougar means to be successful, no matter what it takes. It means to respect other people and help them achieve their goals. To be a Cougar is a source of pride. A lot of tradition, a lot of loyalty, a lot of honesty, all the characteristics that go into being a person of well-being—that's what it meant to me. It wasn't just given. I had to learn it. I had to earn it.

My junior and senior year I was a captain on defense. As a captain, we were expected to take charge of the team—to lead by example. That's what I learned from teammates who were captains before me. LaVell trusted us, but what made him such a great coach is that he made sure we earned that trust—that we were going to do the right thing and make the right decisions at all times.

I was really close to Leon White. We had great chemistry. I knew exactly what he was going to do on the left side, and he knew exactly what I was going to do on the right. He played at the varsity level before I did. He basically showed me the ropes—what to do in certain situations and how to handle different formations. It was a real pleasure, playing linebacker with him, Cary Whittingham, and Marv Allen. We had great respect for each other. It was like family.

Playing in front of the home crowd at BYU is unbelievable. I remember coming out of the locker room, running onto the field behind the flag, and the crowd was going crazy—65,000 people cheering you on. That's the college spirit. It's just an unbelievable feeling. Not even the NFL has that feeling. I played with the Washington Redskins and won two Super Bowls. When we would come out of the chute at RFK, the crowd would be rocking, and the stands would be vibrating. It was close to being at LaVell Edwards Stadium. Almost. Not quite.

After winning the 1984 Holiday Bowl to complete the undefeated season, it was just chaos on the field. We were celebrating, having a good time, and congratulating each other. It was exciting. I had the opportunity of going through that feeling two more times in winning the Super Bowl. It was just like that. All the hard work from camp and spring ball. The sweat and tears and the sacrifices you make. It's just emotional. It was a tremendous achievement to go undefeated.

When we beat Michigan, it wasn't for sure that we'd be named No. 1, but I think in our hearts we had already won the national title. I know the whole team felt that we deserved to be national champions. No question.

I learned so much while I was at BYU. Respect. Loyalty. Honesty. Dedication. Trust. I learned it from the school and my teammates. I took it with me to the NFL. The qualities it takes to be a good human being and a champion I learned at BYU.

Kurt Gouveia played varsity linebacker for three seasons at BYU, from 1983 to 1985. As a junior in 1984, he was a co-captain of the national championship team. In 1985 Gouveia led BYU in tackles, was named first-team All-WAC, and received All-America honorable mention. The Washington Redskins selected him in the eighth round of the 1986 NFL Draft. Gouveia played 13 seasons in the NFL for the Redskins, San Diego Chargers, and Philadelphia Eagles. He won two Super Bowls with the Redskins, in 1988 and 1992.

LEON WHITE

LINEBACKER

1982–1985

ABOUT THE THIRD GAME of the 1984 season, my mom called me and said, "Your dad has cancer, and they're not giving him very long to live." I knew he wouldn't be able to watch me play anymore because he couldn't travel. So making it to the Holiday Bowl that year, so I could return home, was extremely important to me.

Before the bowl game the guys were saying, "We're playing this game for the national championship." The championship was the furthest thing from my mind. I knew this was going to be the last time my dad would ever see me play. Nothing was going to keep me from playing the best game of my life for him. The championship was secondary to me. I was just happy that he was able to see me play.

The Holiday Bowl Committee and the BYU administration made it possible for him to be on the sideline. They put him on a lift and propped him up about 10 feet in the air so he could watch the game in his hospital bed. That was the biggest thrill for me.

During the game, it was so fun to be able to make a great play and then come back on the sideline and see him give me the thumbs-up and say, "Good job, son." He had always taught me to do my best, regardless of the situation—to give 100 percent. Every time I came to the sideline, he would say, "Keep pushing. Don't let them stop you." Those were his words of encouragement.

After the game we went crazy. The team was jumping around and celebrating. It was amazing. Dad was on the sideline when they presented me the Defensive MVP trophy. I'll never forget that night.

Growing up in San Diego, I was a baseball player. It's really the only sport I played until I got to Helix High School. The only reason I started playing football was that my friends were playing. I was a tight end and linebacker my freshman year. My sophomore year I actually got a recruiting letter from Dartmouth. That was the most exciting thing that had ever happened to me. I couldn't believe it. I started to think, *Maybe I have a chance to play football in college.*

By my senior year I was one of the top recruits out of San Diego. USC, Arizona State, and San Diego State were very interested. It was a pretty exciting time. BYU didn't come in until late. I wasn't even really on their radar until Coach Ted Tollner, who was the offensive coordinator at San Diego State, left to coach at BYU. He was a friend of my high school coach. He said, "You should talk to Leon and see if he'd be interested in going on a recruiting trip to BYU." I said, "Sure, what the heck?"

I knew BYU from the Holiday Bowls, but I had never given it a serious thought. When I went on my trip to BYU in January, it was snowing, and I loved it. Jim McMahon was my recruiting host, and we had a ball. He showed me around and said he loved it. "You've got to come here. The people are great. We'll go to the Holiday Bowl every year and have a great time."

I also took trips to USC and, of course, San Diego State. USC was definitely a dream school, but at the time they were on probation for four years, so they couldn't go to a bowl game.

After talking to LaVell Edwards, I decided to go to BYU. He said, "We're going to play in a bowl game every year. You'll play in San Diego in front of your family at least twice during your career, and I think you'll have a chance to play right away." That was it. I committed and headed to Provo for the summer camp.

The plan was to redshirt my freshman year in 1981, but I got hurt and was granted a hardship year. The biggest adjustment for me at BYU was the weather. I had never really been in the snow. I was scared to death to drive in the stuff. Even just walking to class was scary to me. One day I was walking down a slight slope, and I slipped and fell on my butt. The next day I went and got my turf shoes out of my locker and wore them to school.

I was lucky to learn from some great linebackers. Glenn Redd had just graduated. I'd watch his film and try to emulate the way he played. I wanted

Leon White played four seasons at linebacker for BYU, from 1982 to 1985. As a junior in 1984, he was named second-team All-America, helped lead BYU to a national championship, and was the defensive MVP of the Holiday Bowl. White went on to play eight seasons in the NFL.

to be like him because everybody talked about him. That's one of the reasons why I wanted to wear his number—41.

I learned from guys like Todd Shell, Kyle Whittingham, and David Aupiu. Shell is one of the greatest all-around BYU linebackers. He could do it all. He was such a good athlete, he could have played safety. As a freshman, I watched those guys perform and was amazed at what they could do.

Later I played with guys like Marv Allen, one of the smartest linebackers I ever played with. He was the quarterback of our defense and ran the show on the field. Kurt Gouveia was outstanding in every aspect—such a great athlete. Cary Whittingham followed in the footsteps of his dad and his brother—just a tough, solid player. We had guys who could do a lot of things, and we spent a lot of years together, so we trusted each other. That's what made our defense so great.

Every time I drive by Qualcomm, I think about that year. I remember the games we played at that stadium, especially the '84 Holiday Bowl when we won the national championship. I have a lot of great memories of that year—right from the first game against Pitt. I think they were No. 3 in the nation, and we dominated that game on both sides of the ball. It was the start of one of the greatest seasons ever at BYU. Definitely a game I'll always remember.

Another memory I'll never forget was the game at Hawaii. The play Kyle Morrell made in that game to save the touchdown was just amazing. I show people that tape because it's just so incredible. I remember being in the NFL and having people ask me about it.

They were down on our 1-yard line, or even less than that. I remember thinking, *Gosh, our whole season is going to come down to this one play.* Knowing if we didn't stop them, and we lost, we were going to drop in the polls. Nobody really wanted us to be up there, anyway. I was on the left side, and Kyle was in the middle behind me. I just remember seeing something flash in my peripheral vision before the snap. I'm thinking, *Oh, my gosh, what just happened?* I thought somebody had jumped offside.

Next thing I know, Kyle's grabbing the quarterback and pulling him back, while doing a flip. I'm thinking, *What the heck is going on?* I didn't really realize what had happened or how amazing the play was until I saw the tape. It was the most amazing play I'd ever seen in my life. It was going to be a quarterback sneak, and he was just going to dive into one of the gaps for a touchdown. I think Kyle knew the only way we could stop him was to do something extreme, and he did. I think that play basically won the championship for us.

After we won the national championship my junior year, I got this itch to play baseball again. I always thought it would be cool to play baseball at BYU, but it was right during spring football. I finally drummed up enough courage to go ask LaVell.

First I asked Coach Pullins, the baseball coach, and he said, "I'll let you try out, but you need to go talk to LaVell." So I walked into LaVell's office, and he said, "Hey, how're you doing, Leon? What's going on?" Anybody could walk into his office at any time and ask a question. He was really easy to talk to. I said, "Hey, Coach, I've got a question. What would you think of me missing spring ball this year?" He kind of looked at me with a puzzled look. "What do you mean miss spring ball?" I said, "Well, I want to go out for baseball. You know I played in high school, and I want to try out for the team at BYU. Pullins said he'd let me try out if it was all right with you."

So we talked about some of the challenges, like missing school, keeping up with homework, and missing all of spring camp. I told him I could handle it. Finally he said, "Well, can you hit the curveball?" I said, "Yeah, Coach, I can hit the curveball." So he said, "All right. Go ahead."

So I went out for baseball and made the team. I wasn't a starter, but I got some playing time at DH and filling in. We ended up winning the WAC championship that year. It was a blast. I had a great time. I might be one of the few players who won a WAC championship in football and baseball.

Playing for LaVell Edwards was a real honor. He is one of the best men I've ever known. He was the greatest teacher I've ever had. BYU owes him a lot. He has done so much for the university, the community, and the Church. I don't think there will ever be another one like him. I have great respect for everything LaVell Edwards has done.

When I think about being a Cougar, I think about the closeness I felt with my teammates. We had a special bond that you just don't find on too many teams. We were a close-knit group, and we knew we could count on each other. That's what made that national championship team so special, more so than any other. We had some guys who were really talented, and it showed on the field. I think there were other teams that may have been more talented, but they didn't play as well together as a team. Those are the memories I have. The fun that we had on road trips, the camaraderie, and the close-knit family—that's what made it so great. It doesn't matter where you are, or how long it's been since you've been at BYU, there is pride in being BYU blue. It's a special place.

Leon White played four seasons as a linebacker at BYU from 1981 to 1985. He helped the Cougars win the national championship in 1984 and was named Defensive MVP of the Holiday Bowl. White was named second-team All-America as a junior in 1984 and received All-America honorable mention in 1985. He was selected in the fifth round of the 1986 NFL Draft by the Cincinnati Bengals and later played in Super Bowl XXIII. White played eight seasons in the NFL with the Bengals and the Los Angeles Rams. He was inducted into the Holiday Bowl Hall of Fame in 2001.

The NINETIES

CHRIS SMITH

TIGHT END

1988–1990

MY FOOTBALL CAREER started at Columbine High School in Colorado. After my sophomore year, we moved from Colorado to La Canada, California. I didn't play much football until my senior year. I come from a family of 10, and my four older brothers—Kevin, Kenny, Scott, and Brent— all came to BYU. No matter where I went, someone would say, "Hey, you're a Smith!" After my senior year, I thought, *I'm not doing that again.* I didn't want to follow them to BYU.

I had a few schools looking at me but nothing really serious. There was a coach from the University of Arizona who was watching film on a defensive back at another high school and noticed me playing. He asked the coach, "Who's this guy? He keeps beating your defensive back. Where's he from?" He called my coach, and they showed him some of my film. The very first play was this little wide receiver screen. I caught the ball and ran through four or five little defensive backs. He said to my coach, "That's the type of guy we want."

BYU had asked me to walk on, and the University of Arizona said, "We're going to give you a scholarship." I said, "Sweet, I'll go to the U of A." At that time, UCLA was recruiting me a little bit, but for whatever reason I never wanted to go to UCLA. The wide receivers coach would call me and come see me play, and I just kind of blew him off. My dad couldn't believe it. As we were driving to Arizona, he said, "Son, seriously. Why were you

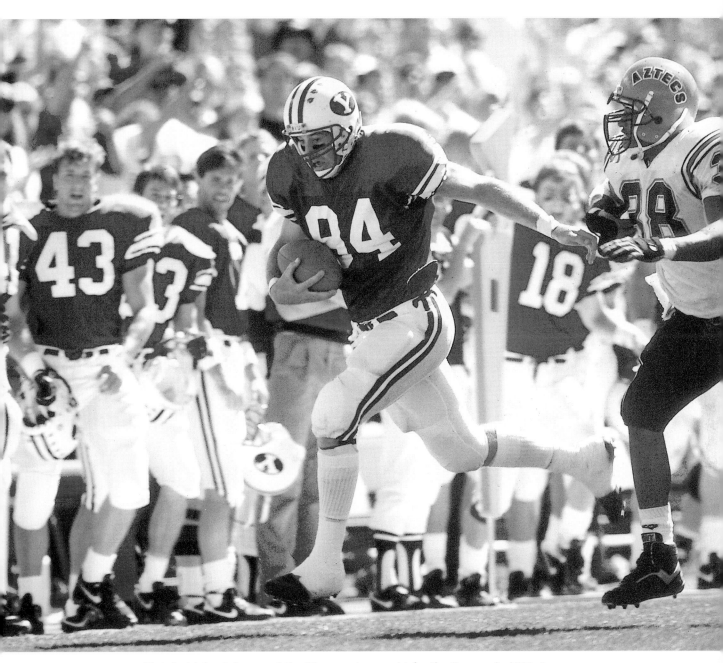

Chris Smith hauls in one of the 68 passes he caught for the Cougars in 1990. As a senior, the two-time consensus All-American set an NCAA tight end record with 1,156 yards receiving.

not interested in UCLA?" I said, "I don't know, Dad. I just feel like there's somebody at the University of Arizona that I'm supposed to meet."

Three weeks later, after training camp ended, I called my dad and said, "I'm redshirting, and I found the person I was supposed to meet." He said, "Really?" I said, "Yeah, I met this girl. She's wonderful. You're going to love her." So that's how I met Sarah—whom I later married—on a blind date after a football game while I was a Wildcat at U of A.

After my freshman year, I got called on a two-year Church mission to Albuquerque, New Mexico. My first area was Silver City, New Mexico— literally two hours away from Tucson. I was saying to myself, "Come on guys, really?" My mission president must have been inspired, he said, "Elder Smith, it seems like you're kind of having a hard time. What's going on?" I said, "Well, I'm two hours away from my old life and the girl I really love and just baptized before I left on my mission. My heart aches for her."

He told me, "You're either a missionary or you're Chris Smith the football player. Who do you want to be?" I said, "You're right." So, at that moment, I had to decide what I was going to be. I chose to be a missionary.

While I was serving, my head coach announced he was leaving U of A to go to USC. I'm thinking, *Wow. What happens to me now?* Three days later he called me on my mission and said, "Hey, Chris, we want you to transfer over to USC. We like you." Sarah was graduating from the University of Arizona, so I figured, "I'll go to USC, not a big deal." Two weeks later, the SMU football program was given the death penalty by the NCAA, and USC gave my scholarship to a tight end transfer from SMU.

So, when I got off my mission, I didn't know where to go to school. Pasadena Community College said, "We'll give you a scholarship," but I didn't like that option. I called the University of the Pacific and San Diego State, but no luck. This was June, and I was barely off my mission. I wasn't going to have a lot of luck finding a scholarship mid-summer.

One of our family friends had a son playing at Utah. He called Coach [Jim] Fassel and said, "You've got to see this kid. He played football at Arizona before his mission. He ran track in high school and is fast." So Coach Fassel flew me up on a trip, and they offered me a scholarship.

So I was just off a mission with no opportunities to go anywhere, and the U was offering me a scholarship. Sounded good. My older brother, who had played football for BYU, talked to LaVell and said, "Hey, remember Chris?

He doesn't have a place to go right now." At that time BYU didn't have a scholarship available, but LaVell told my brother, "Tell him he can walk on."

I didn't have the money to walk on, so I was leaning toward the U. The day before camp started, I was ready to call the Utah coaches to tell them I was coming. It wasn't like I was a huge BYU lover or was holding out for BYU, but going to Utah just didn't feel right. I came home from work that day, and my dad said, "Chris, if BYU offered you a scholarship right now would you take it?" I said, "Yes." He said, "They called."

One of the BYU tight ends had gotten in trouble and couldn't get cleared to get back into school. BYU told me, "You have a scholarship."

I literally threw all my belongings in this duffel bag and said, "I guess I'm out of here." I called Sarah and said, "Sarah, I know I'm supposed to come down this weekend"—she lived in San Diego, and I was in Pasadena—"but I'm going to BYU." She said, "What?" I told her that BYU had called and offered a scholarship, and that I was going.

If you look at how the whole thing came about, I can't argue the fact that I was supposed to come to BYU. I had a good career at BYU, and it was a lot of fun.

Coming down the ramp onto the field at Cougar Stadium on game day is one of the coolest things ever. During warm-ups there were usually about 12 people there. I'd be thinking, *Where is everybody?* The locker room was right underneath the stadium, and as it got closer to the game, I'd start to feel the energy, hear the stadium filling up, and sense the excitement. I would walk out, look up, and see all these kids hanging over the sides wanting a high five. I thought, *This is cool.*

Even to this day, I remember the first time I ran onto the field. I looked around and said, "Wow!" Sixty-five thousand people screaming, yelling! It's exciting. It's electric. It is just one of those things that I'll never, ever forget.

I'll always remember the Miami game. We beat No. 1 Miami, and we had all these fans running onto the field. But at no time did I think, *Wow, I'm in danger.* We were out there just screaming and yelling, and everyone was jumping up and down. College football was fun. Those memories of playing at BYU will always be there.

I remember prior to the 1990 season, someone in the media asked me, "So what does it take to win a Heisman?" I said, "Well, first of all you have to have a winning team—because the Heisman is never given to a player on a losing team. You have to have a structure in place. You have to have players who can make plays on defense. You have to have a great offense and players who can make plays. You need a great offensive line." Ty Detmer never forgot that. On Heisman announcement day, the whole team gathered around the pool at the hotel in Hawaii. When the announcement came, Ty said, "We got it!" How cool is that! You have to know Ty, just a humble guy from Texas. *We* got it. Not *I* got it, but *we* got it. It was just one of those cool things. Even when you talk to him today, it was about the team.

Because a lot of my experiences here revolved heavily around sports, no matter where I was, I was Chris Smith the football player. I remember being in an airport one day, and out of nowhere this little kid came up to me and said, "You're Chris Smith. You play football for BYU." At that moment I realized that you never really know who's watching, who needs you to be the example, who needs you to do what is right. BYU taught me that.

LaVell was a great coach. He taught me a lot of important lessons. My first time on the field at BYU, I was in a drill, and coach Roger French was barking and yelling at me. Being the confident player that I was as a freshman, I yelled back. LaVell was standing there, and he looked at me and said, "Excuse me? What did you say?" I told him what I said. He said, "You get off my football field right now." I looked at him, and he said, "I mean it." He didn't yell, but you knew he meant it. At that moment, I knew who was in charge.

Also being the stupid freshman that I was, I was thinking, *That's it. What do I do now?* I thought I was gone. I thought I was done. I thought I was packing up my duffel bag and going back home to play at Pasadena Community College. Afterward, Lance Reynolds said, "Hey, Chris. Now you know to show the coaches respect. Don't do that again. See you at practice tomorrow, and come ready to go."

But with LaVell it went both ways. Against Navy my junior year, we had one drive where my mistakes, from start to finish, literally cost us the drive. I jumped offside. I had a holding penalty. I dropped a pass. When I got off the field, my position coach was so mad. He was just ripping me. He said, "You could have cost us the game." He really let me have it. When we got to the airport, I called my wife, "Sarah, I'm done. I'm packing my bags, and I'm done." While I was on the phone, I saw LaVell talking to my position coach. It wasn't a very long conversation—maybe 10 or 15 seconds.

After that, my coach came up to me as I was talking to my wife and apologized. It had come full circle. It didn't matter what your role was on the team, he was the same with everyone—"This is my team. Show people respect." It changed the way I looked at LaVell forever. The man was so consistent. He respected you, he trusted you, and he wanted you to have respect for the game, yourself, and for everyone. That's what I loved about him.

When you play at BYU, you have that feeling of "I am here not just because I'm a good football player. I'm here because, in a lot of ways, I'm supposed to be here." Austin Collie got a lot of grief for saying, "When you do the right things, magic happens." But it's true. BYU is different. It really is. BYU is a place where you come, you learn, you go to class, and you represent not just yourself. You represent BYU. You represent the Church. That means something.

When you ask, "What does it mean to be a Cougar?" The answer is a lot. Because when you're an LDS kid and you're idolizing players from BYU, you have an instant connection. "He believes what I believe. We have something in common. We're the same. We are BYU."

Chris Smith set an NCAA record for tight ends with 1,156 yards receiving as a senior in 1990 and became the first Cougar to be named to every All-America team in the same season. He was named consensus All-America as a junior and a senior. His 2,367 yards receiving is the ninth-highest career total in BYU history. The Cincinnati Bengals selected Smith in the 11th round of the 1991 NFL Draft.

TY DETMER

QUARTERBACK
1988–1991

M Y DAD WAS A HIGH SCHOOL football coach, and as a kid I was a ball boy for his teams. I got to sit in on some of his coaches' meetings on Sunday evenings around the house, watching film on the old projector. I thought this was pretty normal, but later I found out that I was around football a lot more than most kids.

I enjoyed all the sports growing up. I played baseball, basketball, and soccer. Whatever season it was, that's what we played. In high school, I ran track and played on the golf team in addition to football.

My junior year I had some big games in football. I broke the state passing record and started getting a lot of interest. Back then, recruiting was a lot different than it is now. We didn't go to football camps and all the stuff kids are doing now—getting on college campuses in front of college coaches. Your exposure was sort of whatever came out in the media.

Back then nobody was really throwing the football much in high school. We threw it quite a bit. My dad ran a pro-style offense—split back, two backs, two receivers, tight ends. He liked to spread people out a little bit. My junior year we had a tight end who was small but could really fly. We had good receivers and used our backs coming out of the backfield a lot. It was pretty unique for the time. We threw it probably 30 times a game, not 60 like some of these kids are now, but at the time it was a lot for high school football.

In one of the greatest games in BYU football history, Ty Detmer completed 38 of 54 passes for 406 yards and three TDs to upset No. 1 Miami 28–21 in 1990.

We had an assistant basketball coach at our high school who was LDS. He talked to my dad about BYU. We knew BYU had won the national championship in 1984. We had watched some of the games and knew that the offense looked really similar to what we were running. I'm not sure if my dad made contact with them or if it was our assistant basketball coach, but BYU came down in the spring and watched me throw during our athletic period and saw some game film.

As I was looking at options, BYU kept coming up first on my list as far as the offense and obviously the quarterback tradition. So my dad said, "Well, why don't we take a family trip this summer and go tour the West. We'll stop by BYU first, then Arizona State, and some of the other schools that are interested that run a pro-style offense." So BYU was our first stop. It was really the first school on my list. When we got there, we sat down with Coach Edwards. He said, "We'd love to have you. There will be a scholarship waiting for you when you're able to sign if you want to come here."

Obviously going in we knew the quarterback tradition and that the school was nationally known and all those things. I don't think there was much said afterward other than, "This is where we want to go."

I loved the area and the school, with the campus right there in the mountains. I just felt like it was the place for me. We fished the Provo River for a few days and messed around and then headed home. So we didn't actually go to any other schools. It was a family vacation. If BYU hadn't been interested, we probably would have gone on maybe to Arizona State or UCLA. Since BYU was really my first choice, and they wanted me, we came to an agreement.

I love being outdoors. I love to fish and hunt. I think it was a real combination of both—the football tradition and the Provo area. I don't think I would have been able to fish much in Westwood or Phoenix.

The thing I loved about Coach Edwards was that he was really low key. He seemed really personable and easygoing. He's not a car salesman, putting a big pitch on you. I had obviously heard a lot about him. I felt like he would be great to play for and knew he would be there for my whole four or five years. The program was really stable, and I just felt like you knew what you were getting when you went to BYU.

Other schools called during my senior year after I had already committed. I let them know that I had made my decision that I was going to BYU. Miami and Michigan expressed that they wished I had at least given them a look, but wished me luck. Nobody with a really hard sales pitch came in and tried to sway me, I think probably because I just let them know right up front that I'd already made my decision.

I was 6' and 170 pounds coming out of high school. I redshirted my first year at BYU. I think the coaches thought I would come in and they would try to put some weight on me and let me get to know the system. The weight part didn't work really well, but going in, that was their plan.

The transition from high school to BYU was pretty easy for me. I don't really recall ever thinking, *Man, this is a lot different than what I thought it would be*, or anything like that. It was really a perfect fit. My roommate was Dave Henderson from Longview, Texas—so two Texas guys. I lived in the dorms the first semester. We really just had a great time and kind of got to know the school and the area.

Probably the biggest adjustment was when I went deer hunting. We got up early, a friend and I, and drove up to South Fork in Provo Canyon. We parked along the road with a lot of the other cars and hiked up the mountain. It was pitch black. We hiked for a while, sat down, and thought, *Okay, this is probably high enough*. It started getting light, and we were about 100 yards from the road. Here we thought we'd hiked all the way up to the top part of the mountain, and we had barely gone anywhere. The altitude and the steepness of the mountains were probably my biggest adjustments coming from the Texas flatland.

I ended up getting a deer and an elk while I was there at BYU. We hunted pheasants. It was something we did fairly often, maybe once a week or every two weeks, something like that. Sometimes we had to get out and go.

My first year at BYU, we opened the football season at home versus Pittsburgh. It was an ESPN night game. I had been playing in front of a few thousand people in high school. We came out on the field that night with 65,000 fans, and the lights were on; it was like, *Man, okay, this is for real now. This is the big time*. It was an awesome place to play—a great stadium. The grass was always perfectly manicured. Those types of games and those types of crowds are really what you are looking for when you leave high school. You want an opportunity to play in front of your fans and have the stadium full every game. It was always something special.

I have a lot of great memories at BYU. Obviously beating Miami, with all the media attention and everything surrounding that game, is a great memory. The fans just couldn't wait for that game. That was probably the most memorable game. There are not many times you have a chance to play the No. 1 team in the nation, and then to beat them on a national stage was something I will always remember. That one probably sticks out more than others just because of the magnitude of the game.

Obviously winning the Heisman was another great memory. It was a pretty nerve-racking day. To me, the Heisman is one of the best-kept secrets in the country because you really don't know who will win until they open that envelope. It just builds all season long. I really didn't think I was going to win the Heisman until the *USA Today* weekend edition came out on Friday,

I think, and it had me as the front-runner in some sort of a straw poll. At that time, I thought, *Man, this could really happen.*

We were in Hawaii to play our final game of the year. We gathered by the pool after our walk-through, and all the team was around. I had an earpiece so I could hear the announcement, but no one else could hear because there was no volume on the TV. When they read the announcement, I just remember saying, "We got it!" Everybody went crazy. It was just great.

I was happy for the program, for the players who had come before. I really felt like they were a big part of it because they put BYU on the map. With the season we had, beating Miami, it all kind of came together that year. But it would not have ever been possible without Nielsen, Wilson, McMahon, Young, Bosco—those guys earned the notoriety and put BYU on the map. It was great, and I was really happy for LaVell. He had come close several times, and he finally had a Heisman winner.

I announced I was coming back to BYU for my senior year at the Heisman ceremony. I told people, "I'm coming back and looking forward to it."

Ty Detmer and LaVell Edwards share a quiet moment prior to the 1990 Heisman Trophy announcement. The Cougars were in Hawaii preparing to take on the Rainbows on December 1, the night of the Heisman announcement.

That was kind of it. There wasn't a big press conference or anything like that. There was no sit-down meeting with LaVell. We didn't even talk about it.

To me it wasn't about, "Well, I won the Heisman, and I should go to the NFL. This is my chance." I was really enjoying what I was doing and having fun at BYU. I just felt like I wanted to have a senior year at BYU and continue the great experience I was having.

I had a great experience at BYU. You learn a lot about life there. I think college is where you really start shaping what you want to do, who you want to be. With the influence of the Church, and the standards at BYU that are expected, it shaped me as a person. The whole experience there helps you keep things in perspective. It is not just live or die with football. You are learning life lessons. You're going to school. You're taking religion classes. You're improving yourself overall rather than just as a football player.

BYU is a little different that way. You're expected to hold certain standards. They are trying to develop the best men, not just the best football players. Overall, it was a great experience. It taught me a lot about myself, about what I wanted to be, and how I wanted to be seen by other people.

I am proud to say that I am a BYU graduate and played for the BYU football program. I think people around the country have a lot of respect for what is going on at BYU. Again, not just football-wise but the type of people BYU produces. You're representing a lot of people, through the Church, all across the nation. We had fans everywhere we went. A big part of that is the Church, so it's something I'm proud to say I'm a part of. I will always try to represent the program in the right light.

Ty Detmer won the Heisman Trophy as a junior in 1990. He was named consensus All-America in 1990 and 1991 and won the Davey O'Brien Award both years. Detmer also won the Maxwell Award, the Sammy Baugh Trophy, and was named 1990 UPI Player of the Year. During his BYU career, he set 59 NCAA records and finished his college career as the NCAA all-time leader in pass completions, passing yards, touchdowns, total offense, and passer rating. He was selected in the ninth round of the 1992 NFL Draft by the Green Bay Packers. In 14 NFL seasons, Detmer played for the Packers, Philadelphia Eagles, San Francisco 49ers, Cleveland Browns, Detroit Lions, and Atlanta Falcons.

ERIC DRAGE

WIDE RECEIVER

1990–1993

COMING OUT OF HIGH SCHOOL, I was being recruited by Stanford, Washington, and BYU. At least those were the three top schools that I was considering. BYU got involved pretty early. Being from Tucson, I was hoping to get a little more interest from the University of Arizona, but they tried to get me to walk on as a receiver. Interestingly, Ron McBride was one of the U of A coaches who was talking to me.

I didn't grow up a BYU fan. We lived in Maryland, North Carolina, and Arizona, so I didn't know much about BYU. My first introduction really was during the recruiting process. Ultimately, the decision of where to go to college came down to football. I'd like to say that it was because I was LDS, but football was the main reason.

My goal was to play in the NFL. That was it. So I looked at BYU, and they threw the ball 40 to 50 times a game. As a receiver it's hard to not like that. Plus BYU had LaVell Edwards, and I knew there was stability. I felt he was going to be there forever.

I made my recruiting trip in January, and when I got to sit down and talk with Coach Edwards in his office, he offered me a scholarship. I pretty much accepted right there on the spot. I called and canceled my trip to Stanford after that.

There were a lot of talented wide receivers in our freshman class of 1989. There were a bunch of guys who were players of the year in their state—

Micah Matsuzaki from Hawaii, Jason Cooper from Utah, Nati Valdez from Texas, and me from Arizona. There was obviously a lot of competition. During fall camp Norm Chow told me they were going to redshirt me. I wasn't happy about that at all, but I redshirted and played on the scout team. That was a difficult year for me, not being able to play.

The next year I got to travel as a redshirt freshman, and I roomed with Chris Smith, who was an All-American. I hung out with Andy Boyce, who was a stud receiver. They took me under their wings and taught me a lot. Gradually I got playing time.

Norm was technically the receivers coach, but he was also the offensive coordinator and helped with the quarterbacks. So I always felt guys like Andy, Chris, and Jeff Frandsen were my receivers coaches. I learned so much from them. Just watching them on the field, how they carried themselves, how they handled different situations. Later I tried to help younger guys like Tim Nowatzke and Kaipo McGuire. The older guys mentored the younger guys. That's the way we did it.

The best part of that 1990 season was I got to play with Ty Detmer the year he won the Heisman Trophy. I'll never forget the Miami game. I got to play about 10 plays in that game. The atmosphere that night was just electric. I don't know if it will ever be replicated. To beat the No. 1 team in the nation was just amazing.

Ty was a lot of fun to be around. He was also probably the smartest player I ever played with. We would watch film, and he would know what the defense was going to do before the play began. I would be sitting there thinking, *You haven't even seen this film yet, how do you know?* Sure enough, he'd be right. He was amazing. Ty was also a fiery competitor.

That's what I remember most about the 1991 San Diego State game that ended in 52–52 tie. At halftime we were down by two or three touchdowns. I remember in the locker room Ty was telling everybody, "Hey, we're going to win this game." It wasn't like he was screaming or yelling. He just said, "We're going to win this game." In fact, he was calm about it, and we believed him. We all said, "All right, maybe Ty knows something we don't."

We came out in the second half and scored 35 points and could have won the game. I still wish we had gone for two and won the game. We just needed a tie to clinch the conference championship, so we kicked the extra point. I got quoted after the game saying, "You know, they say a tie is like kissing your sister, but tonight she looks pretty good."

Eric Drage led the Cougars in receiving for three straight years, from 1991 to 1993. He finished his BYU career as the leading receiver in school history with 3,065 yards and was named CoSIDA Academic All-America in 1992 and 1993.

I have a lot of good memories of my sophomore season. The UTEP game that year was a breakout game for me. I remember one play when I ran a curl and go. Ty underthrew me, so I had to come back for the ball. It ended up getting tipped three or four times before I was able to catch it in the end zone. It made the ESPN Plays of the Week. After that game, Ty started having more confidence and trust in me. He started looking my way more and more, which gave me a lot of confidence.

Another memorable game for me was at New Mexico. I had a huge first half with more than 100 yards receiving. In the second half they switched and put this little defensive back on me. He immediately started talking trash, "I'm gonna shut you down, Drage." I didn't like to talk a lot of trash, so I didn't say anything. The very first play I caught a curl route for about 12 yards. I got up, looked at him, and said, "Don't talk." He didn't say a word the rest of the game.

I loved playing in the Utah game. We beat them four of the five years I was at BYU. In the 1991 game we started off slow. We were backed up on our own 3-yard line. Chow called a play where Ty would drop back and then sprint out. It was a long developing play, and Ty threw me a corner route. The safety must have fallen down because I caught the pass and turned up the sideline and no one was there. I actually saw Ron McBride put his hands on his knees. I took it 97 yards for a touchdown. Usually you would celebrate at the end of a play like that. I just remember hoping we had oxygen on the sideline. I wasn't used to running a 100-yard sprint. That was a memorable play.

To me, being a Cougar meant winning games. We took a lot of pride in winning, and winning the right way. Some people would say that we were arrogant. Yeah, there might have been a bit of that, but to me it was more of a confidence that, "Hey, we can play with anybody." We expected to win. We expected to beat Notre Dame. We expected to beat Penn State. It didn't matter whom we played. It was instilled by Coach Edwards and by veteran players like Ty Detmer. Every time you put on a Cougars uniform and went out on the field, you expected to win. It was a cool feeling.

Nothing beats coming down that ramp onto the field at Cougar Stadium. To this day I have withdrawal because I just miss that feeling. My senior year there were some guys in the stands who were Drage fanatics. They had my name—D-R-A-G-E—painted on their chests. I remember seeing them for the first time and thinking, *Are you kidding me?* There's just nothing like that.

187

The other cool thing about BYU is we played big-time teams at home. Penn State, Notre Dame, Miami, UCLA—we had some big-name programs come through Provo. In all those games, the atmosphere was just electric. It's hard to describe. It's a high. It's a rush that you just can't get anywhere else.

I loved my time at BYU. The university had a lot to offer. From a young age I was always concerned about my grades. So when I got to college nothing really changed. It was important to me, so I worked hard at it and had a great experience in the classroom.

I'm not sure the casual fan realizes how much work goes into football. It's pretty much a full-time job with all the meetings and practices and film work. During the season it's not easy for players to stay up on their grades. You're traveling and missing classes.

I was first-team All-WAC a couple of years, and from a football standpoint that was a big deal for me. But being able to tell my kids that I was a two-time Academic All-American probably makes me as proud as anything. When you work hard at something and then get recognized for it, it's a cool thing. I didn't go to BYU just to play football. I wanted to be successful in the classroom and get a good education.

I was fortunate to play for some of the greatest minds in college football. Norm Chow had a great football mind, and LaVell is a legend. LaVell hired great people to surround him, and he let them do their job.

I never saw Coach Edwards get on his coaches and say, "Hey, we need to do this or that differently." Now, in their coaches meetings that may have happened, but he never undermined his coaches in front of the players. We had great coaches, and LaVell let them do their jobs. That's one of the reasons why BYU football was so successful for so many years.

Eric Drage played four seasons as a wide receiver at BYU, from 1990 to 1993, and led the Cougars in receiving for his last three (1991–1993). Drage finished his BYU career as the all-time leading receiver in school history, with 3,065 yards. That record held for 15 years before being broken by Austin Collie in 2008. Drage was named first-team All-WAC in 1992 and 1993. He was also named a CoSIDA Academic All-American both years and was the recipient of an NCAA Postgraduate Scholarship as a senior. Drage played one season of professional football with the Toronto Argonauts of the CFL.

JAMAL WILLIS

RUNNING BACK

1991–1994

I STARTED PLAYING TACKLE FOOTBALL at the age of six. I never played anything but running back. I grew up in Las Vegas, and sports were what we did. I played basketball, baseball, and football.

I really loved basketball, but about my junior year in high school I figured I wasn't tall enough for basketball. When I started getting a lot of recruiting letters for football, I realized that was probably my best opportunity to play athletics in college. Football just came naturally because of my size, speed, and knowledge of the game. Nebraska was recruiting me very hard. Eventually, it came down to Washington, a few other Pac-10 schools like Arizona and Cal-Berkeley, plus Nebraska and BYU. Nebraska was kind of the front-runner, but I started to consider BYU more after I took a recruiting trip to Provo.

I really knew nothing about BYU, and my parents didn't know much, either. My dad said, "Let's give them a chance. Let's take an official visit and see what BYU is all about." At the end of all the recruiting trips, I was try-ing to figure out where I wanted to go. My dad scheduled home visits from LaVell Edwards and [Nebraska head coach] Tom Osborn back to back. So while LaVell was talking with me at our house, Tom was waiting in the car. LaVell walked out, and Tom walked in. It was an interesting contrast. LaVell didn't pitch football much. He pitched everything that BYU represents. With Tom Osborn it was all about football, football, football. It was about the national championships and really nothing else.

I had kind of committed to Nebraska, but at the last minute my dad said, "I really believe you need to consider BYU." We kind of battled back and forth, but at the end of the night, I said, "Dad, where do you want me to go?" He said, "BYU." So I said, "Okay, I'll go." As a 17-year-old kid, I was looking at different things than my parents were. They were looking for the whole gamut—good education, environment—not just great football.

Looking back, if I had not listened to my dad, my whole life could have gone in a different direction. He helped open my eyes to other things. Now, as a dad, I can see what he saw. He was looking for the whole package, and I think LaVell sold him big time. Even after I signed to go to BYU, there were doubts. I had thoughts like, *Is this going to work out for me? Am I going to feel comfortable there? Am I going to play? Am I going to feel a part of the community since I'm not LDS?*

When I started to play my freshman year, I knew I'd made the right decision. From there, my life was kind of bolstered, whether it was in football or other things. Ty Detmer had just won the Heisman, yet he made me feel welcome—a part of the team. Peter Tuipulotu was another player who helped me fit into the environment and feel a part of the team.

I didn't grow up in a religious background. I grew up in inner-city Vegas where anything happens, anything goes. So there were adjustments at BYU, like going to religion classes. The interesting thing is it sort of opened my mind. My dad would say, "Get what you can out of the school and out of the community that will help you in your life." So I took the approach of, "How can I benefit from this? What can I learn from the people at BYU?" I tried to just embrace everything. If I had it to over again, I would do the exact same thing, because it helped me develop as a person.

I met my wife at BYU. She was on the gymnastics team. We started dating when I was a freshman. She played a big role in my life because she kept me on the right road. She was one of the people who brought the Church into my life. Another guy who played an important role is Lance Reynolds. He was big-time. Growing up, I looked at my coaches as coaches. They weren't really my friends, but Lance was different. He helped me fit in, feel a part of the culture, and motivated me to reach my potential.

The other person was LaVell. He was like my dad. LaVell was one of the reasons why I am who I am today. He helped me to understand that life is more than just football. LaVell was the catalyst in helping me reach a lot of goals in my life.

Jamal Willis finished his BYU career as the leading rusher in school history with 2,970 yards and 40 touchdowns. He went on to play two seasons with the San Francisco 49ers and was a member of the 1995 Super Bowl team.

LaVell's genius was to motivate you by helping you understand that he cared about you. The door to his office was always open. He was certainly there as a leader but, more importantly, as a father figure. He was a unique, one-of-a-kind coach. You wanted to play for him because you knew he cared. As a freshman and new to the culture, he made me feel like, "Jamal, I don't care if you're not LDS. I care about you." He didn't have to say that. I knew it.

I think my dad saw that right off the bat. He saw what took me a year or two to see. I've talked to dozens of players over the years who have the same story. Whether they're black or white, LDS or from another religion, they have the same story. It takes a unique person to bridge the gaps. LaVell is one of a kind.

I remember my first time running out of the tunnel at Cougar Stadium. It was such an eye-opener for me. We had 65,000 fans screaming and hollering, and I'd come from a high school where barely 100 people would watch our games. I remember thinking, *This is big-time.*

When I started to play well and get more carries, the fans would start chanting, "Give Jamal the ball! Give Jamal the ball!" That was cool. When that happened, I thought back to my dad. He was right.

To me, being a Cougar, being BYU blue, is deeper than just football. It's how you represent yourself. It's a way of life. It's how we live our lives. Every football player who walks off that field is changed by their experience at BYU, even guys who were a little rough around the edges.

LaVell always said, "I don't care who you are or where you come from, but you represent this team. You represent BYU on and off the field." I hear from so many former players who still live the standards regardless of who they are, where they live, or what religion they belong to. They are still BYU guys. That is amazing. That's the really unique part of being a BYU Cougar.

I have a lot of great memories of BYU. One of my favorite moments was the 52–52 tie at San Diego my freshman year. That was kind of a breakout game for me. It was a high-scoring affair that seemed to go all night. Marshall Faulk and I were battling back and forth. That game sort of put me on the map at BYU.

I felt like I had something to prove. Faulk was a freshman putting up big numbers, so I wanted to do the same. The game was on ESPN, so we had the national spotlight. There was not much defense played in that game. They would score, and then we would score. It was one of those magical games where I was in the zone and felt like I couldn't do anything wrong.

Another great memory was the Notre Dame game—another big game on the national stage. South Bend was an amazing environment in which to play. Some places are like that—you just smell football in the air. You could feel it when you walked on that field. That was a great football crowd that appreciated football. They wanted their team to win, but they wanted to see good football, too.

The odds were against us winning that game. But to go down there and walk off that field with a victory on national TV was huge. When I look back, I have a lot of great memories, but that afternoon at Notre Dame was a defining moment.

When I think about my time at BYU, the first thing that comes to mind is tradition. To me, there's a lot wrapped up in tradition. To know every time you step on that field you represent that Y on your helmet, and you represent the university. You represent all those great players who came before you. When you walk in that locker room and you look around, you know that you're playing for a greater cause. You know when you walk out on that field that you're going to give it your all, regardless of what happens. There is this brotherhood with your teammates that goes way beyond football.

For me, that's what being a Cougar is all about. To this day, I bleed blue—win or lose. I believe in what BYU and the football program is all about. That's why the program is so successful. We get the type of athletes who have the mind-set to look beyond just themselves.

When I came here, all I wanted to do was leave my mark, and hopefully that would pave the way for others. I think that's an important part of being a Cougar—leaving your mark. It's about reaching your potential, helping the team win, and adding to the tradition. We played to represent BYU and to leave a legacy for others to follow and continue the success.

We've had some great backs come through the program, so I was proud to hold the career rushing record for as long as I did. If I had to pick someone to break my record, I would probably have picked Curtis [Brown]. He was a lot like me. When he was closing in on my record, I put some pictures of me in his locker with a note that said, "Until you break my record, you're going to have to look at me every day. When you break the record, you can take the pictures down." The night he broke the rushing record, we talked on the sideline before the game. He told me, "Jamal, this is going to be the game." When he broke off that long touchdown run and set the new record, the crowd went wild. I was as excited as if he were my brother or my son. I was proud of him.

He came over afterward, and we gave each other a hug. Monday morning Curtis showed up at my office with all my stuff. That's what it's all about. I think he probably felt the way I felt about BYU—"I made the right decision. This is a great place to be."

Jamal Willis was a four-year starter at running back, from 1991 to 1994. His career 2,970 yards rushing and 40 touchdowns are both third-highest in BYU history. As a senior in 1994, Willis rushed for 1,042 yards and was named first-team All-WAC. Willis went on to play two seasons in the NFL with the San Francisco 49ers.

CHAD LEWIS
TIGHT END
1993–1996

M<small>Y FIRST YEAR OF FOOTBALL</small> in pads was seventh grade. I had three older brothers who all played football before me, so that's what you did. I couldn't wait to get my No. 22 jersey and play football. That was my brother Dave's jersey number. He was the oldest, so it was like, "All right, give me No. 22, and let's get rolling."

I was a big-time BYU fan growing up. In seventh grade we'd sneak down to the games. We would scalp tickets when people gave us a couple extra. We'd sell those for lunch money. If we didn't have tickets, we'd sneak in. I loved BYU football. I can remember Adam Haysbert catching the winning touchdown pass against Pitt. I was in the Marriott Center watching that game on the big screen. I was in eighth grade the year we won the national championship.

I was a sophomore at Orem High School when my brother Mike started to get recruited by Utah. He was a good player, but I didn't dream he was going to get a scholarship to play college football. Then all of a sudden Wayne McQuivey from Utah started showing up at our house, and I thought, *Wow, Mike might play college football!* To me, college football was a pretty big deal.

BYU was not recruiting him at all. He was a late bloomer, as I was. He was a 210-pound defensive end out of high school. Utah offered him a scholarship, and I was out of my mind with excitement that he was going to be

Chad Lewis hauls in a pass in a 34–28 victory over UTEP in 1994. While at BYU, Lewis was named honorable mention All-America and CoSIDA Academic All-America. He went on to play nine seasons in the NFL and was inducted into the BYU Athletic Hall of Fame in 2007.

playing college football. I started wearing all of his U of U paraphernalia and painted the U logo on my school notebooks.

At the same time, this is when Ty Detmer was at BYU. You could not watch college football and not love watching Ty Detmer. During Mike's red-shirt year after his mission, the BYU vs. Utah game was the same week as Orem High School's state championship game. We were at Orem High practicing, and some media showed up. One of them asked me, "Hey, who do you think is going to win, BYU or Utah?" We were getting ready to play Alta for the state championship game, and they were asking me that? I said, "Even though my brother's playing at Utah, I think BYU because I love Ty Detmer." Boy, did I catch crap for that! The Utah coaches were on the phone that night saying, "Dude! Your brother plays up here! We need you to be our ambassador down there in Utah Valley." I just couldn't get BYU out of my system.

I always wanted to go to BYU, study, and become a doctor. When I came home off my mission, a good friend and former mission companion, Larry Harmer, talked me into walking on at BYU. He was an All-America defensive lineman out of Olympus High School. He kept pestering me, "Hey, have you talked to the coaches yet?" I'd say, "No." Finally he came to me and said, "Look, Chad, just pray about it. If you'll do that, I will never bug you for the rest of your life." He was different in that conversation than any other we'd had for two years as missionaries. I said, "I'll do it."

So for two weeks I prayed about playing football at BYU. At the end of two weeks, in my parent's basement lying in my bed, I had a total answer to my prayers. No question. Confirmation. Period. The next day I went in and talked to Coach Pella and Coach Chow. I said, "I want to walk on to this football program." I wasn't bubbling over with confidence, but I had a quiet confidence because my prayer had been answered. I knew what I was supposed to be doing. I owe a lot to Larry Harmer.

I love what BYU represents. I love everything about BYU. So for me to be on campus, to walk on to the team, to have some BYU gear, and to be on one of LaVell's teams was almost too much. I revered LaVell growing up. To get to know him and play for him—it was more than I could handle. It was too good to be true.

I have so many favorite LaVell Edwards moments. My junior year, in 1995, I broke my ankle in the seventh game against Hawaii. I had to miss the last four games. I remember being in the training room, and LaVell was always in there checking on the injured guys. He had this way of letting you know how much he cared about you. He came over and told me how sorry he was that my ankle was broken. I remember just feeling so grateful to have a head coach who cared about me personally more than football. I would do anything for LaVell and his wife, Patti. There are thousands of players who feel exactly as I do about LaVell.

My freshman year, in 1993, we had a solid group of returned missionaries who were great leaders. We had Tom Young, Bryce Doman, Greg Pitts, Hema Heimuli—guys whom I thought the world of. I seriously felt I was surrounded by greatness at BYU. I was so pumped to be friends with those guys.

Tom had just played in the Aloha Bowl and was the BYU MVP of the game. He took me under his wing and threw me the ball all spring and summer long. He threw me the ball almost every day. Every time Tom was lifting, I was lifting. I loved everything he stood for, how he treated me. We were running 69-H Option all summer, and I was thinking that I'd died and gone to heaven to have a quarterback who wanted to throw to me all the time. It was like Austin Collie years later. He was beating down Max Hall's door at 10:00 at night, saying, "Dude, let's go throw." That's how you have to be if you want to be great. That was Tom.

I had a pretty good spring camp and caught a touchdown in the spring game. The whole time Coach Chow was telling me to be patient. I told him that I was willing to dedicate one year of my life to BYU football as a walk-on. If I wasn't going to get a scholarship at that point, tell me, because I'll do something else with my life. He would just say, "Be patient."

I went through spring ball, all through summer workouts, and worked my butt off. On Thursday, the first week of two-a-days in the fall, LaVell said, "I'd like to see Chad Lewis and Tom Baldwin after practice." I was walking off the practice field, and Norm Chow looked at me and said, "If this is what I think it is, you owe me a steak dinner." I said, "Okay!"

I went into LaVell's office, and he said, "You're doing a great job. We've decided to put you on grant-in-aid." He told me, "Don't stop working hard. Don't slow down. Don't take your foot off the gas pedal." I promised him right then I would keep it up!

I knew how much school cost. I was working to put myself through school. My dad had suffered a massive stroke. My parents had lots of hospital bills. They couldn't afford to help me at all through school. When I was given that scholarship, it meant everything to me.

The first time walking out on the field wearing the uniform was unforgettable. We played the opening game my freshman year at New Mexico. With two minutes left, and the game on the line, Coach Chow just threw me out there. He said, "You're the tight end." I said, "Okay, let's go!"

Just to travel with the team, to be issued sweats, to be a full-fledged member of that team was a dream come true for me—a kid who grew up in Orem, Utah, just a few minutes from campus. I was wearing the jersey. I was playing in the games. I had the "Y" on my helmet. That was sweet.

BYU is a unique place. It's a special place. The campus is like no other. I loved going to class. I studied Chinese and communications. I loved going on campus because of the feeling and the people who were there. I felt like I was surrounded by greatness. Once a month it seemed like an apostle of the Church came to speak. The opportunities, the doors, were just wide open for things that I cared about, the things that I loved. I loved my Book of Mormon teachers. Susan Easton Black was one of the greatest teachers ever. I would go into her class and just be inspired. I would come out of classes thinking, *How did I get so lucky to be at this school?* I have a total appreciation for what BYU stands for in a crumbling world. That's one of the things I loved the most.

I met my wife, Michele, at BYU in the training room. She was an All-America volleyball player and captain of the first BYU team to advance to the national semifinals at the NCAA Tournament. We got talking, and over the course of the next month or so, we got to be friends. Then one day it just hit me, "I want to ask her out!" So we started going out, and the rest is history. I was smitten from that point on. I wanted to be around her and no one else from then on. If only for that, I love BYU. I thank BYU for letting me run into Michelle Fellows.

To me, it means more now to be a Cougar than it even did then. When I played, I gave my heart and soul—so to say that is saying something. When I think about what colleges represent around this country, most of it is superficial—drinking, partying, hooking up. It's crazy. Unfortunately, that is celebrated more than the academics or anything else.

To have a school like BYU that has its mission aligned with the Church of Jesus Christ of Latter-day Saints is special. There is nothing like it in the world. As a missionary for two years, I was a soldier on the front lines sharing the Gospel of Jesus Christ. To come to a school that gets hammered by the world for what it stands for—which are important things—I love it. I love that my kids have the association with BYU. To have them grow up around BYU, standing up singing the fight song, saying, "Rah, rah, rah, rah, rah, goooooo Cougars"—I love it.

One of my favorite memories of playing at BYU came in my freshman year after playing Utah. They beat us at home in Cougar Stadium for the first time in forever. Their players tried to tear down our goal posts, and some of us ran down there and put an end to that idea. I couldn't believe they were trying to tear down our goal posts in our stadium. It was bad enough that they beat us. It just was a total reaction. I ran into the middle of their team and stopped it. That's one of my favorite memories of my early days at BYU.

Later on in my career, beating Kansas State in the Cotton Bowl—LaVell Edwards' first New Year's Day bowl game—meant something to every one of us on that team. That was a sweet team. It was special. The week of the bowl, Steve Sarkisian, our quarterback and leader, was so focused. He wanted more than anything to win that game. He rallied our team to dig deep and win that game.

I'll never forget the memories I have of that week. Steve Sarkisian being our leader. Legendary LaVell Edwards as our coach. Itula Mili and I had been this great two–tight end tandem all season long. Then he shattered his knee against Wyoming in the WAC Championship Game in Las Vegas. I felt terrible for him. His injury was horrific. We were so comfortable playing with each other. We knew how to get each other open. Playing that game without him was hard. I had his number written on the back of my helmet. Playing for him meant something to me, and it meant something to everyone on that team.

It had been bitter cold all week in practice, and then on game day it was hot and humid. I remember being so tired in the fourth quarter and thinking, *I have got to suck it up!* Our whole team felt that way. When K.O. Kealaluhi caught the touchdown pass to put us ahead toward the end of that game, it just felt right. When the game clock ticked to zero, after Omarr Morgan's amazing interception, I can't describe the feeling. That's one of my all–time great memories of BYU.

Chad Lewis played four years at BYU, from 1993 to 1996. As a junior, he received All-America honorable mention honors. In addition to his success on the field, Lewis was a three-time Academic All-WAC selection and was named Academic All-America in 1996. He also earned a spot on the College Football Association All-Academic Team. Following graduation from BYU, Lewis signed a free agent contract with the Philadelphia Eagles. He spent nine seasons in the NFL with the Eagles and the St. Louis Rams. Lewis was selected to the Pro Bowl three times, led all NFL tight ends with 69 catches in 2000, and helped lead Philadelphia to Super Bowl XXXIX in 2005. Lewis was inducted into the BYU Athletic Hall of Fame in 2007.

I went to the BYU football camp the summer before my junior year. The coaches all thought I was going to be a senior. When they found out I was just going to be a junior, they were surprised because I was so big for a 16-year-old. I went again the summer before my senior year. One of the things I was worried about was getting hurt and not having a scholarship. At the BYU camp, Claude Bassett told me, "If you'll commit to LaVell right now, he'll promise you a scholarship, and that way it's kind of insurance for you."

So I did. I committed to LaVell before my senior year. During the camp I went and met with him. I just told him, "I'd like to commit, but because of what's going to happen later with recruiting, I'd kind of like to keep it a secret." He said, "That's fine. I trust your word. I'll give you my word that if anything happens, you'll have a scholarship at BYU." I never told anybody. I eventually told my parents. They were upset because they wanted me to go to Arizona State so they could watch me play, but, in the end looking back, it was a good decision to go to BYU.

I have tremendous respect for LaVell. He was this legendary, revered coach. I don't think he ever said one word to me coaching-wise the whole time I was at BYU, but he would always call you in, see how you were doing. He was a father figure in a lot of ways. He wanted to make sure that everything was going okay for you.

Even though he wasn't out there doing a lot of active coaching, there was never any question as to who was in charge and who was calling the shots. I think what made him successful was his ability to delegate to his coaches. He was able to get a group of guys around him who were extremely capable and talented and let them do their thing. There are a lot of head coaches whose egos wouldn't allow it. He had a really good system. He had Norm Chow on offense and Ken Schmidt as the defensive coordinator. I think the trust that he had in his assistant coaches was something pretty special.

I felt the same trust as a player. He expected you to be a man and to make good decisions. You never felt like you were being spied on or he was checking up on you. There was an expectation of what you needed to do, and you didn't want to disappoint LaVell.

I arrived at fall camp my freshman year in 1993 thinking I was going to be great. That was my plan, "I'm going to play my first year!" Then reality set in, and all of a sudden I was thinking, *Oh, my gosh, what's going on? Maybe I'm not that good.* We had Mike Empey and Eli Herring. Where was I going to play? I think they determined to redshirt me right away.

207

John Tait blocks a Tulane lineman in the 1998 Liberty Bowl, his final game at BYU. From 1996 to 1998 Tait started all 37 games he played as a Cougar. He was taken in the first round of the 1999 NFL Draft and went on to play 10 seasons in the league.

At the time, I hated being on the practice teams and getting beat up every day. It was tough. You feel like you're back on the bottom of the heap. I was just young. I had my mission coming up and was thinking, *Get me out of here. I'm ready to go on my mission.* Looking back, I think it built character, just sticking to it, going to practice, stuff like that.

I served in the Tennessee Knoxville Mission. I got back in December 1995, right before Christmas. I was back in school two weeks later. The mission experience was an important part of my life. You go out and serve other people and learn a lot about yourself in the process. You have a lot of situations that are difficult, and you come through them. Your faith grows, you learn about the Gospel, and it sets the foundation of what kind of a man you're going to be later in life. As far as football goes, there is a higher maturity level when you come back—being able to focus on studies and juggle football and your personal life.

When I came back, I was working hard to get ready for the 1996 season, lifting weights and stuff like that. My goal was to start right away. The first game against Texas A&M, I was scared to death to play those guys. I was going against an All-American in my first college game. Before the game I was in the locker room, and Lance Reynolds came up to me while I was getting dressed. He said, "Good luck today. You're a great player. Just remember, if things go wrong, if you start giving up sacks, don't panic." I said, "Okay, Coach, thanks." It was good advice, but at the time I was thinking, *Okay, right before the game you're telling me, "If you start giving up sacks, don't worry and don't panic."* I didn't give up a sack, and the offense played really well. When the game ended, the crowd rushed the field—there was just a sea of people. It was really cool. It was just a great feeling.

That was a special team. It started with Sarkisian at quarterback. At the time I thought that was how all quarterbacks acted, but now I look back and realize that the guy was a great leader. You had other veterans like Itula Mili, Chad Lewis, and Mark Atuaia. It was just a great group of guys. I remember being in the huddle and kind of looking into everybody's eyes and knowing that we were going to get it done, even in games when it looked pretty grim.

It was a long season. I had never played college football, and the first season I played was 15 games. Looking back, it was a special team and a special season. They just don't come around that often in any league. So when things are going good, you try to slow down, smell the roses, and just enjoy the ride.

Playing at Cougar Stadium was great. That stadium is a special place. The fans are great and are very loud. There is excitement and electricity in the air. Going out on the field and knowing that you're going to score a ton of points is pretty cool. It was great being part of a play where your block springs somebody or the offense has a long drive and scores. Everybody shares in the excitement. Even though, as an offensive lineman, you may not get your number called on a touchdown, we understand the importance of our role. I always enjoyed the emotional reaction of the fans when we'd do something great—when we scored. We'd look over in the stands and make eye contact with some random person and see how excited they were—it was great.

I'm proud to say that I played at BYU. I look back at my experience, and like a lot of things in life, you don't realize how good it was until you leave and experience something else. When I tell people that I played at BYU, the first question is usually, "Wow, was it hard to go to school there?" I'll say, "Oh, no. I'm a member of the Church. That's one of the reasons I went there." Then the Church conversation comes up. There's an expectation of what you're about if you played at BYU.

You learn a lot of life lessons at BYU. Just living on your own, making decisions for yourself, and having to deal with the good and bad consequences from your decisions—just being accountable to yourself. There are some great teachers and professors at BYU. I loved taking a class that opened my eyes to something new that I hadn't learned before.

There were a lot of people at BYU who made a huge difference in my life. Claude Bassett was one and Roger French, of course. I had a really cool relationship with Ollie Julkunen, one of our trainers. There were certain athletes who gravitated toward him, and he really took care of us. He was my guy. I love George Curtis, too—he's the best. I really appreciated people like that because they made BYU a special place.

John Tait played three seasons at BYU, from 1996 to 1998. He was named Freshman All-America by the *Sporting News* in 1996 and first-team All-America by *Football News* in 1998. He was also a two-time first-team All-WAC offensive tackle and started all 37 games he played in his BYU career. After his junior season, Tait was selected in the first round (14th overall pick) of the 1999 NFL Draft by the Kansas City Chiefs. He played 10 seasons in the NFL for the Chiefs and the Chicago Bears.

ROB MORRIS

LINEBACKER

1993 ★ 1997–1999

Coming out of high school, I was recruited mostly as a running back, although I played linebacker, as well. I told everyone, "Look, I want to play running back. I don't really want to play defense." Mostly the Pac-10 and WAC schools recruited me. I took a recruiting trip to Stanford and loved it. Bill Walsh was the head coach. While I was meeting with Coach Walsh, I asked him, "So, if you guys are going to offer me a scholarship, when would you do that?" He said, "How about right now?" I said, "Heck, yeah!" I shook his hand, and I was committed. I was going to Stanford. Tom Holmoe was the defensive backs coach; he gave me the spiel of how a good Mormon boy could go to Stanford and thrive. So I was all set to go.

My dad came with me on the Stanford trip. He was all fired up because it was Bill Walsh and Stanford. They were just coming off a 10-win season. When we got home, my dad was wearing his "Stanford Dad" sweatshirt, and I told my mom, "I'm going to Stanford." She started crying. I was like, "What? This is supposed to be a happy moment."

I had a trip scheduled to BYU, but I called them and said, "I kind of decided I'm going to go to Stanford. I'm not going to come on the BYU trip." I think LaVell called me and said, "Just come on the trip, anyway, and see what you think." So I came on the trip to BYU and really liked it. I loved LaVell, and I really liked Coach Reynolds. If it hadn't been for Lance Reynolds and LaVell, I probably wouldn't have come to BYU.

I went on three official trips—Utah, Stanford, and finally BYU. I also took unofficial trips to Washington and Washington State. After BYU, I canceled all my other trips. Eventually, Lance came to visit me in Nampa. He said, "So, are you ready to be a Cougar?" I said, "Yeah," and then I signed. So the reality is I probably committed to three or four different schools. Ultimately, it was the people and the long tradition of success at BYU that made the difference. You knew if you came to BYU you were going to win.

When I got to BYU, I played running back for Lance. A large part of my BYU story is Lance Reynolds and his family—we grew really close. I spent a lot of time at his family's house and became close with his daughter, Brittany. John Tait and I would go over there and play Nintendo with Dallas, Matt, and Houston. We spent a lot of time at the Reynoldses' house. Those are some of my fond memories of BYU.

When I arrived, I didn't think I was actually going to be playing. I thought I would probably redshirt. Tait and I were roommates. We remained roommates our whole career. I remember when I found out that I wasn't going to redshirt and was actually going to travel. The guys who traveled got sweet warm-up suits. I thought, *I've arrived, I've got a warm-up suit. Are you kidding me? I bet Stanford doesn't have these sweet warm-up suits!* I remember putting that warm-up suit on and walking from Helaman Halls to the Smith Fieldhouse to catch the bus. I had my matching travel bag, and I was thinking, *People will know that I'm traveling on the football team.* That was a huge deal.

Although I started out playing running back, LaVell was always in my ear about switching to linebacker. I just didn't want to do it. One day in practice, I was on offense, and LaVell was driving around in his golf cart. I always thought he looked like a golf marshal, not a coach. He wheeled up to me on his cart. I don't remember who was in the cart with him, but he kicked them out and told me to jump in. So I sat in his cart. I was a freshman, so if LaVell talked to you, it was a big deal.

I'll never forget this. He said, "I know you want to play running back. I think you can be a really good college running back. If you switch to linebacker, you'll play on Sundays." That was it. I was never a running back again. My running back days were over. I thought, *Okay, this guy clearly sees something that I'm missing.* So I switched to linebacker, and that was it. I think every linebacker wants to be a running back—to score touchdowns. But he was right. I think my mentality is a little more suited to playing on defense. The interesting part of that story is that I actually listened to his advice.

As a senior in 1999, Rob Morris was named first-team All-America and was a semifinalist for the Butkus Award. He was drafted by the Indianapolis Colts in the first round of the 2000 NFL Draft. Morris played eight seasons in the league and helped the Colts win Super Bowl XLI in 2006.

My first game in Cougar Stadium was against Hawaii in 1993. The crowd was going crazy. I was playing a lot of fullback, but mostly just blocking. I remember we ran a bootleg pass, and I was lined up kind of as a tight end. John Walsh hit me, and I ran it for like 30 or 40 yards. I think Eli Herring held on the play. It seems like athletes always have these great stories, but mine always end with a penalty or something bad happening.

Game days were always exciting. My family would drive down from Idaho. Hearing your name on the loudspeaker was a thrill, "Rob Morris on the tackle. Rob Morris with the catch." It was fun. It's a great stadium. It's a great setting. Nampa is a small town, small school, but we had a nice stadium. We played Jake Plummer's high school, and we were both undefeated. There were about 8,000 people there, which was a pretty big deal for Nampa, Idaho. Then at BYU we're talking about 65,000 people. It was exciting.

As I look back, it seems like I have memories from each year. Most of the things I remember are the stupid, ridiculous things. My freshman year we played at Colorado State. I remember it was really raining hard. On special teams there was a kickoff or a punt, the CSU returner was going down the sideline, and I hit him so hard that he was done. They had to cart him off the field. That's how I loved to play.

In the San Diego State game in 1998, I had an interception that I took back for a touchdown. It was raining hard. When I got to the end zone, I fell down and did a snow angel in the grass. It wasn't planned—it was a natural reaction. There was also the moonwalk I did after a sack. I never planned to do those things, they just happened. I think I was just so excitable in college that stuff like that happened. After the game the media asked me about the moonwalk, and I told them, "I'm going to do a dance move from every decade." Ha-ha. I loved the media attention in college. It was fun. A lot of it was just building a reputation or image that matched football.

I think the best part about college is the people—the coaches. I was close with LaVell and Coach Reynolds. Coach Schmidt and I always had a good relationship, also Barry Lamb. There were a lot of people I felt like I could go talk to about things that weren't necessarily football-related.

I also got to interact with a lot of great people. I remember President Rex Lee. He was such a gung-ho, diehard BYU sports guy. His excitement and attitude trickled from the top down. He would come and talk with you. I remember we had L. Tom Perry come to the locker room one time, as well. When I got hurt my senior year, I was on crutches getting on the elevator to

watch one of the games from the coaches' box. There was an elderly couple
I let go in front of me. The guy turned to me and said, "Hey, Rob, do you
need any help? How are you feeling?" I realized, "Hey, you're Neal A.
Maxwell. You know my name?" On Monday I went to check my mail slot in
the football office, and there was a book there. Inside, it said, "To Rob. It
was nice to meet you. —Neal A. Maxwell." I thought, *Wow, a General
Authority's book is in my mail slot? He's probably got 10 billion other things to do,
and he took the time to send me his book.* That was very cool.

After I left BYU and went to the NFL, there was a time period—and I'm
not trying to bag on anyone—where I just didn't feel like a BYU Cougar.
There wasn't a lot reaching out going on. When Bronco got the job, I didn't
know him. But he reached out and welcomed guys back. He would send
somebody out with gear, some "Band of Brothers" T-shirts. It made us guys
in the NFL feel good. I thought, *Hey, this guy didn't play at BYU, but he gets
it.* He's trying to recognize LaVell's legacy and build on it. After that, I would
work out at BYU in the off-season.

When I was trying to decide whether to retire from the NFL, I went and
talked to LaVell, a couple of close friends, and Bronco. He was one of three
or four guys whom I went to, to ask his opinion, because I thought that
highly of him. Tom Holmoe is the same way. I like the alumni events that
Bronco has. I've been to them a couple of times. It makes you feel like you
are still part of the program.

When you get to know Bronco, he is a funny guy. He's a good guy. I think
the general public thinks, *This guy's hardcore.* But you know what, LaVell was
the same way. The public knew LaVell as this scowling coach who stood on
the sideline with his arms folded, but he's one of the funniest men I know.

I'll tell you a funny LaVell story. My freshman year, we were at Air Force.
I was still a running back and was standing next to Robbie Bosco, waiting to
get the next play and run it to the huddle. We were about to score, and Steven
Christensen, one of the other running backs, did something wacky. He came
off the field, and Bosco started yelling at him. Steve had a temper, so he was
yelling back at Bosco. Robbie took the headset off and threw it down. Mean-
while I was standing there waiting to get the next play. The game was still
going on, and our quarterback John Walsh was looking at the sideline for a
play. Finally, LaVell picked up the headset, put it on, turned to me, and said,
"Uhh, uhh…pass it. Yeah, pass it." Then he took the headset off and gave it
to Robbie. So here was a legend of the game, one of the innovators. We're

about to score, and I was thinking he was going to call something like, "Red right motion, flip to go right, Rhonda," and he said, "Uhh...pass it." That was just vintage LaVell. He let the other guys coach, but he made the important decisions.

The players nowadays are so much smarter than we were. We had just some different cats who would do crazy stuff. I kind of miss that. I don't know that I miss much in between the whistles. I miss the locker room and the bus rides and the times with teammates. Those are the things I miss from playing football at BYU.

Rob Morris played four seasons at BYU, in 1993 and from 1997 to 1999. As a senior, he was a semifinalist for the Butkus Award and was named first-team All-America by the Associated Press, *Sporting News*, and *Football News*. Morris was a two-time first-team All-WAC selection and was the conference Defensive Player of the Year in 1998. He was selected in the first round (28th pick) of the 2000 NFL Draft by the Indianapolis Colts. He played eight seasons in Indianapolis and helped the Colts win Super Bowl XLI.

The
NEW
MILLENNIUM

CHRIS HOKE

DEFENSIVE LINE

1994 ★ 1997–2000

I DIDN'T START PLAYING FOOTBALL until I was a freshman in high school, but I wanted to play ever since I was a little kid. I grew up in Southern California, so I used to go to the Holiday Bowl every year when I was young. I was eight years old sitting in the end zone when Kelly Smith caught that touchdown pass that won the 1984 Holiday Bowl.

I wanted to be Jason Buck. I wanted to be Shawn Knight. I wanted to be those guys. It was my dream to play at BYU. When you get recruited, you have to play the game so you can take other trips, but in my heart it was always BYU. That's where I wanted to go. That's where I wanted to be. I always wanted to play for Coach Edwards. That was the dream. I dreamt about that my whole life.

I went on my recruiting trip to BYU, and I didn't see Coach Edwards until Sunday. I had a great time. I was hanging out with my host, Travis Hall, going snowmobiling—all that fun stuff. My dad was with me, and before we went to the airport to head home, we went to LaVell's office. Right there he offered me a scholarship. It was really, really cool.

There was something special about Coach Edwards. They don't call him "the Closer" for nothing. He knew what he was doing. That guy was the best. You just knew that you wanted to play for that guy. Although I wanted to be at BYU, I didn't commit right then. I promised my dad that I would fly home with him, and we'd talk about it. A couple of days later, Ken Schmidt,

Chris Hoke helped BYU to 10-7 victory over UNLV in 2000. As a senior that year, he led all BYU linemen with 51 tackles. Hoke has enjoyed a 10-year career in the NFL with the Pittsburgh Steelers, where he's won two Super Bowls.

the defensive coordinator at BYU, called me and said, "What's your decision?" I said, "I don't know yet." He said, "Come on, Chris. You're not going to choose Utah over us, are you?" I said, "No, I'm coming to BYU, Coach. I just don't know how I'm going to tell the Utah coaches." He said, "I understand, just call them."

So I got off the phone and called Coach McBride and told him I was going to BYU. It was hard. Fred Whittingham was at Utah at the time. The Whittinghams were family friends from the days when he coached with the Rams in L.A. I was good friends with their youngest daughter, Julie, so it was hard to tell them no. But the bottom line was, it was BYU all the way. That's where I dreamt of going my whole life.

I didn't take any other trips. I was supposed to go to UCLA and Colorado State. I called Colorado State and told them, "I'm going to BYU." Then when UCLA found out that I was going on a mission, they called me and canceled everything. They told me, "Hey, if you change your mind about going on a mission, we'd love to have you, but if you go on a church mission, we're not set up for that."

It was always my plan to go on a mission. When I was getting recruited, my high school coach told me that I was dumb to try to go on a mission, that I was hurting my career. It was kind of a test of my faith, but I knew I needed to go on a mission. You grow up singing the song, "I Hope They Call Me on a Mission," right? It was part of the plan.

In my very first training camp at BYU, I remember being in the dorms in Helaman Halls. I remember checking out the other freshmen who were reporting and thinking, *How do I compare size-wise to these guys?* I remember going into the old locker room in the Smith Fieldhouse for the first time. It was awesome—unbelievable.

I'll never forget the first time running out of the tunnel at Cougar Stadium with the "Rise and Shout" song playing. I don't even remember whom we played. I know I got chills, and there were literally tears rolling down my face. Everyone was cheering. It was a dream come true. It was what I wanted to do since I was a little kid—eight years old. I remember thinking, *Man, this is the best!* I still get chills right now just thinking about it.

My senior year was Coach Edwards' last year. I'll never forget the final game at Utah. We weren't having a great year. We were 5–6 at the time. I remember guys on the team saying, "We've got to win this game so that Coach Edwards can go out not having a losing season." I don't remember feeling a lot of pressure. I just remember wanting to win the game for him.

It didn't look very good late in that game; in fact, it looked bleak. Brandon Doman drove us down the field, and we won the game. To win at Utah in my senior year was great. It was one of the best moments of my career. I'll also always remember President Hinckley coming into our locker room before LaVell's final home game and then being right there on the field when they named the stadium after Coach Edwards. That was an experience I'll never forget.

I was actually the only Cougar to play in the final game he coached. Most people don't realize that. LaVell was an assistant coach in the Hula Bowl in January 2001, and I was the only BYU player in that Hula Bowl. It was great. Just being there with him over in Hawaii was really special. He is a great man.

There were so many people at BYU who had an impact on my life. First of all, my position coach, Tom Ramage, was the best. He made you want to play hard because you loved the guy so much. I knew he always had my back. He was always there for me.

There was one time, my senior year, when we played Mississippi State at home and we got beat. I didn't have a very good game. For me it was always team first, but I knew the NFL scouts were watching that game, so I wanted to play well. Coach Ramage knew I was frustrated and upset.

On Monday after practice we watched film, and then I went back in the locker room at the Smith Field House and showered up. I was walking to my car, and Coach Ramage was waiting for me in the parking lot. He was sitting in his old yellow truck. As I walked out, he rolled down the window and told me to hop in. We drove around for a few minutes, and then we parked by my car. We talked for 25 or 30 minutes. He told me I was a great player, that he wouldn't want anybody else beside me at my position.

I gained so much respect for the guy because he didn't have to do that, and you know what, coaches don't do that. That's what's so special about BYU and what's so special about Coach Ramage. He really, really motivated me and built me up and made me feel like I was going to be okay if I just kept working.

He was a great coach. He knew how to teach. He taught me lessons off the field, too. We spent a lot of time with him. He taught me to be true to myself, be who I am, and work hard—things will work out.

As a player/mentor, I really looked up to Chad Lewis. He was a returned missionary and, I think, a sophomore when I was a true freshman. I remember Chad was a very hard worker. One time Chad was back from the NFL working out with us in the off-season. He had just got back to the weight room from running steps in the stadium. He was wearing a hat that said, "It Ain't Free." So I went up to him and asked him, "What does 'It Ain't Free' mean?"

221

He said, "Bro, it ain't free! Nothing's free! You've gotta go chase it. Nobody gives you anything. Whatever you want, you've got to go get it." I thought, *Whoa!*

Another time I saw him in the training room, and he said, "Hey, Hoke, how are you living your life?" It kind of caught me off guard for a second, but that's Chad. I said, "I'm doing fine." He said, "Just know that there are a lot of LDS kids looking up to you. Make sure you're living your life right." And he was right. I admired him for those kinds of things. He made me think and look myself in the mirror. In 2010, before we played the Tennessee Titans, he texted me and said, "Hey, I hear you're starting. Good luck." Then he texted me a couple of scriptures. That's the type of brotherhood we have at BYU.

There were a lot of good people at BYU. I never took anything for granted. I always dreamed about playing in the NFL, and I got that chance at Pittsburg as an undrafted free agent. I never take anything for granted. That's how it was at BYU. I knew that I was lucky to be there. I knew that there were thousands of kids in the country who would love to be in my position. To be at BYU and be a part of the football program, to go to school there, it was something that I was totally grateful for.

I take a lot of pride in being a BYU Cougar. I love the school. I bleed blue. My kids love BYU, too. My oldest son has it all planned out. He thinks he's going to play at BYU, so we have to watch the BYU football games whenever they're on. We DVR every game and watch them together. I am never embarrassed to say I went to BYU. I'm proud of it. I'm never embarrassed to stand up for BYU and what it represents. In my family, we are all about BYU.

Chris Hoke played four seasons at BYU and was named Academic All–Mountain West Conference twice. As a senior in 2000, he was named second-team All-MWC and led all BYU linemen with 50 tackles. Hoke finished his BYU career with 135 tackles and 13 sacks. The Pittsburgh Steelers signed him as a free agent in 2001. Hoke has played 10 seasons for the Steelers and won two Super Bowls.

BRANDON DOMAN
RECEIVER/QUARTERBACK
1998–2001

I HAD THREE OLDER BROTHERS play at BYU. I just didn't think there was any other way. I figured you played little league football, then you played high school, and then you played for BYU.

I remember watching my brother Bryce play for BYU at Rice Stadium. I was sitting with a bunch of my buddies who were Utah fans, and Bryce scored a touchdown. He came running across the back of the end zone, pulled up right in front of all the Utah fans, and pointed at me. I'm sure the whole section thought he was mocking them, but I knew he was pointing specifically at me. He was letting his little brother know that "this was for you."

I have always held that memory dear to my heart just because it was my big brother. I looked up to him so much, and in the middle of all that was going on, he came running over to acknowledge me. That was a neat moment.

Later, my brother Cliff and I got to play football for two years together at BYU. Being roommates and traveling together was a pretty memorable time for me. We were in the huddle together with me as the quarterback and him as the receiver. I was a triple-option wishbone quarterback in high school, so most of the schools in America that ran the option were looking at me—Notre Dame, Texas A&M, the service academies. I actually took a trip to Notre Dame, which was really neat at the time. When I got back, I visited BYU and committed. I didn't want to go anywhere else. My goal as an eight-year-old boy was to play for BYU. I had written it down as a goal several times.

Brandon Doman looks to the referee for the signal after diving into the end zone for the go-ahead touchdown in LaVell Edwards' last game as head coach, a thrilling 34–27 come-from-behind win over Utah on November 24, 2000.

I think BYU was scared to death to play me at quarterback, and I don't blame them. Now that I'm a coach, I can see why they would have had reservations playing me at quarterback. They recruited me as an athlete. I played safety in high school, and I think they really wanted me to play free safety. I fought that pretty hard.

My sophomore year was Kevin Feterik's senior year, and I was kind of a third- or fourth-string quarterback. I think the coaches wanted to figure out how to get me on the field. I think I actually played in almost every game as a receiver that year, but I didn't catch very many balls.

The next year was the turning point in my whole career. Feterik had graduated, and now it was Charlie Peterson and me as juniors—Bret Engemann and Matt Berry as sophomores. I knew I was fourth on the depth chart. So I went to see LaVell Edwards before the 2000 season and said, "Okay, Coach, I'm ready to make the switch to safety."

He said, "Matt Berry just came in to see me last week, and he told me he's going on a mission, so we can't afford to have you change positions now. We need to have three quarterbacks." I said, "No way. I'm not going to be the third-string quarterback, because I know what type of reps that guy gets. I know what type of attention he gets in meetings. I've been around the block now long enough to know that's not what I want to do."

LaVell said, "Well, what would we need to do to keep you as a quarterback?" I said, "I need as many reps as the other guys. I need to have the chance to improve as a player. If I can see that I'm getting better, then I'll stay at quarterback." So LaVell said, "Okay, you've got it." Sure enough, they invested a ton of time and energy into me, and I started to get better.

That fall ended up being Coach Edwards' last season. We got off to a rough start. Engemann hurt his shoulder in the Syracuse game and was out for the year. All of a sudden, I was the backup quarterback by default. With three games left, we were 4–5 and headed to Fort Collins to play Colorado State. The night before the game, I got a phone call in my hotel room. It was my grandpa on the phone. He said, "This is Clifford Gledhill, the grandfather of Brandon Doman, the starting quarterback of BYU." Click. He hung the phone up. He didn't say hi or anything. He was calling to basically remind me, "Brandon, you've grown up your whole life wanting this. You need to believe that you can be the starting quarterback. Get yourself ready."

It was a freezing cold, rainy game. We were losing 38–0 at halftime. Charlie Peterson got injured, and I played the second half. I think we lost 45–21. We headed back to Provo at 4–6. LaVell Edwards hadn't had a losing season in something like 27 years. We had two games to play and were on the verge of sending LaVell out with a losing season.

We had a bye that week before facing New Mexico in LaVell's final home game. There weren't any other quarterbacks, so I took every snap. I was it.

The week of the game, on Wednesday, they realized Charlie wasn't physically ready. LaVell named me the guy. I went to practice that day as the starting quarterback at BYU.

Here I was, third-string guy. We were 4–6. The team was worn out. We were beat up, and it was my first chance to start. I was running around, hitting guys in the head, saying, "Here we go! Let's get going!"

Before the New Mexico game, President Hinckley came into the locker room. He said, "You have one chance to send LaVell out a winner. Don't muff it." We didn't know they were going to rename the stadium after LaVell. We walked out onto the field and, sure enough, they dropped down the banner on top of the press box—"LaVell Edwards Stadium." That was cool.

All I ever wanted to do was run out of the southeast corner at Cougar Stadium as *the* starting quarterback at BYU. Then, when I finally got that opportunity, the Prophet of the Church comes into the locker room five minutes before kickoff to address the football team. It was remarkable because, here we were, a bunch of young men who believed he was a Prophet of God, and we're playing for Brigham Young University. There wasn't a sound in the room. It was reverent like a Church meeting. We sat there surrounding him, and there was such genuine love for that man. It was amazing. Where else in the world are you going to have that experience? I certainly wouldn't be who I am today without those types of experiences at BYU.

I was really nervous before that game. Bronco Mendenhall was the defensive coordinator at New Mexico. They were the No. 1 defense in our league, and I was panicking. Fortunately, we ended up playing great and winning the game.

Then we went to Salt Lake City the next week, miraculously came back, beat Utah to finish the season 6–6, and carried Coach Edwards off the field. I was proud we sent LaVell out a winner. It was a really memorable time for me.

Just look at the reality that took place for me. LaVell Edwards was the head football coach at BYU for nearly 30 years—the icon of this institution. I got to be the starting quarterback for his last home game, the game they named the stadium after him. Then I got to play, as his quarterback, in the last game he ever coached at BYU.

It changed the course of my life forever, and I mean that. LaVell's decision to keep me at quarterback has taken me down a path I would have never imagined. My friendship with him is unique. I feel really fortunate that I had the chance to be with him in those last moments as the head football coach at BYU—forever memorable.

LaVell's final game was a typical BYU-Utah battle. We were up 16 in the fourth quarter, and all of a sudden Utah started making plays. Every ounce of momentum we had was now going their way. They scored 17 unanswered points in the fourth quarter to take a one-point lead with about two minutes to play.

There was 1:13 left in the game. It was fourth-and-13. We were backed up to about our own 15-yard line. We ran this sprint-out dash play where I just sprinted out to the left, and Jonathan Pittman ran a little stutter and went out on the edge. I remember seeing a little pocket of dead space toward the middle of the field and just threw it there. He kind of maneuvered his way back into that spot and made the play. It was unbelievable.

The very next play was a Red-Right 64. It was a two-minute-drill play. Basically, the two receivers run 10-yard outs, catch the ball, and get out of bounds. The clock was still rolling. Coach signaled me the play, and I signaled it out to Ben Horton and Jonathan. All of a sudden, Jonathan shook down a number eight, which meant 58, or he was going to run a fade. I was looking at him like, *No, you're not*. I was yelling, "Four!" and he was shaking his head, saying, "I'm running a 58."

So, consciously in my mind, I said, *Forget him, I'll hit Ben on the 64*. As I snapped the ball and took my three-step drop, I was planning to throw to Ben. For some unexplainable reason, almost instinctively, at the last second, I planted my foot and I threw the fade down the left sideline to Jonathan. Somehow he caught the ball and dragged a foot in bounds. It was an unreal catch.

We ran downfield, and I got everyone set. I handed off to Luke Staley, and he ran it down to the 4-yard line. We called a timeout, and Coach Bosco came running out into the huddle. He said, "Were not going to take any chances on an interception or a missed handoff. We're running a quarterback sweep right." We didn't even have that play. We'd never run it before. He said, "Brandon, just snap the ball, run a sweep to the right, and go score. Everybody else, block like you've never blocked before in your life."

We had Luke Staley in the backfield for goodness' sake, and he decided we'd do this little QB sweep right. Our guys were so juiced at that point, I don't think Utah had a chance of stopping us no matter what we did. So we lined up, ran this quarterback sweep right, and I fell in the end zone. I have that picture in my office. You can see the ball was just barely over the end line, and I was looking up at the referee to see if he'd signaled touchdown.

The funniest part about that story that no one knows involves my brother Bryce. He was up in the bleachers, and when we scored, he jumped onto the field and met me in the end zone. He head butted me, and then security got him and kicked him out of the stadium. Ha-ha.

In the end, we carried Coach Edwards off the field. It was pretty remarkable and a memorable experience for me. I don't know that I enjoyed winning a football game anywhere else more than in that stadium.

Something happened after that game that was pretty cool. Steve Young called my brother Kevin and said, "I want to talk to Brandon as soon as he comes out of the locker room." So, after doing all the media interviews and getting showered, I came back on the field and got on a cell phone with Steve Young. He said, "Did you capture the moment in your mind? Because you need to right now, so you'll never forget it." He told me, "I want you to walk out on the field again and just look around. Capture everything that happened. Even if your career continues and you play in the NFL, it will never, ever feel like it did tonight. Super Bowls, all those other things don't feel like it just felt for you tonight. Capture this moment so you'll never forget it." That was pretty cool.

A few years later I was in the 49ers locker room, and in walked Ron McBride. I said, "Hey, Coach McBride, how are you?" He said, "Brandon Doman. Unbelievable." He turned to some of the 49ers coaches and said, "Hey, let me tell you something about this guy. Brandon Doman made me think for a moment, after playing him, that God was Mormon." Everybody laughed. He said, "Here I thought I'd beaten LaVell in his last game, and all of a sudden Brandon Doman just takes that game away. I figured, God must be a Mormon and wanted LaVell to win."

That was probably the most memorable football game I've ever played in.

The thing that makes BYU so unique and so great is there is a culture and environment for young men and women unlike any place in the world. I was surrounded by greatness everywhere I went. If I walked into the equipment room to get some socks, there was Floyd Johnson waiting for me, genuinely interested in what was going on in my life. He had a great impact on my life. When we would get banged up in practice and games, Ollie Julkunen and George Curtis were there to take care of us. They cared so much about the off-the-field lives of the players.

Then I'd go to class and be taught by people like Alex Baugh, Norm Nemrow, Susan Easton Black, and others—teachers who just blew me away sitting in their classrooms, listening to what they taught, and feeling the spirit of campus. It had such a great impact on me.

The spiritual aspect of the BYU campus is incredible. The Sunday night before the Utah game my senior year, I was driving by the Utah Valley Hospital headed home when my cell phone rang. It was about 11:00. I answered the call, and it was Reno Mahe. He said, "Brandon, I'm in the hospital. I just had my appendix removed and I need a blessing." I said, "Which hospital?" He said, "Utah Valley, in the emergency room." I said, "I'll be there in two minutes." So I parked my car, walked in the hospital, and gave him a priesthood blessing that night. Remarkably, he played that Saturday.

Where else are you going to have that type of experience in an academic or football setting? I would argue that probably nowhere, except BYU. Those types of things changed my life in a far greater fashion than just playing football. To me, being a Cougar means a number of things. It means faith—what I hold dear, and what I represent. It's bigger than just being a football player. There is an importance in representing the institution at a very high level. That is a great responsibility.

Being a Cougar to me is deep-rooted in family. Part of what I knew growing up was, "Rise and shout, the Cougars are out." For me, my parents, brothers, sisters, and grandparents are all part of the experience. It also means friends. It means people who impacted my life in such a way that they're going to be friends forever.

For me, faith, family, and friends are what it means most to be a Cougar.

Brandon Doman was a unanimous first-team All-MWC quarterback as a senior in 2001. As a team captain, he guided BYU to a 12–2 record and a MWC championship. Doman and teammate Luke Staley were both on the Heisman Trophy watch list for much of the 2001 season. He was selected by the San Francisco 49ers in the fifth round of the 2002 NFL Draft, where he spent the majority of three seasons. He also played for the Buffalo Bills and Washington Redskins. Doman returned to BYU as the quarterbacks coach in 2005 and was named offensive coordinator in January 2011.

RYAN DENNEY

DEFENSIVE LINE

1998–2001

MY DAD PLAYED FOOTBALL at BYU from about 1970 to 1973. He was on the team when LaVell Edwards was named head coach. When I was playing at BYU, my dad would walk into LaVell's office, and Coach would know his name and remember details like where he played high school. I was always amazed because that was 30 years earlier.

We always followed BYU, even though we lived in Colorado. On Saturday mornings my dad would take us to the church where we watched the satellite feed of the BYU games. Then usually once a year, we'd go to Fort Collins, or Laramie, or even the Air Force Academy to watch the Cougars play. We had a copy of the 1984 BYU highlight tape, and we probably watched that thing 10,000 times growing up. So I grew up cheering for BYU.

During my senior year of high school, I won some awards in Colorado, and I was being recruited pretty heavily by a lot of schools to play football. I was receiving a bunch of letters and phone calls. It was exciting, but I was always kind of waiting for BYU to come around. They were a little bit late in the process.

LaVell made a trip out to watch one of my basketball games. Afterward, he came to my home and told me, "Congratulations on your basketball game." My mom asked if he wanted apple or peach pie, and he said, "Both, please." It was his way to break the ice and be himself. It was great. To me the man was a legend—that stoic, stern face I always saw on the sideline.

Ryan Denney returned this blocked field goal attempt 82 yards for a touchdown in a 59–21 victory at San Diego State in 2001. As a senior that year Denney was named a CoSIDA Academic All-America. He went on to play nine seasons in the NFL.

While we were talking, he said, "Ryan, we'd like to have you at BYU." I said, "You know, Coach, I want to commit." It was such a thrill for me to have a legend like LaVell say how excited he was for me to come play for him. It was a real boost for a young teenager and a pretty exciting night for our family.

When I arrived at BYU in the fall of 1995, I was 6′7″—a big, tall guy—and weighed about 225 pounds—pretty skinny. We had some great big guys playing D-line at the time, like Henry Bloomfield and the Raass brothers. There were also guys like Daren Yancey and Ed Kehl just coming off their missions who were 6′5″ and about 290 pounds.

I was just not quite ready to play at that time, and so I spent that first year on the practice squad as a redshirt. At that time, the practice players didn't get a Y on their helmet unless they got to dress for a game. I was able to suit up for a game or two that season. Just to be part of the program was exciting at that point. Having that Y on my helmet was awesome. I still have a photo of me from that first game that a friend of mine took to help me remember that experience.

After my freshman year, I served a Church mission to Buenos Aires, Argentina. I returned for the 1998 season. I came back with a desire to do well in school and to work hard with my studies. I think student-athletes are capable of putting equal time into both schoolwork and their athletic pursuits. I would always take about 12.5 credits so I could focus on the classes and not get too burned out.

One of the great things about BYU was having solid peers, either teammates or classmates, who you could look up to and were examples of hard work. Some of the older players I watched as a freshman and sophomore were good leaders. They worked hard on the practice field and demanded effort from their teammates. That really helped develop my work ethic and especially gave me the tools to succeed in the NFL, having been around players who were quality guys as well as good players.

There was also a lot of great support at BYU, like our trainers George Curtis and Kevin Morris. They were always there to take care of us and keep us healthy so we could be successful.

As far as coaching goes, I learned a lot from Tom Ramage. He is one of those guys who, if you were playing well, would let you know and, if you weren't doing as well as you should, would remind you that you could be better. He would have all his players to his home once a week for ice cream sundaes. I had a lot of good times at his home with the other defensive line-men. It was fun to play for him.

I remember returning a blocked kick back 80-something yards for a touch-down against San Diego State. To be able to score is a pretty special moment for a defender. There's a highlight video of that play where Coach Ramage is jumping in celebration. I think he got about two inches off the ground. That always brings me fond memories of playing for him.

I miss being at BYU. I played nine years in the league after I graduated, and I think it would be more fun to get out on the field in Provo again than it would be to be still playing in the NFL. At BYU it was all about playing for your coaches, your teammates, and the school. A lot of that is lost at the pro-fessional level. At BYU, the fans would live and die by the wins and the losses. There was so much hope, even when the team was down, that we would be able to come back and win the game. It's something that I think only exists at the college level, and BYU has some of the best fans in the country.

For me, it was an honor to be a Cougar. It meant a lot to be a part of that brotherhood and be associated with the university. When I was in the NFL, I didn't meet one player who had played with another BYU guy who had anything bad to say. It was such a privilege to be associated with an organi-zation that stands for so much.

During my career at BYU I had a bunch of great experiences. I was on the field the night President Gordon B. Hinckley renamed the football stadium LaVell Edwards Stadium. It was quite memorable to be a part of that night. It was an honor that LaVell clearly deserved, and I was very happy for him. He brought BYU football to the highest level.

His greatness was the ability to develop a strategy that worked at BYU. He was also wise enough to have a good supporting cast in his assistant coaches and coordinators. Some of those guys had been together a long time—Norm Chow, Ken Schmidt, Lance Reynolds, Ramage. They worked well together and trusted each other. That's why he was so successful.

One of my favorite memories was LaVell's last game. All the talk leading up to that game was about would he go out with a victory or a loss. We played the game at the University of Utah, and I remember feeling a lot of pressure as a player to send LaVell out with a win. There was such a sway in momentum at the end of that game. Utah came back in the fourth quarter to take the lead, and we had to find a way to win. The game looked pretty bleak there for a little while. After Brandon Doman and the offense scored to give us back the lead, I remember feeling a huge amount of pressure to go out there and keep them from scoring. When the game was finally over, I was standing right next to LaVell, and I thought, *How can you not carry him off the field to finalize his great career, especially after such a big win?* It was just a natural reaction as part of our celebration to pick him up and put him on our shoulders. It was a pretty neat experience being one of the guys who helped carry Coach off the field.

My senior year was a lot of fun. We won our first 12 games, and there's nothing more fun in football than winning. We had a lot of good players on defense, but we weren't ranked very high statistically because the offense was so good. We were having a lot of fun winning games and climbing the national polls. It was a really good experience for me.

Serving a mission and playing football at BYU really helped prepare me for the NFL from a maturity standpoint. The NFL demands quite a bit of maturity. It's really easy to get squeezed out, to succumb to the pressure that exists to succeed and make the team year after year. I saw a lot of talented players have a hard time with their self-confidence or their maturity level. They had a hard time making the adjustment.

I wouldn't trade my experience at BYU for the world. To play there and to have been a part of some great seasons was incredible. I had great teammates and made lifelong friendships in Provo. It really was a great experience, and if I had to do it over again, there's nothing that I would want to change about my time at BYU.

Ryan Denney played four seasons as a defensive end at BYU, from 1998 to 2001. Following his senior year, Denney was selected as a CoSIDA Academic All-American and was also named first-team all-conference. The Buffalo Bills took him in the second round of the 2002 NFL Draft. Denney played nine seasons in the NFL with the Bills and the Houston Texans.

RENO MAHE

RUNNING BACK/RECEIVER

1998–1999 ★ 2001–2002

M Y DAD WAS AN AMAZING rugby player. To this day people tell me that he was a better athlete than I was. I tell them, "Come on, I played in the NFL." And they will say, "You've got nothing on your dad." Even when I was a sophomore and junior in high school, he would challenge me to a 40 and beat me. He was just a natural athlete.

He had a huge impact on me playing sports. Football was second to none in our house growing up. Most kids growing up do chores—cleaning the yard, taking out the trash, cleaning their room. My chores were to work out—pushups, sit-ups, running. He wanted me to play football. He felt it was the thing that would open doors for me and change my life.

We moved to Utah when I was 12. We lived in a rough area on the west side of Salt Lake City. Before my sophomore year we moved to the east side just down the street from Brighton High School. He wanted to give me a better opportunity to play football and be in a better neighborhood, where we would stay out of trouble.

By the time I was a senior, I was being recruited by BYU, Utah, and Utah State. My older brother, Sione, is six years older than me. He played football at Utah, so our family became University of Utah fans. Because of the rivalry, if you were a Utah fan, you hated BYU. I would attend both Utah and BYU football camps during the summer and wear my brother's Utah jacket at the

BYU camp. The camps are where I made a name for myself, not necessarily my high school stats. That's where I really started getting noticed.

At the end of my senior season I took a recruiting trip to both schools. It was set in stone that I was going to Utah. But on my trip to Utah they were flip-flopping on my position. The coaches weren't sure if I was going to play on offense or defense. I thought that was really weird. At BYU they told me I would play offense. They really did the recruiting part right.

The last thing I did on my trip to BYU was meet with Coach Edwards. I was with my parents. When it was time to leave, my mom stayed behind and kept talking to Coach Edwards. When she came out from his office, she told me, "I want you to go back in and tell Coach you are coming to BYU."

I said, "What?"

She said, "You're coming to BYU."

So I went back in his office and told coach I was coming to BYU. I can't say that I made the decision to go to BYU, but I did make the decision to listen to my mom.

When I came to BYU, I had a plan. I wanted to make a name for myself as a freshman. I wanted people to know I could play. Then I would go on a Church mission, come back, take my redshirt year, and have three years left to play.

In fall camp my freshman year, little by little, I got opportunities to play. The more plays I made, the more the coaches said, "Hey, this little guy can play." By the time we started the season, I made the travel squad. We opened at Alabama. I won't lie; I was scared. I didn't know if I wanted to play. In the second half we had a couple guys cramp up, and I think one of the guys fumbled. Eventually they put me in, and I actually scored a touchdown. From there everything just started to fall into place. I actually started to make a name for myself and eventually ended up starting in the bowl game my freshman year.

On the way back from the bowl, people started asking about my mission plans. Would I go? Would I stay and maybe have a chance to start the next year? Rather than sticking to the plan, I started thinking more about football than the plan and what I was supposed to do. That spring I made a decision to stay and play, even though I knew I was supposed serve a Church mission. By July, I got kicked out of school. I violated the honor code, something I had signed and agreed to abide by.

I still had my redshirt year, so I went to Utah Valley State for a year. The plan was to get my life in order and get back to living the standards I knew I should be living by. Then I would come back to BYU. But when that time came, BYU felt I had not grown up enough yet—and rightfully so. I hadn't.

At that point I was struggling with life. I didn't know where I was going. I was on hiatus from life and just lost. I decided to bag BYU. So I took a recruiting trip to North Carolina State because Norm Chow, my former coach at BYU, was now there. On that trip I was actually hosted by Philip Rivers, who is now in the NFL. After returning, I decided to just go to Dixie so I wouldn't lose a year of eligibility and still keep my Division I options open. It was also close to home. I remember sitting in the driveway with my dad the day I left for Dixie and promising him that someday I would play

Reno Mahe led the Cougars in receiving as both a junior and senior. His 1,211 receiving yards in 2001 is the third-highest single-season total in school history. Mahe went on to play five seasons in the NFL with the Philadelphia Eagles.

237

professional football. I would go to Dixie, and then to a Division I school, and then go pro. Somehow things worked out.

At Dixie things were a lot different. At first, I played running back, but teams would stack nine guys in the box and just try to stop the run. I went to Coach Croshaw and told him that I had played some receiver in high school. We had several other good backs, and I felt if I played receiver it would give us a second option and our team wouldn't be so one-dimensional. That's how I switched from running back to wideout.

It worked out. I had some success and had a lot more options for football. I came really close to going to USC—I can't tell you how close. But there were a lot of other factors to consider, including Sunny, who was an All-America volleyball player at BYU I was dating.

One day I was sitting in an LDS Institute class at Dixie. I was thinking about where I wanted my life to go, what I wanted to accomplish, and suddenly it all came clear to me. I had this feeling like, "I want to go back to BYU. I want to marry Sunny, and I want to finish what I started." I had tarnished my family name and I wanted to go back and bring honor to my parents and my name. I wanted to prove to myself that I could go to a school like BYU, live up to the standards, and do what I'm supposed to do. A lot of it had to do with Sunny and the quality person that she is. I knew I wouldn't be able to find someone like her at any other school.

There were so many people at BYU who really had an impact in shaping my life. I got to play for Coach Edwards. He was a legend. When I came back I got to play for Gary Crowton on one of the best teams to ever play at BYU. Coach Mike Borich was my position coach, and he really taught me how to be an athlete.

Then there were three guys I played with who really taught me a lot by their example. Brandon Doman taught me about leadership. The way he carried himself on and off the field inspired me. I hoped I could be like that. Gabe Reid was a guy who taught me about trust and respect. Finally, my friend Naki Maile. Although he's gone now, I think about him a lot when I have tough life decisions. I wonder what he would do.

Every Saturday I had a chance to run out of the tunnel at LaVell Edwards Stadium was like a dream come true. It reminded me how lucky I was to have the opportunity to play football at BYU. The stadium is awesome. The fans are amazing. I can picture every moment. It's a cool feeling. I get the chills just thinking about it.

There are two memories I'll never forget about playing at BYU. One was my first touchdown after coming back. I knew I was on my way to finishing something I started. The other memory will always be the Utah game in 2001. I had an emergency appendectomy on Monday and played in the game five days later. We were still undefeated at the time. When they told me I needed to have my appendix removed, I had no doubt I would find a way to play in that game. I didn't know what was involved in the procedure. I didn't know how long the recovery should take. I just knew I had to play.

Later I had a priesthood blessing that confirmed to me that I was going to be okay. I didn't take any pain medication for the next four or five days, and I knew when I could live with the pain I could play. I caught a touchdown in the third quarter to help us come from behind and win the game.

It means a lot to me to be a Cougar—I will forever be indebted to BYU for numerous reasons. One, I was able to find someone like my wife, who inspires me and makes me want to be a better person. The school itself is inspired. It has high standards. It makes you want to be a better person. The bar is set very high, and they don't bring the bar down so you can easily clear it.

Being able to take that standard of excellence and implement it into my life is something I'll never be able to repay. BYU is a school that athletically, academically, and spiritually inspires you to be so much more than you are or even more than what you think you can become.

Reno Mahe was named first-team All-MWC in 2001. He led the Cougars in receiving in 2001 and 2002, and his 1,211 yards receiving in 2001 is the third-highest single-season total in BYU history. Mahe signed as a free agent with the Philadelphia Eagles in 2003. He played five seasons with the Eagles. In 2005 he led the NFL in punt-return average with 21 returns for 269 yards, an average of 12.8 yards per return.

LUKE STALEY

RUNNING BACK

1999–2001

GROWING UP, I REMEMBER idolizing BYU players like Ty Detmer, Brian McKenzie, and Ronnie Jenkins. In Oregon I wasn't able to watch the games on TV, but I was able to pick them up on the radio. I would grab my Walkman, some headphones, and go out to mow the lawn while listening to BYU beat Notre Dame. It was always something that I wanted to be a part of.

My brother Dustin is about five years older than I am, so I didn't play on the same team with him in high school. Ultimately, that was one of the reasons why I chose to go to BYU. Dustin was a very good high school player and got a lot of exposure. He opened a lot of doors for me. I went to the BYU football camp prior to my senior year in high school. I wanted the coaches to see firsthand what I could offer.

Most of the colleges at that time were recruiting me to play defense, so at camp I was spending most of the time working out with Barry Lamb. A day or two into camp, Coach Reynolds came over and said, "Hey, come spend some time with the offense." That's where they wanted me to play, which was another big factor for me to go to BYU.

I love Coach Reynolds. There are not very many people like him. He is very easygoing. I've maybe heard him raise his voice once or twice. I think the world of Lance—the way he handles himself and the way that he leads by example.

At the camp LaVell pulled me aside and said, "Hey, we want you to come to BYU, we're offering you a scholarship." When BYU offered the scholarship, it really wasn't a question for me. It was a decision that was already made.

Dustin was just coming back from his mission, and was a redshirt sophomore when I was a freshman. He was always my idol. He was my hero growing up. At BYU I just watched what he did and followed him around. He was able to show me where to go and how to do things. My freshman year was a lot easier with him there.

I remember the night before the Washington game my freshman year in 1999. I couldn't sleep, so I went to the stadium. I hopped the 10-foot fence and sat in the stadium for about an hour or two. Every time I ran out of the tunnel onto that field I felt like Rudy. It was something that I worked so hard for. I would get chills. It was probably the greatest feeling that I had at BYU.

Football doesn't necessarily define who I am, but it helped mold who I am now. I learned that, if you have a goal in mind and you put in the hard work, you could find a way to succeed. The only person who can stop you is you. Not everything in life is going to go smoothly. Things are going to change. Accept the change and make the most of it.

I have a lot of great memories of playing with my brother at BYU. One that stands out is his interception against Air Force my freshman year. I remember giving him a hug when he came off the field, and then running onto the field with the offense.

Another cool memory was seeing my jersey hanging up in the locker room. It didn't just say "Staley" on the back—it said "L. Staley." There were a lot of little things that stand out to me. Like him coming up during games and saying, "Hey, good job!" For both of us to have an impact on the success of the team the way we did was something special.

My sophomore year was somewhat frustrating. At that time, LaVell had had a run of 26 straight non-losing seasons, and we obviously didn't want his last season to break that string. I remember being 4–6 and knowing we had to win the last two games to avoid a losing season.

We beat New Mexico in LaVell's last home game. That night was something neat to be a part of. I'm sure everybody remembers it differently and has his own favorite experience. It was a defining moment in not only LaVell's history and legacy but also the stadium's history.

242

Luke Staley led the nation in scoring and yards per carry as a junior in 2001. He was named a consensus All-American and won the Doak Walker Award, awarded to the nation's top running back.

That final win at home and the Utah victory the next week kind of erased a lot of the negative things from that season. LaVell showed a lot of emotions after those games, and you usually didn't see that from him.

We were in control of the Utah game for three quarters, but in college football that can change very quickly—which happened. For me, I don't think there was necessarily a question that we would win. Maybe that is just the mentality I had for every game, but there were some tense moments for some of the players and fans, wondering if we would pull it out.

The game came down to one drive, and that was it. If we didn't succeed on that last drive, the game was over. I think I can probably remember every play of that drive. Of course, there was the questionable call on whether or not I fumbled on the third-down play. I've actually gone back and looked at that play and tried to analyze if I fumbled or not. It could have gone either way. We were fortunate it went our way.

After that, Brandon Doman basically completed the same play to Jonathan Pittman twice. Then I ran the ball to about the 4- or 5-yard line, and Brandon called a timeout. The coaches said, "We're just going to keep it simple. We don't want any screw-ups. Let's minimize the risks of throwing an interception or having a bad quarterback–running back exchange. Brandon, just keep the ball, run to the right, and find the end zone."

It was basically student-body right and go get it done. Everyone did his assignment, and Brandon made a good play getting into the end zone. It was memorable for me to be a part of LaVell's legacy and to be there in the locker room that night, because at that time, for me, BYU football was synonymous with LaVell Edwards. The two went together. We wanted to send him out on the right note.

My junior year in 2001, there were a lot of expectations among the team and myself. A lot of it we put on ourselves because of the prior year. There was a lot of good energy. I remember sitting in a running backs meeting at the beginning of the year and writing down my goals for the season. That was one thing I always liked to do, write down goals. If anybody were to see those goals prior to that season, they would have looked at me and said, "Are you kidding yourself?" One of my goals was to be the best running back in the nation and win the Doak Walker Award. I didn't tell anybody.

That 2001 team was one of the most complete teams that BYU has had. We were a very explosive team. As an offense, we had a lot of expectations.

We knew we could be good, and we had a lot of leadership. We also had a common goal that we were going to find a way to succeed.

Going into the Utah game in 2001, I kind of knew it was probably going to be my last home game. I obviously wanted to go out on a good note. It's something that I will always remember and cherish. At that time we were undefeated. We had a lot riding on that game with a chance of being a BCS buster.

From a fan's point of view or from a player's point of view, that game was one in a million. It was a classic BYU vs. Utah rivalry game. I remember being in the locker room before the game, hearing the fans stomping their feet and feeling the bleachers shaking. When I scored the go-ahead touchdown and also when Jenaro had the interception at the end, that is by far the loudest and most electrifying crowd I've ever heard.

Before our second-to-last series, Brandon and I looked at each other and said, "We're going to win this game. I don't know how we're going to do it, but somehow we're going to pull this off." I remember it was a long touchdown drive, more than 90 yards. Then the defense had a huge series and left us some time to score the go-ahead touchdown. It was just one of those things where there was no question we were going to win that game.

I'll always remember that winning touchdown. It was a basic option play to the right. I think we caught them in a corner or safety blitz. If everyone did their job on the play, which they did, it should score a touchdown. Brandon froze the corner or linebacker and dished the ball. Soren Halladay had a great block on the defensive back, and there was nothing but green grass in front of me.

Finishing the season by winning the Doak Walker Award is something that I'll cherish all my life. I broke my ankle in the Mississippi State game, so I didn't travel with the team the next week to Hawaii. I was invited to attend the ESPN College Football Awards Show, and someone told me I should go because it was a once-in-lifetime experience. So I flew out to Orlando the same day as the show. I went to my hotel room, showered, and headed to the event.

I had no idea that I was going to win. There's nothing like being in a setting where you don't have any control of the outcome. Sitting there on the second row waiting for the announcement was maybe one of the most nervous moments of my life.

The one thing I do regret is that the Doak Walker is an individual award. The trophy only has my name on it, but it really should have been a team award. That was a special team and a memorable season. It was always something that I wanted to be a part of—to help a program that I loved to be successful.

BYU is certainly a great chapter in my life. It provided some of the fondest memories I have.

Luke Staley played three seasons at BYU, from 1999 to 2001. As a junior, he led the nation in scoring and yards per carry, while finishing third in rushing yards. Staley was named consensus All-America and became the only Cougar to win the Doak Walker Award, given annually to the nation's top running back. He was selected in the seventh round of the 2002 NFL Draft by the Detroit Lions.

CURTIS BROWN

RUNNING BACK

2002–2006

WE MOVED TO PALMDALE, California, when I was 10. I didn't even know Pop Warner football existed. During my first year of football, my dad bought me some Payless cleats that ended up being baseball cleats. I was slipping all over the place. At the end of the season, I was going to quit. My coach talked me into playing one more year. Fortunately he did, because I ended up excelling the next season.

I went to a private Catholic high school and was fortunate to be able to play varsity football as a freshman. During my four years of high school football, our team won the league championship every year. Because of the success, I had good enough credentials that BYU gave me a look.

Teams like Washington State, UCLA, and Clemson recruited me, but what sealed the deal for me was the consistency at BYU. I knew the coaches cared about me from their approach. The closer I got to signing day, some of those schools shied away. I knew BYU wanted me from the time they contacted me after receiving my recruiting tape. That's the way it should be. It shouldn't take that long. Either you want me or you don't. It shouldn't take someone else turning down a scholarship for the school to then decide they want you.

BYU was the first to invite me on a recruiting trip, so I took advantage of the opportunity. My parents have always had high expectations for me. They helped me evaluate each of the schools and opportunities. It was weird, but I knew after my recruiting trip to Provo that BYU was the place for me.

was closing in on my record. But I love Harvey, and there is no one I'd rather see break my record than him. I think Jamal was proud to pass on the torch to me, and I was proud to pass it on to Harvey.

I remember Jake Kuresa saying to me in the huddle that day, "You're only a couple yards away from breaking the record. I don't want you to break the record by one yard or something. If you're going to do it, do it big." They called the play, and the safety went with the motion. I got the handoff and saw the hole open up, and I remembering thinking, *Man, this is it.* What a way to break the record, with a 49-yard touchdown run. In a way it was a relief, because I had tried to keep the attention on the team, not me.

The biggest lesson I learned at BYU was the concept of "unless you believe in something, you'll fall for everything." BYU is about faith. It's about believing in something you can't touch or see, but something you feel inside emotionally and spiritually.

It wasn't until I bought into everything that BYU stands for that I really understood it. Gaining an appreciation for the academic program, the service aspect, the religious and spiritual side. That's when I really started to get the full benefit as a player and as a person.

My experience at BYU was priceless. I wouldn't trade it for the world. There is a responsibility that goes with being a graduate of BYU, being a football player, being a Cougar. Not everyone can make it at BYU. There are a lot of high expectations that the school and program has for you as a person first, and also as a player. I have a lot to be grateful for. I have great parents who raised me well. I had great coaches and players around me who kept me focused. I feel really blessed to have been given the opportunity to be at BYU.

Curtis Brown finished his career at BYU as the leading rusher in school history with 3,193 yards. He was named first-team All-MWC in 2005 and 2006 and was a second-team selection as a sophomore in 2004. He was the first BYU running back to rush for more than 1,000 yards in back-to-back seasons. Following his BYU career, Brown signed an NFL free agent contract with the Cincinnati Bengals.

BRYAN KEHL

LINEBACKER

2002 ★ 2005–2007

I STARTED PLAYING FOOTBALL when I was eight. I had four older brothers, and they all played. It was just something I was going to do. I remember them always asking me from a young age, "What position are you going to play, Bry?" I used to say, "Running back." Obviously, that didn't work out.

I'm not sure how my immediate family became BYU fans, because even today most of my extended family are University of Utah fans. For one reason or another, we became BYU fans and started going to the games back in the early 1990s. Even before my brother Ed went there to play football, we were BYU fans. We were season ticket holders. We went to the bowl games. So, basically for me, it was never even a decision where I would play. It was always, "I'm going to play football for BYU someday."

Coming out of high school, I really didn't get recruited that much. The first school that actually called me was Utah, then BYU called later. The only other football coach who called me was from Harvard. After BYU started calling, Utah offered me a scholarship a couple weeks later. A few days after Utah offered a scholarship, BYU did, as well. I called BYU back the next day and told them, "I'm coming." This was after my junior year and before my senior year of high school. After that, I didn't get letters or phone calls from any other coaches. I guess they all knew.

In high school our coach would only let us play one way, so I just played defense. It made me mad because I wanted to be a running back. But that's how I became a defensive player. I reported to BYU on August 4, 2002. I still remember it. I had high expectations. It was Gary Crowton's second year as head coach. BYU had just come off a 12–2 season, flying high. We started the season ranked, and I was really excited. I had a late birthday, so I had a whole year before I would turn 19 and could serve an LDS mission.

My plan was to play that year, go on a mission, and then come back and redshirt when I got home. So I came in with the expectation to play. I played a bit as a true freshman, not nearly as much as I think I should have played, but I'm sure everybody has that opinion as a freshman. We had a terrible year. We were 5–7, but I really enjoyed playing college football. I liked Coach Crowton; he was really good to me. Aside from the losing record, it was fun. I really loved it—it was BYU football.

I left on a Church mission on May 7, 2003. Like playing football for BYU, it was something I knew I was going to do. It was never a question. My four older brothers went, and my dad went. It was something I had planned on doing for as long as I can remember.

I got back July 1, 2005. I went down and met with Coach Mendenhall the next day. He had arrived at BYU in January 2003 as the defensive coordinator. I was with him from January until I left on my mission, so I'd gone through spring ball with him. When I was on my mission and heard that he had been hired as the new head coach, I was pumped beyond belief because I loved him. I was only with him for a couple of months, but he had won me over.

Coach Mendenhall was always big on helping us realize that it wasn't just about football. School mattered. Church mattered. Our family relationships mattered. Our community service and friendships mattered. He taught us that, if we took care of all those things, football would take care of itself. If you look across the country at other football coaches, especially at the collegiate level, I don't think they're teaching that same message. Some might say they are to be politically correct, but I don't think there are too many who actually believe it as Bronco does.

I worked hard to stay in shape on my mission. I ate really well and took care of my body. I always had a jump rope. It allowed me to keep my legs in shape. For nine months I lived in a big high-rise in Toronto. It had 46 floors, so I would run those stairs everyday. A lot of guys come back and they have lost a step, but I was able to come back and just pick up where I left off athletically. I lost a lot of muscle mass because I couldn't lift weights, but as far as speed and quickness, it was no problem. I weighed 235 when I left. When I came back, I was 217.

I can't even describe how excited I was to get going after I got home. The team was off that week because it was the Fourth of July. Consequently, I only had three weeks to lift and work out with the team before fall camp started. I thought I was going to redshirt, but I guess I came back in too good of shape because they threw me right in there as a sophomore, basically a month back from my mission.

At the beginning of fall camp, Coach Mendenhall took us to the stadium and had us lie on the field. While we were lying there, they played audio highlights over the stadium speakers—Greg Wrubell, Paul James, and some of the other broadcasters calling the different miracle moments of BYU

Bryan Kehl was named academic all-conference three straight years, from 2005 to 2007. He was taken in the fourth round of the 2008 NFL Draft by the New York Giants.

football. I had tears in my eyes lying there because it was so close to home for me. I had lived many of those great moments. I wasn't just a kid who got recruited to come to BYU. I wasn't just an average BYU fan. I was always a diehard. For most of those great BYU moments, I had been there at the game or had watched on TV. I remember that night in the stadium like it was yesterday. I was so glad to be at BYU and have the opportunity to make some of those same moments as a player.

There are several moments at BYU that I'll never forget. There is nothing like coming out on the field at LaVell Edwards Stadium. Right above the locker room, all the fans are stomping their feet on the stadium floor, and everything is just rattling. You're with a group of guys you spent eight months in the off-season sweating, bleeding, and crying with. You're so bonded to this common goal, and then you have the opportunity to run out on the field and work toward a single purpose together. Nothing compares to it.

During my sophomore year in 2005 against Utah, we came out and played a terrible first half. We battled back and actually tied the score at 34 to send the game to overtime. Right before overtime, there was probably about a minute left, and Utah was driving downfield to try to win the game. There was a timeout or something, and we were in a huddle. I remember looking around the stadium. It was a beautiful November day in Provo, Utah. The stands were packed in blue and red—the mountains in the background. The game was tied. BYU vs. Utah, game on the line. I looked over at Cameron Jensen and said, "Dude, where would you rather be than right here, right now? This is just awesome." I can't remember exactly what he said, but something along the same lines. That moment stands out.

My final game at BYU against Utah in 2007 was the perfect ending to my career at Edwards Stadium. I had so many emotions that day. I remember as a kid being one of the first to storm the field after a big BYU win. I loved that, dodging the security guys so I could get onto the field. So when we beat Utah 17–10, I knew what it was like for the fans when they stormed the field and then lifted me up on their shoulders. It was my last game in that stadium that I had grown up coming to for so many years. It was against my favorite opponent, and we won in prototypical miracle BYU fashion. Sports-wise, I don't think anything can even come close to that moment.

The coolest thing about BYU is that it has the proper balance of what's important in life. It's a prestigious academic institution. It's always among the

255

top schools in the country as far as rankings and the quality of education, but the fact that the school puts so much emphasis on growing spiritually makes BYU special. There is a great emphasis on being well-rounded in all phases of life—most importantly spiritually, academically, but also socially and physically. That's one of the things that makes BYU unique, the quality combination of all those different phases of life. Consequently, the average student on campus is very happy and positive. That's another unique aspect of BYU—that everybody is just glad to be alive, glad to be there, glad to be working, glad to be toiling, glad to be studying, glad to be facing the daily challenges of life.

Being a Cougar is a tremendous privilege and something that I'm just so grateful for. With that comes a great responsibility. Bronco used to always remind us that the mission of the football program is to be "the flag bearer of Brigham Young University, through football excellence, embracing virtues like truth, tradition, honor as a beacon to the world." I agree with that 100 percent.

So for me it's a privilege and then a responsibility. I think about that in everything I do. Everything I pursue for the rest of my life will be reflective of the fact that I went to BYU—that I'm an alumnus, that I am someone others will look to, and when they look at me they will also identify the university. So everything I do needs to be reflective of those qualities, virtues, and characteristics.

Bryan Kehl earned Academic All-MWC honors as a sophomore, junior, and senior at BYU. Following his senior season in 2007, he was named first-team All-MWC and BYU defensive MVP. Kehl was selected in the fourth round of the 2008 NFL Draft by the New York Giants. He has played professionally for the Giants and the St. Louis Rams.

DANIEL COATS
TIGHT END
2003–2006

M Y FIRST GAME AT BYU was against Georgia Tech—the home opener in 2003. Coach Mike Empey was joking with me all week that it was my first game and I was going to be so scared. I told him, "No way, Coach. In fact, I'll bet you I'm going to score. Then, after I score, I'm going to do a dance in the end zone."

So when I actually scored in the game, the dance just happened. Boy, did I hear about that later. The whole team let me have it. The next day at practice, it was the biggest joke. A couple of guys got quoted in the paper saying it was the worst dance they had ever seen. That was a great memory.

Another game that sticks out in my mind was the next week at USC. They had recruited me out of high school, and I really wanted to have a good game. I ended up having a bunch of catches [eight] for about 100 [114] yards and scored another touchdown. We lost, but it was a fun to go to a place like USC and try to take it to them.

I began playing Pee Wee football when I lived in Tucson, Arizona. My family moved to Layton, Utah, when I was in the seventh grade. In high school I played any sport they'd let me play—football, basketball, baseball, and I ran track. I tried to do it all.

As a sophomore, I played the last half of the season as the varsity free safety. The next year I started varsity at free safety and at wide receiver. I actually had a really good junior year. I was named MVP in the state and received All-America honors. After that, I started to get recruited. That's when I realized I could possibly go to college through football.

I was talking with USC, North Carolina State, Utah, Colorado, and BYU, of course. A lot of colleges wanted me to be a strong safety or some kind of a linebacker. All the schools except BYU were talking to me about playing defense. That kind of helped in my decision to go to BYU.

I liked the whole feel at BYU. I felt like BYU was competing at the highest level, against the best teams, but I also felt like it was still a home atmosphere. I wasn't a party guy, so the whole Honor Code thing kind of appealed to me. I was getting engaged at the same time, so I thought BYU would be a great place for me.

I redshirted my freshman year at BYU and played wide receiver on the scout team. Late in the year, one of the tight ends got hurt, and they didn't have anybody to fill in. I was a big receiver, so the coaches asked me to give it a try. Our tight ends coach, Mike Empey, used to always mess with me, saying, "Time is on my side. Coach [Jay] Omer is going to put more weight on you, and you'll be with me before you know it." I would always fight it and tell him, "No way! I'm never going to line up with one of my hands on the ground."

That spring they officially moved me to tight end. When it first happened, I was a wreck. Coach Empey told me, "Being a tight end here at BYU is a good thing. You'll get to catch a lot of balls." I thought it was going to be horrible.

I'll tell you what, he was right. It was awesome. You're definitely going to get your share of balls as a tight end in the BYU offense. Yeah, you have to block, but so do the receivers. In a way, it was really an advantage for me. I was used to going against corners and smaller safeties. Now I was going against linebackers. I felt like I had a huge speed advantage. It just worked out awesome for me.

My first couple of years at BYU, Reno Mahe took care of me. I can't think of a better way to put it than that. If I needed anything—if I had a problem with something—he was there to help. He showed me how to be a good person. He means a lot to me.

After Reno left, I became really close to Phil Niu. That was interesting, because Phil and I were competing for the same position on the field. We had our heated moments of competition, but all that got put aside because of true friendship. No matter what happened on the field, we were always friends.

Daniel Coats was a freshman All-American who started four straight years at BYU, from 2003 to 2006. He has been in the NFL since 2007 with the Cincinnati Bengals and Denver Broncos.

He would look after me, and I would look after him. I learned there is more to life than football.

After my sophomore season, Coach Mendenhall took over the program. I was sad to see Coach Crowton go. He was a big part of why I came to BYU, and I really respected him. He was always great to me. As a tight end, I was a little worried that we might change to an offense where the tight ends were just big fat guys who tried to push people around and never got to catch the ball. It didn't take long for us to see that the new offense was going to be exciting and that we were going to be throwing the ball like crazy.

We've had a lot of great tight ends come through BYU. I think we've had more talent than any other school in the country, and it shows by all the guys who came through the program. I'm proud to be part of that tradition. Everybody refers to BYU as the quarterback factory, but we've had so many great tight ends that I'm thinking we need to start calling it the tight end factory.

BYU was a place where I felt like my teammates were truly my brothers. I still talk to many of the guys I played with. We don't talk every day, but once we have a chance to talk, we catch up like we're old family members who haven't seen each other in a while. I know all of us are still deeply rooted in the school and in the football program. That's just the way it is at BYU— a family. That's our lifestyle.

One of the main things I learned at BYU is that there's a right way of doing things and there's a wrong way of doing things. There are no cutting corners. If you're going to do something, you have to do it right. If you're not prepared to do it right, you're not going to get the results you want, and it's really not worth doing. I am who I am as a person and as an athlete because of that.

I also learned that integrity is important. It's not just something you talk about. It's not just something you think about. It's something you show in your actions. You are who you are. Your word is one of the most precious things that you have.

Coach Mendenhall taught us the importance of representing ourselves. He taught us we represent the team. We also represent the school. There was a lot that we stood for. It was going out there and playing football the right way, with the right kind of players. It was always a great feeling to know what we represented.

Coming out onto the field at LaVell Edwards Stadium was always something special. You knew the whole community was excited. The fans truly, truly loved you. They lived and died by what we did on the field. So everything we did felt important because people truly cared what was going on when we played.

I have a lot of great memories, but I'll always remember the Utah game my senior year. Being from Utah, that's the game you want to win. I remember that game was such a roller coaster of emotions. We scored early, then they scored to take the lead. Toward the end of the game, it was a back-and-forth deal. I scored a touchdown in the fourth quarter and thought I was going to be the hero of the game. There wasn't a lot of time left, and I remember thinking, *Everybody's going to be talking about that winning touchdown.*

After Utah went down and scored, I thought, *Okay, we have time to get another one.* Lo and behold, we drove the length of the field, and Jonny caught the winning touchdown. I have to admit I had a little selfish moment of, *Dang, he stole my glory.* Ha-ha. I was actually more excited that we got the win and in such a dramatic fashion. What a way to go out.

I remember the final drive was total confidence. Nobody was worried about how much time was left or how far we had to go. Our only thought was, *Okay, how are we going to get this done?* That was one of John Beck's strong points. He was one of those great leaders who got us all going. Sort of like, "Okay, fellas, let's hurry up and do this real quick, so we can celebrate and go home." It was like we all knew a secret that the whole stadium didn't know. That was a special thing about that team. I felt like everybody on the team knew it was going to happen.

I'm always going to be a Cougar. I'm always going to be a BYU football player. It means a lot to me. One of the things that brought me to BYU was the legacy of all those great players who played here. You know they're not just names on the wall. When I was there, a lot of those guys came back and helped us. They tried to help us improve on the football field and in life, also. It was cool that the tradition was real, that somebody was there to encourage me. I can't wait until I get a chance to come back and help the next generation of players, the way someone helped me follow in his footsteps. You are never done with BYU or being a Cougar.

Daniel Coats started four years at tight end for BYU, from 2003 to 2006. He set a BYU freshman tight end receiving record with 30 receptions for 378 yards and four touchdowns and was named a *Sporting News* Freshman All-American in 2003. Coats signed as a free agent with the Cincinnati Bengals in 2007 and has played four seasons in the NFL for the Bengals and the Denver Broncos.

JOHN BECK

QUARTERBACK

2003–2006

I GREW UP IN MESA, ARIZONA, and I went to Mountain View High School. I couldn't wait for my opportunity to be the quarterback for the Toros. My senior year we went 13–1, won the state championship, and, I believe, were No. 14 in the country. I was named the Arizona Player of the Year and had some offers from Pac-10 schools like Oregon, UCLA, and Arizona State.

When I told them that I was going on a mission, many of them backed off. I remember my coach telling me, "John, Oregon is going to offer you a scholarship, but they're not going to give you a scholarship if you're going on a mission." I told him there was no way I was going to tell someone I wasn't going on a mission. I've always planned on going. If they really wanted me, they could offer knowing I was going.

About that time Chris Pella at BYU starting recruiting me. My dad ran track at BYU. I grew up on campus as a little kid. I used to be around the football players in the weight room and on the track while my dad was training.

My mom tells a story—I obviously can't remember it—about me being in the Smith Fieldhouse when Coach Edwards came walking over and bent down to my level and said, "What are you doing, buddy?"

I guess I took the hat off of his head and put it on my head and said, "I'm going to be your quarterback." I had a speech impediment, so he didn't understand what I said.

As a senior in 2006, John Beck was named second-team All-America by the *Sporting News*. He concluded his BYU career with 11,021 yards—the second-highest total in school history.

My mom explained, "He's telling you that he wants to be a BYU Cougars quarterback."

Coach Edwards reportedly said, "Sounds great. When he grows a little bit, tell him to find me."

Arizona State was also recruiting me hard. I felt it was going to come down to either Arizona State or BYU. I wanted to make a decision before going on my mission. Growing up, my dad had taught me, "If you face a hard decision, you get down on your knees and you pray about it." I was praying about it a ton but wasn't necessarily getting an answer. On conference weekend, President Gordon B. Hinckley got up and gave the opening address, and I had this feeling like I had my answer. I knew Heavenly Father wanted me to go to BYU. It was kind of a fulfillment for me of a childhood dream.

I called Coach Pella and told him I was coming to BYU. Then he put me on the phone with LaVell Edwards. A little while later, LaVell sent me a letter saying that he had made the decision to retire and that my scholarship would be there when I returned from my mission.

While serving a mission in Lisbon, Portugal, I actually got recruited more heavily than when I was in high school. Washington, Arizona State, UCLA, and Miami all wanted me to take visits. Miami was really pushing to get me. I'll admit that was pretty cool to have the Miami Hurricanes interested in me. I told everyone recruiting me that I had committed to BYU before my mission. They were telling me that I was crazy to go to BYU because LaVell was gone and it wasn't the same program as before.

When I got home, I went to BYU for a visit. It was November 2002. I still wasn't sure what to do because I had all these offers. One day I was walking across campus to visit a friend who taught at the Missionary Training Center in Provo. It was fall, and the leaves were falling. I decided to cut across the practice field. I could see the stadium in the background. It was one of those moments that was an answer to my prayers. I had this feeling come over me that I was supposed to go to BYU, and as long as I worked hard, great things were going to happen.

It's funny because, during tough times at BYU, I thought back to that moment walking across the practice field. I'll never forget it. It was my "Rudy" moment. I could hear the theme song from the movie *Rudy* in my head. I always loved the movie. I never felt like an underdog or anything like that, but I loved it because of his determination and how hard he worked. In that moment I realized I could achieve all my goals at BYU. That afternoon I called my dad and said, "I'm definitely going to BYU."

When I arrived in Provo, I hadn't played any college football. I had no previous redshirt year, nothing. I went right from high school to my mission and missed three football seasons. I knew I had a lot of ground to make up. A lot of stuff was foreign to me—taking a snap from the shotgun, multiple reads, and audibles at the line of scrimmage. I had no idea how crazy it was going to be.

I was always in Coach Crowton's and Coach Bosco's offices, trying to learn plays, learn terminology and schemes. Coach Crowton was awesome about teaching me everything. I'm sure there were times when he was probably thinking, *I would like to go home and see my family*. I appreciate all the time he spent working with me.

I loved playing football at BYU. I loved coming out of the locker room and onto the field. I would try to high-five as many of the kids as I could because I knew it would mean something to them. As a kid, I got to slap hands with Ty Detmer and get pictures with him. That meant something to me.

Coming onto the field and playing football at BYU was something I dreamed of as a kid. When you hit the field and the fight song is playing, it's awesome. I get teased for not having a very good voice, but after we beat Oregon in the 2006 Vegas Bowl, they handed me the microphone, and I wanted everybody to sing the fight song because that song meant something to me. My mom would sing it to me when I was a little kid.

BYU is a special place. For me, BYU is a place where I gave everything I had, mentally, emotionally, and physically. It was not the easiest of times. The program went through some tough times for a while. It was hard on me, but I learned and grew so much. Who knows if the Utah game my senior year would have turned out like it did if we had not gone through all the tough times together. Because of those difficult times, I know that, when the clock showed three seconds, I had this feeling, *I'm so ready for this. I've done everything possible to prepare. I've worked as hard as I can. I know I'm going to make this play.*

My group of guys, we had to battle through a lot. To be able to share that moment at the University of Utah in 2006 was unforgettable—despite adversity, we came together and won the biggest game of our careers. We had already won the conference championship, but if we had lost to Utah, it would have tarnished the season. To be able to end in that fashion will be something I'll remember forever.

The best part about it was celebrating with the seniors. Guys like Jake Kuresa, Curtis Brown, Jonny Harline, Daniel Coats, Zac Collie, and Matt Allen. Guys who had been there the entire time together and had put in the extra time to be great. Dan Coats had three kids, including twins. He was getting about four hours of sleep a night. Every time I called Dan to throw, he was there. Zac Collie and Nate Meikle were the same way. Those guys made us great because they were willing to put in the extra time.

For the fans, the University of Utah game was a big win, against our rival, on a last-second play. To us on the field, especially those guys in the senior class, it was way more than that. It was the culmination of a lot of hard work. It was so special.

There were a lot of little plays in that final drive that led to Jonny's winning touchdown. I threw a check-down pass to Curtis. I knew we were taking a chance because we only had one timeout and he didn't have an easy path to get out of bounds. Somehow Curtis shed two tacklers and got out of bounds to stop the clock. In the game of football you have to have guys make plays like that if you're going to do something great.

Then there's the fourth-down play later in the drive. They rushed just three guys, and our offensive line kept them away from me. I sat back there for easily six seconds before I found Jonny to convert the fourth down. Another big play was McKay Jacobson's deep in-route for 19 yards to set up the winning touchdown. He was a true freshman in his first college football season, and he came up with a huge catch like that late in the game.

I get asked all the time about the final play, "What were you thinking? What happened?" For some reason, I have never been so calm as I was before that play. When we broke the huddle on the sideline, Jonny came to me and said, "What do you want me to do?" I said, "If they man-blitz us, and it's one-on-one, look for a jump ball. If not, just buy yourself time in the end zone and try to get open."

When we got to the line of scrimmage, I looked up at the clock and thought, *Okay, three seconds left.* I looked back down, and I had this feeling that we were going to make a play—exactly like that feeling when I made my decision to come to BYU. I felt that something great was going to happen.

When I dropped back, I knew they were only rushing a couple of guys. I thought, "I'm probably going to have to buy time with my feet." So I started to go left, and then the linebacker brought pressure. As I started going back to the right, I could just feel everyone moving with me. I also saw Jonny's long jersey cutting back across the flow. When I threw the ball, I knew we were going to win the game.

People have no idea how much goes into it. The sleepless nights, the long talks sharing my frustrations with my wife, the extra time on the practice field or in the film room. I would tell the guys, "Hey, we're not doing this to go beat teams 55–7. We're putting in the extra effort so when we really have to make a play, we make it."

For me, it was awesome to be a part of a return to what BYU was all about. To go back to the traditional BYU jersey and helmet—that was huge. I remember as a kid going to the stake center with my dad to watch BYU football games. I also remember going to San Diego for the Holiday Bowls. Ty Detmer was my childhood hero. When I thought of BYU, it was that jersey and the Y on the helmet.

I was pretty close with Mick Hill, our equipment guy. We would always share fishing and hunting stories. I remember one thing he said that really meant a lot to me. After the bowl game my senior year, I had just finished an ESPN radio interview when Mick grabbed me and said, "Johnny, this is what BYU football feels like." To have someone who had been around the program for so long and knew the history grab me with a big smile on his face and say, "BYU football is back, Johnny. This is what BYU football feels like." It was awesome!

There is such great history at BYU. LaVell Edwards established a place with such rich tradition. To me, being a Cougar means living up to that tradition—being everything that tradition stands for. When you play in that stadium on Saturdays, it means something to you. You feel it inside. When you look up at those mountains that overlook the stadium, you get chills. When you look at the Y up on the mountain, that's what you work for. Being a Cougar means living up to everything the Y stands for.

I found the love of my life, my wife Barbara, at BYU. It was a huge blessing to be able to meet her. I married her after my freshman year. She was there for everything—the hard times, the good times. The other great thing about BYU is that there is no other campus, I believe, where you can feel the Spirit like you can at BYU. Being of the LDS faith, that is something I wanted to be around. I was able to play football on Saturday and then attend Church on Sunday. It's a very unique place.

John Beck finished his career at BYU as the Cougars' No. 2 all-time passer, with 11,021 yards. As a senior, Beck was named second-team *Sporting News* All-America and received honorable mention citations from CBS Sportsline.com, *Pro Football Weekly*, and *College Football News*. The Miami Dolphins took him in the second round of the 2007 NFL Draft.

JONNY HARLINE

TIGHT END

2004–2006

I STARTED PLAYING FOOTBALL in the ninth grade. My parents were worried about me playing because no one in my family had really played football. Every fall my friends would have football games, and I'd think, *Man, I don't even know how you sign up for that*. I found out later my parents intentionally never told me when the sign-ups were for football.

I finally started playing football at Orem High when I was a freshman. I played wide receiver all throughout high school, and defensive end. When I got to Ricks College in Idaho, they moved me to tight end. I've always been kind of a go-with-the-flow guy, so I said, "Well, whatever you think I'll be best at." We had another all-conference tight end at the time, so we went with a two–tight end set, and somehow I played well enough that BYU offered me a scholarship partway through my freshman season.

I actually tore my ACL right after Coach Crowton offered me a scholarship. I have to give BYU credit, they stayed good on the offer and had a scholarship for me when I got off my mission. I came down to BYU that next semester and did some rehab and then went on a Church mission to New York in May 2002. I got home from my mission and got right into workouts with the team. I still had missionary legs and was a lot slower than before my mission. I didn't play much my sophomore year, just a little bit on special teams.

My first game in LaVell Edwards Stadium was against Notre Dame. I remember running out of the tunnel. I had never been in front of that many people before. We were in warm-ups, and I couldn't stop smiling. I remember thinking, *Man, I must look like an idiot. I have this big old grin on my face.* It was pretty cool. Then we went out and beat Notre Dame. So my first experience as a BYU Cougar was awesome. I didn't play in the game, but I'll never forget that feeling.

My dad taught at the University of Idaho for a few years before he got a job teaching at BYU. My brother and I loved the Idaho Vandals, and we were upset when we had to move. When we moved to Utah, we were actually against BYU because my dad's job there was the reason we had to move. When I got to high school, I started pulling for BYU, especially when I realized I might have a chance to play in college.

When BYU starting recruiting me, Brandon Doman and Luke Staley were playing. It was a lot of fun watching them. I came down to the Utah game where Luke Staley scored that touchdown along the sideline late in the game. The crowd was going nuts. I remember thinking, *Man, that would be so awesome to have a moment like that!* Coming out of Ricks, I wasn't getting offers from other places. I probably would have seriously considered them, but BYU offered me, and I thought it would be a good place to go, so I accepted right away. Maybe other schools just assumed that I would go to BYU.

My dad definitely had a big influence on my life. While I played at BYU, he was down at practice almost every day. He got to know the practice field security guys on a first-name basis. Now that I have a little daughter, I can see how he just wanted to watch everything that I was doing, but at the time I was like, "Come on, Dad. No one else's dad is out here." It was kind of like that in high school, too. He would volunteer to drive on every trip that we would go on as a basketball team. He was always there supporting me.

When Coach Mendenhall took over the program, right off the bat you could tell his focus was on the little things—doing the little things right. Things were different from the first day we went out there to do warm-ups. If we didn't do the drills correctly, he would send us back, and we'd have to start over. Things were going to get done exactly how they're supposed to be done. At the time, I thought, *Man, is he serious?* But I'll tell you he was right on the money. When I was with the Indianapolis Colts, they were coming

In one of the legendary moments in BYU football history, Jonny Harline hauled in this 11-yard touchdown pass from John Beck to give BYU a 33–31 victory over rival Utah in 2006.

270

off the Super Bowl win and had been dominant for a decade. If you didn't break the huddle right, you started over. You did it right every time.

Observing a football team on the surface is so much different than being involved in meetings and in the program on a day-in, day-out basis. If a team is losing, usually the media or the fans will point to certain things they think are wrong—play-calling, not playing with enough heart, or not showing enough passion. More often than not, it's just little mistakes that do a team in—jumping offside, a false start, dropping a pass, missing a block, etc. The little things are usually the difference. That was the difference between being a .500 team my junior year to being an 11–2 team as a senior in 2006. That's why Coach Mendenhall is such a great coach.

When I first started becoming a big part of the offense, it was pretty cool. I really didn't think I was doing anything special. I kept thinking, *How long until the other teams catch on and realize that I'm not that good?* I probably didn't give myself enough credit. My whole outlook was to just get my job done. My focus was to work hard in practice every day, so in games it was the same thing.

My first big play was against TCU my junior year. I caught a pass going over the middle. I had to reach up and go get it. I turned sharply up field, broke a couple of tackles, and got down to the 2- or 3-yard line. It will always be one of my favorite plays because it was my first highlight-type play.

Then of course you couldn't have scripted a better ending for my career than the Utah game in 2006. I had three touchdowns in the game—they were all sort of highlight plays. I get asked a lot about the final drive at Utah. Not daily, but pretty close, someone will make a reference to, or ask me about, the winning touchdown catch.

I'm sure, if Hollywood made a movie about it, there would be a very dramatic speech before we went on the field for that last drive, but there was nothing of the sort. We just went out there. No one needed to say anything. Everyone knew what needed to be done. We had done it—the two-minute drill—a million times.

Here's how it went in my head. I remember they scored, there was about 1:20 or so left, maybe less. I remember thinking, *Oh, great, I cannot believe that we're going to lose this game!* At the same time, I was always the kind of player who really didn't worry too much. I'm not going to say I didn't care, but my mind-set was always just focus on what I could do, what my responsibilities were, and then just go execute. I just wanted to go out and get my job done.

I remember thinking, *Whatever happens, happens. I'm going to run my route, and if I'm open, I'll catch the ball.* That's just kind of how my mind-set was. You don't want to complicate it too much more than that. The one thing that I do remember saying to John [Beck] when we came out for that final play with three seconds remaining—and I don't know if he heard me or not—was, "If you get in trouble, just throw it up to me." They had me double-covered on the play. There was a cornerback on me, and they played the safety over the top so we wouldn't throw a fade.

At the snap they dropped everybody into coverage, so I knew there wasn't going to be anyone open right off the bat. John kind of looked to his left then rolled that way a little bit. You're taught when a quarterback scrambles, you follow where he goes, so I ran with John and tried to find an open spot. I was at the back of the end zone behind everybody when John got flushed the other way.

My natural inclination was to follow the quarterback. That's what we were taught to do, but when I realized there was nobody with me, I thought, *If he can see me, I'll be wide open.* So I just stayed put when everyone flowed back with John. I knew he had a strong enough arm to make the throw. Then he turned and just chucked it at me. When I realized the ball wasn't going to make it to me, I had to come up fast and slide to make it more secure.

As a fan, watching the game, I probably would have been much more excited than I actually was making the catch. People ask me all the time if I was nervous about it. I wasn't really nervous at all. My whole mind-set was, run my route right, try to get open, and catch the ball when it's thrown to me.

So for me, I didn't have that kind of intense, suspenseful feeling that a lot of the fans had. People ask me all the time if I was afraid I might drop it. As a player, you have such a different mind-set. There was no way I would have dropped it.

One other thing people always ask me is, "What if you had slid out of the end zone?" I knew where I was on the field, and if I'd had to come out of the end zone, I would have just reached down and grabbed it. I played a lot of football over the years. I know the rules.

John told me afterward that he saw me in the back of the end zone. When he got flushed by the linebacker, he was hoping to draw the defense away. I wasn't even sure that he saw me until he threw the ball. It kind of makes sense when you look at the play on tape because he just turns and chucks it. He didn't really have time to see me and then make the throw. He just did it all in one motion.

The football program and its place at the university are just what Coach Mendenhall envisioned. It really is kind of a beacon. BYU was a great place to go to school. There are good people there. It's a place that gave me an opportunity to have my football dreams surpassed from what I ever dreamt coming out of high school. It's a great place, great atmosphere, great coaches and people to work with. I just can't say enough about BYU, what it means to me, and who it helped me to become.

In 2006 Jonny Harline led all tight ends in the nation in receiving yards (935) and touchdowns (12). He was named first-team All-America by the *Sporting News*, ESPN, *College Football News*, CBS SportsLine, and SI.com. Twice he was named first-team All-MWC and Academic All-MWC. Harline was named MVP of the 2006 Las Vegas Bowl after leading BYU to a 38–8 victory over Oregon. Harline spent one season in the NFL before an injury to his Achilles tendon ended his pro career.

AUSTIN COLLIE
WIDE RECEIVER
2004 ★ 2007–2008

WHEN I THINK OF BEING a Cougar, I think of being a leader or being the best at whatever you choose to do in life.

I was eight years old when I started playing tackle football in Folsom, California, just outside of El Dorado Hills, where I grew up. When I was young, I played wide receiver, running back, and quarterback. By the time I got to high school, I was a wide receiver and played corner, as well. I played on the varsity team as a junior and senior. Our teams were pretty good. We won our section each year.

I was being recruited for college as a wide receiver by everyone in the Pac-10 except USC. I was also being recruited by most of the Mountain West schools. Up until about a month before signing day, I was going to Stanford. When my brother Zac got back off his mission, he encouraged me to come to BYU and play with him. We are about three and a half years apart, so we didn't get to play with each other in high school. Playing together was something we had always talked about wanting to do because it would be a unique opportunity.

Also, my dad was a wide receiver at BYU in the early '80s. He would talk about the glory days of playing with Steve Young and Jim McMahon. He would show us some old footage. I wasn't a big BYU fan because we paid more attention to the Pac-10, mostly because the games were always on TV.

In just three seasons as a Cougar, Austin Collie rewrote the BYU record book. As a junior in 2008, he led the nation in receiving with 1,538 yards and set an NCAA record with 11-consecutive 100-yard games.

Ultimately when it came down to making a decision, BYU was a place I felt comfortable with. I also figured, if I didn't like it, I could always go somewhere else after my mission. So I called Stanford and told them I had made my decision to go to BYU. Then I called Lance Reynolds right after that and told him that I was coming. I don't remember exactly what he said, but he was fired up.

I looked up to my brother Zac a lot. I learned a lot of things from him about being a college athlete and a receiver. He made the college transition a lot easier by just being there to walk me through things. All the guys on the team loved Zac, so naturally they warmed up to me. It made it easier in the locker room.

My freshman year was a lot of fun. Probably because I was straight out of high school and playing big-time college football. We weren't that good, but it was still fun. I learned a lot about myself as a player and what it takes to be a top-level athlete. My first game at BYU was the home opener against Notre Dame in 2004. Coming out of the tunnel before the game was crazy. The place was packed. I had goose bumps everywhere. The hair was standing up on the back of my neck. I caught my first touchdown pass in the third quarter of that game. It was a great feeling because I had a goal to begin the season playing wide receiver. To help us win that game felt unbelievable.

Football was my No. 1 priority back then. I had always said I was going to serve a Church mission, but really never gave it much thought until the time came when I had to make a decision. I was worried about coming back and not being as good, or losing the edge. Thankfully, I had Zac to point me in the right direction and let me know that it was going to be the best thing for me. His example played a huge role in my life in a lot of areas. When I got my call to serve in Buenos Aires, Argentina, I was scared. I didn't know what to expect. I was worried about a lot of uncertainties.

Before my mission, I used to think football was the end-all, save-all. Football, and the drive to be the best, sort of ruled my life. A mission really helped me realize just how little football matters in life. How in the grand scheme of things, it's just a game. Now I have a slightly different mind-set. I still love the game, but I feel like I've been given a gift to play professionally, to play at a high level. It's a gift that Heavenly Father has given me. Now I have the mind-set that I want to cultivate the gift and maximize my potential.

My mission really taught me patience. It taught me to be patient with myself and patient with others. After my mission, it took a lot of patience to

275

get back into playing shape and to where I wanted to be as a football player. A mission also taught me how to work hard. I thought I had a pretty good work ethic before the mission, but it was nothing compared to now.

When I got home off my mission in May 2007, I felt I had to prove myself again. I was a little overweight and a little slower. I didn't feel like I was playing my best football. I wasn't playing at the elite level where I wanted to be, so it was kind of frustrating. As the rust started to come off, I started to feel comfortable again. I was able to get that confident feeling back.

I finally felt like I was back to my old self at the Las Vegas Bowl. There was a play in that game where I ran a slant and go. Max Hall threw it over my outside shoulder, and at the last second I wheeled around and caught it. That was kind of a pivotal moment in my college career because that catch was probably one of the hardest catches I've ever made. I just remember thinking, *I'm back*. Winning the offensive MVP award helped cement that feeling.

The reason I worked as hard as I did was to become the best possible me. By becoming the best possible receiver I could be, I knew it would help our team win. Ultimately, I hope people will remember me as a competitor, a guy who always wanted to win.

I still get asked about the fourth-and-18 play against Utah in 2007. I don't remember the play call. I just remember that I got a double-move signal from Max [Hall]. I've never seen a defensive back bite on a double move like that, especially on fourth-and-long. Usually, all they have to do is play back, so I never expected him to bite on the double move, but he did.

Max did a great job of moving out of the pocket and buying some time. When the ball was in the air, I said to myself, *Just catch it and put it away*. The ball seemed like it was in the air a long time. I thought the defense might catch up before the ball got there. It was a great athletic play by Max.

I enjoyed my time at BYU. I liked being on campus with friends and teammates who share common moral values and live by the same principles. Some of the best times outside of football were just getting together with my teammates and their wives and having fun.

There are a lot of good people at BYU. Duane Busby had a huge impact on my college career. He took me under his wing and helped me throughout the entire college process. There were a lot of people at BYU who cared about you and were willing to help. BYU is a unique place. There are so many people going to school at BYU who want to go on and do great things.

Being surrounded by people from all over the world who want to be leaders, who want to be great at what they do—whether it's in business or other professions—helped shape my attitude and mind-set to be great. I think that attitude and passion rubs off on you.

Like I said, to me, being a Cougar is being a leader and striving to be the best at whatever you choose to do in life.

My time at BYU—getting married and moving on to key moments in my life—just solidified the fact that football isn't everything. It really cemented what I learned on my mission. Everything is part of God's plan, and football just happened to be in mine. I try to do my best to be an example for others and succeed with the gifts that Heavenly Father gave me.

I loved my time at BYU. I loved playing football at BYU. It was a special time. The locker room atmosphere, and the type of people you play with at BYU, just does not exist everywhere. We have a great locker room in Indianapolis with the Colts, and we have a great group of guys who play the game because they love it. But the BYU environment, that setting, where you're in the locker room with all your college buddies, is kind of a unique experience, and it will always mean a lot.

The more I play in the NFL, the more I see there are opportunities for me as a member of the LDS Church to showcase to the world what we believe in and what we are truly all about. Playing on national television, and having opportunities like that, presents a unique opportunity for me and others to let people know who we are and what we represent.

Austin Collie played three seasons at BYU as a wide receiver in 2004, 2007, and 2008. As a junior in 2008, he led the nation in receiving with 1,538 receiving yards and was a finalist for the Biletnikoff Award. Collie was named to six All-America teams and tied an NCAA single-season record with 11 consecutive 100-yard receiving games. Following his junior year, he declared early for the NFL Draft, leaving BYU as the all-time leader in career receptions (215, since broken), receiving yards (3,255), and receiving TDs (30). Collie was selected in the fourth round of the 2009 NFL Draft by the Indianapolis Colts. In 2009 he led all NFL rookies in receiving touchdowns and was tied for the most receptions, while helping the Colts advance to Super Bowl XLIV.

DENNIS PITTA

TIGHT END

2004 ★ 2007–2009

Coming out of high school, I was 6′5″ and weighed about 185 pounds. Not a lot of teams were showing much interest. I was getting attention from the Ivy League schools, but mainly because I had good grades in high school. I got letters from some of the Pac-10 schools, but none of them sent anybody to talk to me. BYU was always on my radar because my mom and sister had gone to school there, and I was a member of the LDS Church.

For whatever reason, they didn't have a lot of scholarships that year, and Barry Lamb, who was recruiting me, told me they wanted me to come as a preferred walk-on. I didn't really know what that meant. I remember him making the point that in a normal year they would have a scholarship for me, but they wanted me to come as a walk-on. At that point it was pretty easy. The University of Utah was offering a similar deal. So if it was between Utah and BYU, it was always BYU for me. It was where I wanted to go, anyway.

The plan was for me to gray-shirt and then serve a Church mission the summer after my first year. So I came to BYU in the fall of 2003 as just a regular student. I didn't know a single person on the football team. I didn't even know any of the coaches except for Barry because of our previous contact.

When winter semester began, I was a full-time student and began working out with the team. At that point I was a wide receiver. That's what I played in high school. A couple of weeks into winter semester, before spring ball, Coach Mike Empey called me in and wanted to know if I would switch

Dennis Pitta had seven catches for 90 yards to help lead BYU to a 14–13 upset over No. 3 Oklahoma to open the 2009 football season. Following his senior year in 2009, Pitta was named a consensus All-American.

to tight end. It was okay with me, so when spring practice started, I was a tight end.

Coach Empey had a huge impact on my career because he was the one who really believed in me. I had never played tight end. I had never blocked a soul in my life. He worked with me and became a great mentor and friend my freshman year. He instilled in me the confidence that I could play at that level.

My dad also had a huge influence on my life. He played at Cal, so he knew what it was like to play big-time college football. He knew there were highs and lows, and he was always there encouraging me to keep going, to keep working hard.

I was planning on leaving on a Church mission in the summer of 2004. Right after spring football, I was approached by the coaching staff about postponing my departure time until January so I could play that fall. Apparently, they needed some depth at the tight end position behind Daniel Coates. They told me I would probably contribute right away. So that's what happened. I ended up playing football in the fall and leaving on my mission to the Dominican Republic in early January 2005.

In hindsight, it really worked out great because when I got back it timed out a lot better. Instead of getting back in July and having to redshirt, I was able to get back in January, go through spring ball, go through a summer, and get myself ready to play in the fall of 2007. It ended up being the right decision for me.

My first catch at BYU came in the first game of the 2004 season against Notre Dame. It was kind of a low ball that I had to go down and get. Nothing spectacular, but it was neat that it came against a team like Notre Dame, especially in a winning effort. Running onto the field that day was an unbelievable feeling. Mostly because of the path I took to get to that point was pretty unorthodox. Austin Collie was also playing in his first game at BYU, yet he was a four-star recruit coming out of high school, and everybody knew who he was. He was impressive and took the traditional route, whereas I came in as a nobody and had to make people notice me.

To take the journey that I took and then be able to run out on that field was unreal. Frankly, there were points in my high school career where I thought I would never play at the next level. So to finally take the field against Notre Dame was a dream come true and was just surreal to me at that time.

That freshman year I had some success, and the future looked bright for me at the tight end position. I can imagine that some people in that situation might question the decision to leave for two years on a mission. My parents instilled in me the importance of serving others, so I always knew I wanted to serve a mission. I was excited to go and serve the people in the Dominican Republic.

The mission experience teaches you a lot of things. You learn how to work. You learn how to stay disciplined, stay on schedule, and manage your time. Things that are very applicable to football, to school, and everything else you do in life. Living in the Dominican Republic, seeing the poverty and the hardships people faced, made me appreciate my situation and everything I'd been blessed with. It also made me realize that football was just a game—that there's so much more to life. I love football, but there are so many other more important things in life.

There were a lot great moments on the field at BYU, like catching the game-winning touchdown pass against Colorado State in 2008, or maybe the catch to break the all-time receptions record that my friend Austin Collie had set. Those are great moments that I'll always have with me, but my favorite part of being at BYU was my teammates. Playing with a bunch of guys who shared your values is unique—guys you can trust and whom you care a lot about. That's something I'll always be able to take with me from BYU, the relationships I developed there.

I loved game day at BYU. Taking the field and having everybody cheer for you and knowing that you represent BYU is hard to describe. You represent not only the team, but you represent the school, and you represent a faith. To be able to put that jersey on and run out of that tunnel is so much bigger than just football.

The last play I would ever have on the field at LaVell Edwards Stadium was probably my favorite moment. Playing the University of Utah on senior night, having the game go into overtime, and then pulling it off at the end. What could be better?

Max Hall made the perfect throw, and Andrew George made a tremendous play to catch the ball, split two defenders, and take it in for the winning touchdown.

It was a lot of fun because Andrew and I are really good friends. We are a lot alike, and I think we're similar players. We went through a lot together. We pushed each other, competed against each other, and made each other better. Because of our competitive nature, our friendship, and our chemistry on the field, we were a pivotal part of that offense.

I was really excited when we were both named all-conference our senior year because, up to that point, I felt Andrew didn't get the recognition he deserved. I attributed a lot of my success to him, and he definitely deserved accolades for what he accomplished on the field.

In high school, if you would've told me all the great things that would happen to me at BYU, I would have said, "There's no way." I didn't even know if I was good enough to play college football. I certainly didn't consider myself an elite athlete, so what transpired is pretty amazing. It's not that I didn't believe that I could, but it took others to believe in me, and through hard work I was able to succeed.

To be a Cougar means you take on a lot of responsibility. You not only represent the football team, but you represent the school, and in the bigger picture you represent your faith. What a huge responsibility that is to be an example of someone who tries to live a higher standard. That's what it means to be a member of the BYU football team. To be a Cougar is to be willing to be a role model and be an example of what we believe.

I gained a lot from being at BYU. I learned a lot about myself. I learned a lot about other people. I was able to build relationships that will last forever. I think that's the most important thing. BYU is about helping you progress as a person. Even the football program is centered on Gospel principles. First and foremost, you strengthen yourself spiritually. You are also surrounded by a lot of good people who are great examples, and you learn from them.

Dennis Pitta played tight end at BYU for four seasons. As a senior in 2009, he became the third tight end in BYU history to be named consensus All-America. He was also named All-America as a junior and was first-team all-conference three times. Pitta holds numerous BYU tight end records, including career receiving yards, career receptions, and receptions in a season. His 221 career receptions and 42 consecutive games with at least one catch are both school records. Pitta was selected in the fourth round of the 2010 NFL Draft by the Baltimore Ravens.

MAX HALL

QUARTERBACK

2007–2009

I GREW UP AN ASU FAN. Being from Mesa, I went to Sun Devils basketball and football games with my dad and grandpa as a kid. My Grandpa White and my Uncle Danny are both in the ASU Athletic Hall of Fame. It was cool to go into the stadium and see their names on the wall. I don't know if I wanted to follow in their footsteps, but ASU was the hometown team where I always wanted to play.

I had about 10 Division I offers coming out of high school. I took official trips to ASU, San Diego State, Washington State, BYU, and Utah. My top three choices were Arizona State, BYU, and Washington State. Eventually, I made my decision to go to Arizona State. After redshirting my freshman year, I went on a Church mission.

When you go on a mission and come back, your perspective changes a lot. I just didn't see myself going back to ASU. It really had more to do with the direction I wanted my life to go in, and what I wanted out of life, than it did with football.

During that time, I got a call from Coach Paul Tidwell at BYU. He said, "We know you just got back from a mission, and we've heard that you're considering where to go to school. We want you to know we have a scholarship for you if you want to come to BYU." The timing was perfect. It was like a light bulb went off in my head, and I felt like, *That's where I need to be.* So by inspiration or whatever, I made the decision to transfer to BYU.

Max Hall led the Cougars to 32 victories, the most ever by a BYU quarterback. In 2008 and 2009 Hall was named an honorable mention All-American. Hall and Jim McMahon are the only two quarterbacks in school history to win two bowl games.

When I got to Provo and went to my first team meeting, I knew I'd made the right decision. Being around the players, the atmosphere, and everything that BYU stood for—tradition, spirit, honor, work ethic—I was as happy as could be. At that point I could have cared less if I played a down of football. I thought that, as long as I could be there for three or four years, it didn't matter to me if I started one play. I just wanted to be around those guys and be in that environment. But it didn't take long for the competitive juices to come out in me, and I was anxious to play. BYU was a perfect place for me to play college football.

Obviously, part of it was the religion aspect. It was a place where I could continue representing my faith and continue doing some sort of missionary work. It became more than just football. It became, as Coach Mendenhall puts it, a vehicle to deliver the Gospel to others. That was a cool aspect that I liked. I tried not to mix the two elements too much, but it was fun outside of football to be able to speak at firesides and do service. It was great to have the spiritual experience as well as the physical part of playing football.

When I was in eighth grade, John Beck was the senior quarterback at Mountain View High School. As kids growing up in that area, all we wanted to do was play basketball or football for Mountain View. Because John was the quarterback, he was like a king. I really looked up to him. He set a ton of records and was the state player of the year.

It's funny how things worked out. I ended up following John at Mountain View and also BYU. I wasn't planning on doing that, but it just sort of happened. I'm thankful that it did. John's a really steady guy—a really smart quarterback. Being with him for a year at BYU helped me a ton as far as getting ready to play the quarterback position in college. I still look up to John, and we're really good friends. There is a certain kind of bond and brotherhood between guys of the same faith, especially LDS guys. We played against each other in a preseason NFL game in 2010. After the game we were talking about how weird it was playing against each other.

If you look back at all the BYU quarterbacks, they come in different shapes and sizes. Not all of us are the biggest guys or the strongest guys or have the strongest arms, but all of us competed our butts off and were willing to do anything we could to win. They all had that competitive spirit inside—something that was contagious to the guys around them. That's what I tried to do—compete as hard as I could every time I got a chance. That type of leadership is expected from a BYU quarterback.

I'm thankful that I had an opportunity to play at BYU for three years. The thing I'm most proud of is the wins. I'm proud of my teammates and what we accomplished together—that we beat Utah two out of three years. That would definitely come in at No. 2, because that's such a heated rivalry.

There is no feeling in the world quite like coming out of the tunnel at LaVell Edwards Stadium. There's a certain feeling, or something in the air, when you come running out of that tunnel and you've got a packed house and they're screaming and yelling for you. That stadium has so much tradition. It's contagious. It's something that I already miss.

Honestly, as I look back on my years at BYU, the thing I remember the most is the relationships with the players and coaches. The relationships are what I'll always remember.

The first is probably Coach Doman. We spent a lot of time with each other, and the guy changed my life. He brought out all the best attributes in me and let me just kind of be myself. He knew what was best for me sometimes when I didn't even know it myself—and not only on the football field but also in life. I also really appreciate Coach Mendenhall. He didn't have to give me a chance to be at BYU, but he did. His giving me that opportunity and the relationship we developed are things I'll never forget. The opportunity to be at BYU changed my life.

I have a lot of great football memories. The game against Utah my sophomore year is certainly one of them. It was a game where we were struggling to score points, and we were kicking a lot of field goals. Thank goodness for Mitch Payne, because that guy came to play. Utah couldn't score, either. Finally in the fourth quarter Utah put together a drive, scored, and took a one-point lead.

There was about a minute and a half left, and we needed a score. The drive didn't start too well. We had a couple of incompletions, and then I got the ball stripped and had to fall on it. So now it was fourth-and-18. You could feel the tension in the air. The crowd was quiet except for the Utah section, and I was thinking, *I've got to make something happen right now.*

In the huddle I looked into the eyes of the guys around me. I sensed the same expectation. *All right, Max. Let's make something happen right now.* The play was just a simple trips-right with three guys lined up to the right—the two inside guys find a seam, and the two outside guys run go routes. Right before the snap, I looked over at Austin [Collie]. He was looking at me, and

I think we were both thinking the same thing. I gave him a little signal for a stutter and go instead of just a straight go route.

Austin and I had a special chemistry from the beginning. We are very similar in our personalities, very aggressive, very competitive. He was a guy who, if it was crunch time or we needed a guy to make a play for us, was going to be that guy. Dennis Pitta was the same way.

Utah put three deep, five under, and rushed three guys. The rush forced me out of the pocket about the time Austin began his stutter. It made the corner bite. Then Austin took off down the sideline wide open. I was kind of stunned to see how wide open he was. I wound up and threw the ball as high and as far as I could. I had dislocated my throwing shoulder the week before, so it only went about 40 or 45 yards. Austin caught it and got out of bounds for a first down. I have never been in a louder stadium in my life. I remember my chest pounding and trying to gather myself for the next play. It was an overwhelming experience. That feeling was nothing like I've ever had in my life. From there we were able to score and win the game.

Another favorite memory is beating Oklahoma. When the 2008 season ended, we said to ourselves, "If we're going to beat Oklahoma to open next season, it starts right now." We trained our butts off in the off-season. Every day during training camp we thought about Oklahoma. Normally, I would be kind of nervous for a game like that, but I had been watching film on them for so long that I just remember a certain calmness because I was ready to play.

They were No. 3 in the nation at the time, and we just physically beat them. We took it to them. We knew if we could hang with them early, that we would win it in the fourth quarter. That's exactly what happened. On our last drive, Coach [Robert] Anae said, "Max, let's go two-minute offense and up the tempo on them. You call the plays. Just take it down the field on them." It was a great experience for me. We went right down the field, boom, boom, boom, and on the last play of the drive I found McKay Jacobson in the back of the end zone for the winning touchdown. It was probably the best victory of my college career and one that I'll always remember.

My final home game was a bittersweet feeling for me. I hated the fact that it was my last game at BYU. I didn't want it to end. For the seniors it was kind of a sad thing; but at the same time, we were anxious to go out with a win. In the first half, we jumped on them big time. I think we were up 20–6 at one point, but then we got stagnant offensively, and they came back and tied the score to send it to overtime.

When Utah kicked a field goal on their first possession in overtime, I remember Coach Doman looking at me and saying, "We're destined to win this game. Just go do it! It'll be great!" I remember having this feeling—I knew exactly what he was saying. I looked at our guys and said, "Let's go win!"

The touchdown pass to Andrew George was a play we had run earlier in the game where he was matched up with one of their linebackers. He basically ran a little shake route where he stuttered and then broke back to the inside. Because of their coverage, I knew it was going to be open. Andrew put a great move on the guy, and I just had to hurry and get him the ball. I remember looking at his back as he was running toward the end zone. What an unreal feeling. To go out like that in LaVell Edwards Stadium—with my last throw being a touchdown pass in overtime to beat Utah—was something pretty special.

I haven't been gone very long, but I already miss it. BYU is a special place, and I miss being a Cougar. I'm jealous of the guys who are still there. At the same time, my life has moved on, and there are other things that I want to accomplish. I'll never forget the years that I spent at BYU. I'll always be a big fan of the program. It will always be a special part of me.

Max Hall started 39 straight games for BYU from 2007 to 2009. His 32 career victories are more than any other starting quarterback in school history, surpassing Ty Detmer, who had 29. Hall was named honorable mention All-America in 2008 and 2009. He was also a candidate for the Davey O'Brien Award both years. Hall is only the second quarterback in school history to win two bowl games—the other being Jim McMahon. In 2010 Hall signed an NFL free agent contract with the Arizona Cardinals and later became a starter as a rookie before an injury ended his season.

LEGENDS

DAVE SCHULTHESS

SPORTS INFORMATION DIRECTOR

1951–1988

I WAS BORN IN PROVO but grew up in Los Angeles. I had lots of relatives liv-ing in Utah, and we would visit during the summers. I always loved Provo. I suppose I could have gone to school in California, but I really relished the idea of coming to BYU.

Thank goodness for the GI Bill. After serving three years in the U.S. Army infantry, including some time in the South Pacific, I was released. I wanted to go to school, but I didn't have any money. The GI Bill allowed servicemen like me to get an education. It gave me a chance to go to college. Otherwise, I'm not sure I could have afforded it.

After graduating from BYU, I went to work in Salt Lake City for the *Salt Lake Tribune* and the *Telegram*—the afternoon paper by the same publisher. I worked there for a couple of years, then I had an offer at BYU. They were looking for someone to help at the new university news bureau. It was a great opportunity. I loved it.

It was a dream job in many ways. I loved sports, but I was doing other gen-eral university news, as well. The university was pretty small then. Eventu-ally, BYU hired a full-time sports information director. I was fortunate enough to get the job. It wasn't like it is today. It was a one-man shop for a while.

I thoroughly enjoyed my job. I loved the people I worked with on cam-pus and the athletes. I couldn't be classified as an overachiever, because I

Dave Schulthess was a legend in the sports information community. In addition to serving as the president of the College Sports Information Directors of America, Schulthess was inducted into the CoSIDA Hall of Fame in 1980.

found a job I loved and stayed with it a long time. I was at BYU for nearly 40 years.

For several years we hosted the western regional basketball tournament for the NCAA. Those were big events for us. It was great to get the West Coast media—San Francisco, Los Angeles, Seattle—to Provo. Before then, Provo was just a place on the map that the West Coast media flew over on their way to Big 8 or Big Ten country. Hosting those NCAA events put our athletics department on the map. We worked really hard while the national media was here to make sure they had a pleasant trip. It was a big deal to have press from all over the country come to Provo. In the early years it was hard to get on the national scene. To the national media, Provo was buried in the Rocky Mountains somewhere. It wasn't until we went back east in the 1950s and '60s and won the NIT Championships in basketball that we started to gain some ground on getting national attention.

When LaVell Edwards took over the football team, we started to garner more national attention. There were guys before him that helped establish some national praise, but it was only occasionally. Players like Virgil Carter, Phil Odle, Chris Farasopoulos, and Gordon Gravelle. One of my favorites was running back Eldon "the Phantom" Fortie. We were running the single wing back then—that seems so ancient now. He was our original first-team All-American. He wasn't very big, but he was quick.

Working with LaVell was a real blessing in my career. LaVell was LaVell—he was real. There was nothing phony about him. People liked him. He had lots of friends in and out of the coaching profession. He did a lot consciously to develop friends and contacts. It was natural to him. What a guy to work with. He was the best.

I have some fond memories of all those football trips. We were in Laramie once and had to make the long drive to Denver after the game to fly home. We were in the last car to leave because LaVell had his postgame radio show. They were waiting for us at the airport, but LaVell stopped to get a large drink. I was worried that the plane would leave us. Not LaVell, he was always laid-back. I loved how he was so even-keeled. He was a competitor and hated to lose, but he was also so steady.

I remember going to the first BYU bowl game in Tempe, Arizona. It was so big for our program. We had not been to anything like that. No one associated BYU with a bowl game. It was like a new door opening. It seemed like we had to grind it out to establish the reputation. We were elevated as an athletics program by the football team getting some national attention.

Some of my favorite memories were going to San Diego for the Holiday Bowl. It seemed that we were regulars for a long time. It was always a highlight for me. We would take our families and leave the cold of Provo and go to San Diego for a week. Being a part of all those early bowls was a thrill. The exposure from those games on the West Coast really helped elevate the exposure of the university.

For me, being a longtime Cougar isn't about one person or one thing. It's a lot of parts to the whole—everybody working together, trying to do a good job. Many of the early successes of the football program started to open the door for the university to begin getting respect and recognition.

I loved BYU and stayed for a long time because I sensed that we were building something special. There were so many things going on. It was great to be involved with all those tremendous athletes and great teams. I have strong feelings about the school. BYU is my alma mater. It's where I wanted my children to go to school. To be affiliated with BYU all those years is a real honor for me.

Dave Schulthess served as the sports information director at BYU for nearly 40 years. He reached the pinnacle of his profession in 1980, when he was inducted into the College Sports Information Directors of America Hall of Fame. The following year, Schulthess served as the CoSIDA president. In 1989 he was presented CoSIDA's Arch Ward Award, given annually to an individual who has made an outstanding contribution and brought dignity and prestige to the profession. In 2000 Schulthess was inducted into the BYU Athletic Hall of Fame.

FLOYD JOHNSON

EQUIPMENT MANAGER

1957–1999

I WAS RAISED IN OREM, UTAH, and attended high school in nearby Pleasant Grove. In high school I lettered in track, football, basketball, and tennis. In 1939 I enrolled at BYU. I remained in school until June 1941. During the summers I would work for Robert Wright on his farm.

In June of 1941 I went to work for a contractor who was building the state prison at the point of the mountain. During that summer I felt a strong desire to serve an LDS mission. I was getting to be an old man of 23 years. I had saved enough money to buy my own clothes and pay my way into the mission field.

War clouds were beginning to gather. Canada and England were already at war with Germany. So before I could serve a mission I had to get a release from my draft board, which I did. Eventually, I had an interview in Salt Lake City with Elder Charles A. Callis. On August 27, 1941, I received a call to labor in the Canadian Mission. It was one of the happiest days of my life.

In November 1941, I left Salt Lake City by train for Toronto, Canada. My first area of service was the city of Hamilton, not far from Niagara Falls. While serving in Hamilton, a sister missionary named Anna Gerber was assigned to work in our district. She was a very lovely and faithful missionary.

In May of 1942 in front of her missionary companion and mine, I asked her to marry me at the conclusion of our missions. She accepted. She completed her missionary service in October 1943. I was released from my mission in

November 1943. I met her in Lethbridge, Alberta, on November 8, 1943, and we were married in the Cardston, Alberta, Temple on November 10. It seemed like a completion of a dream—one we had waited for nearly two years to come true.

We journeyed to Victoria, British Columbia, and spent three weeks with her folks. Then we returned to Utah and settled in Orem.

In 1957 I went to work at Brigham Young University as the athletics department equipment manager. My job consisted mainly of keeping BYU athletes outfitted in clean, safe uniforms. I washed their clothes. I sewed numbers on their jerseys. I fixed broken equipment and found shoes to fit their oversized feet.

As jobs go, mine probably wasn't the most glamorous on campus. In fact, if I weren't working with some of the finest young people in the world, I probably would have switched professions. The thing that kept me going through more than 40 years was the chance to share the Gospel with thousands of athletes who played at BYU.

My goal was to help build the Church and build the lives of the student-athletes at BYU, particularly the football team that I worked closely with. Over my years at BYU, I shared my testimony with hundreds of athletes, many who joined the Church.

I guess you could say I was the team evangelist. I spent countless hours sharing my testimony with athletes and counseling young men who were struggling with decisions about missions, marriage, and life. It's never easy to mix religion and athletics—even at BYU.

Up until the early 1970s, most of the coaches discouraged athletes from going into the mission field. They believed mission life would soften athletes and make them lose their aggressiveness. Often opponents said BYU would never be competitive in football because of the missionary program.

Also in those early days, returned missionaries were not considered a welcome addition to the football program. The first returned missionary I remember at BYU was LeGrand Young. He walked on in the late 1950s to prove that a returned missionary could play college football. He was as bull-headed as his son Steve. Most missionaries who left to serve never came back to play. Many of the coaches made them feel so guilty for leaving that they didn't want to come back.

It wasn't until LaVell Edwards became the head football coach in 1972 that returned missionaries were an acceptable part of the football program. LaVell

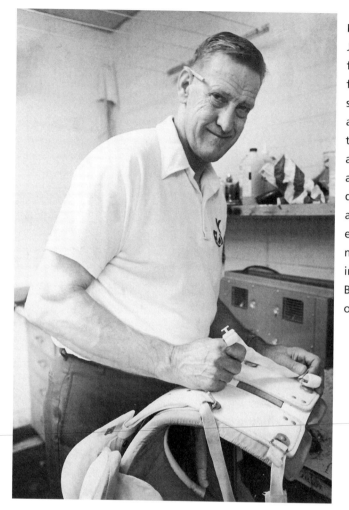

Floyd "Brother J" Johnson was a friend, confidant, father figure, spiritual adviser, and counselor to thousands of athletes who attended BYU during his 46 years as the athletic equipment manager. He was inducted into the BYU Athletic Hall of Fame in 1988.

was a great man. He was much more receptive to the mission idea. He told his players they were free to serve missions if they decided to do so. As a result, more and more football players began leaving on missions.

Many returned fat and out of shape, but Coach Edwards discovered they were more mature. They were more disciplined. Life for these young men was more important than football. Over the years, things changed. In 1984, the year BYU won the national championship in football, there were 52 returned missionaries on the team.

During my years at BYU, I saw the attitude of the football program gradually change to where the team's spiritual qualities allowed the athletes to carry the Gospel message wherever they went. I strongly believe the athletics department has a charge to carry the message of the Gospel wherever it goes—to members of our faith as well as those who are not.

Over the years, I have seen miracles take place in the lives of young men. People always ask, "Brother J, how many athletes have you converted in your time at BYU?" I always respond that I haven't converted anyone. All the credit for any conversion must go to Heavenly Father and the Savior. The rest of us—coaches, teammates, girlfriends, professors, and others—provide wonderful examples and have a powerful influence.

I firmly believe that BYU has a mandate. The coaches may say it's to win championships, but I strongly feel the mission of the athletics department at BYU is to teach the Gospel. Our athletic teams can deliver a message to people around the world by winning the right way and by being an example.

For 40-plus years I met nearly every athlete who competed at BYU. I rubbed shoulders with future Hall of Famers. I washed uniforms and socks of future millionaires. I have counseled all-stars about everything from missions to marriage.

The most inspirational part of my job was watching young men who came to BYU lacking physical skills but exhibited a strong desire to achieve. There have been hundreds of them over the years. These young men believe in themselves. They knew they could succeed.

There are many stories I could share, but Kelly Smith is a perfect example. Those who followed the national championship football team remember the name Kelly Smith. He came from Beaver, Utah, and walked on as a freshman in 1980. He was on the hamburger squad. When you're on that squad, no one appreciates you very much. You get knocked around pretty good.

That's how Kelly was treated. But he had a belief in himself. He believed there were things he could do and some things the Lord expected him to do. He was prepared to give everything he could give. Kelly was probably one of the most inspirational players ever at BYU. After his freshman year, Kelly served a mission in Tampa, Florida.

By the time Kelly was a junior in 1984, he was one of the leaders who inspired the rest of the players on the team to live up to their potential. He came back from an injury and caught the winning touchdown in the Holiday Bowl that secured the national championship. I love his story because he proved that a small kid from a small town could succeed as well as anyone.

I have discovered from my years of associating with athletes that there is a fine line between success and failure. Three ingredients seem to make great athletes. No. 1 is self-discipline. No. 2 is humility. No. 3 is a desire to succeed. When someone with a lot of potential fails to live up to expectations, you can usually trace that failure to a lack of one of those three attributes.

I believe success is made up of 80 percent desire, 15 percent talent, and 5 percent opportunity. Whether that is totally accurate is debatable. I do know, however, that behind every successful athlete or successful endeavor is a tremendous desire to achieve.

When you see an All-American, you know someone didn't just hand him the certificate with his name on it. You have to work hard to become an All-American. You have to have self-discipline, humility, and the desire to succeed. It's a great thing to be an All-American, but to me it's even more important to be an "All-Mormon," whose desire is to serve and touch the lives of other people.

I love BYU. I love to be around the kids. They are all my friends. I've had the best life.

Floyd Johnson worked as the equipment manager at BYU for 46 years. He was perhaps the most beloved individual to ever work in the BYU Athletics Department. Brother J was a friend, confidant, father figure, spiritual adviser, and counselor to thousands of athletes, coaches, and administrators. He was best known for his Christ-like characteristics, devotion to BYU, and for influencing the lives of thousands of athletes who passed through his equipment room. Brother J was inducted into the BYU Athletic Hall of Fame in 1988. He passed away on February 14, 2002, at the age of 83.

Taken from two sources. The personal writings of Floyd Johnson, compiled by his daughter, Ann Johnson; and the book Touchdowns, Tip-Offs and Testimonies *by Floyd Johnson, with Val Hale. Used by permission of Alba Publishing, Orem, Utah.*

GEORGE CURTIS
HEAD FOOTBALL TRAINER
1985–2005

I ATTENDED SNOW COLLEGE and BYU and then graduated from Southern Utah University in 1971. I attended BYU in the summer of 1970 to take a sports medicine class from Dr. Rulon Francis.

I had decided I was going into athletic training, so I thought it would be neat to meet Rod Kimball, the head athletic trainer at BYU. It was a great experience. Rod told me to write down a list of goals—things I want to do in the profession. The following summer I came back to Provo to visit Rod. I had a list of about 10 to 12 items.

Sure enough, Rod remembered me and asked if I had made a list. I told him I had, and then I rehearsed my list with him. The list had things like: work as a high school trainer, work at a junior college, work the Olympics, write a book, and work in pro football.

Rod told me that I really didn't want to work in pro football, that it wasn't the best place for an active LDS guy. I quickly told him that I wasn't planning on finishing my career in pro football. He asked where I wanted to end up. I sheepishly told him it was his job I wanted. He grabbed my shoulder and, with a smile, said, "Well, good, someone's got to have it."

In March of 1985 I got a call from Dr. Clayne Jensen about a job at BYU. I had been with the L.A. Express of the USFL for the previous two years as the head athletic trainer. One of those years I was also the head strength and conditioning coach. I was planning on returning to professional football.

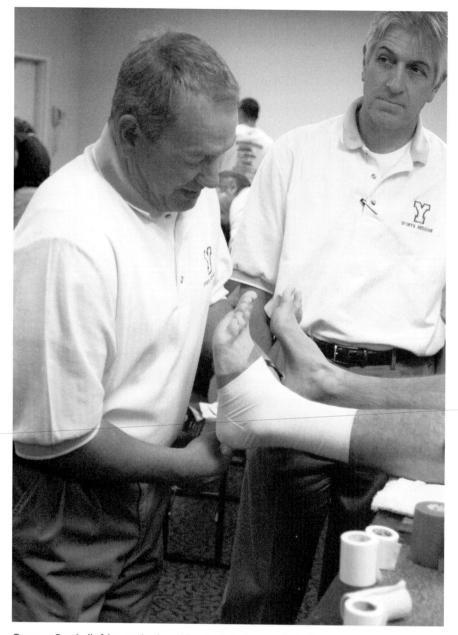

George Curtis (left) was the head football trainer at BYU for 20 years. In 1999 he was named the Outstanding Athletic Trainer of the Year by the All-American Football Foundation. Curtis was inducted into the BYU Hall of Fame in 2009.

I asked Dr. Jensen what the job entailed, and he said he wasn't sure yet. I came to Provo shortly after the phone call and again two more times over the next couple months looking for answers. Finally, in June Dr. Jensen told me that the job was for the head trainer position. He wanted to offer me the position but was wrestling with what to do with Marv Roberson and Ollie Julkunen, two excellent trainers who were currently on staff. So I asked if I could have permission to talk with them and see if they could support me in this move.

Clayne said yes. So I drove over to Marv's home and told him I had just been offered the head job and asked him if he could support me and any changes I was going make. If he could, I wanted him to stay on the staff, but if he couldn't, then I would go back and tell Dr. Jensen I'm withdrawing my name. Marv said he would welcome the help. So I went to see Ollie and went over the same stuff with him. He gave me the same answer, so I went back to Dr. Jensen and told him I would take the job. I felt that I was prepared and sort of destined for the job at BYU.

I met LaVell Edwards in the spring of 1971. When I was finishing up my degree at Southern Utah, I was assigned to Skyline High School for my student-teaching. LaVell was an assistant football coach at BYU at the time, and Ken Schmidt was the head football coach at Skyline. LaVell would come by to recruit some of our players. I had a chance to talk to Coach Edwards often, and I developed a great amount of respect for him during that time.

A year later I was working at Santa Ana Community College when I learned that LaVell had been named head coach at the Y. I called him that very day and volunteered to help with recruiting in any way I could.

When I came to the Y in July of 1985, I was so excited. Not only to be at BYU, but also to work with a living legend in LaVell Edwards was a real pleasure. He always treated me with respect and kindness.

My favorite LaVell story is one a lot people wouldn't know. We were playing at home. I think it was against San Diego State. We played the first half of the game about as poorly as we could and were losing quite badly at halftime.

LaVell was always straightforward with what he told the players before we headed back onto the field for the second half. But he wouldn't yell, because he would treat everyone like the adults he expected them to be. This time, before we left the locker room, I guess he'd had it. He laid into the boys pretty good, but he was dead on with every word he said—and everyone knew it, too.

His voice was loud and clear. He knew exactly what he was saying. He told the team that we were going to get the second-half kickoff and go down and score. Then we were going to stop them defensively and score again. That's exactly what happened. It was truly amazing. He got everyone to believe and perform. He didn't use a single swear word, and no one was singled out or demeaned. It was one of the most inspiring moments I've ever been involved with in sports. We came out in the second half and won quite handily.

Another amazing individual at BYU was Brother J—Floyd Johnson. He was a living legend long before I came to the Y. Brother J was the real deal. I would often visit him in the equipment room and find him with his scriptures opened, teaching the Gospel to someone or giving council to help a young person. He touched a lot of lives.

My favorite memory as the BYU football trainer was the 1996 football season. There was so much talent on that team—guys like Steve Sarkisian, Chad Lewis, Itula Mili, and others. Beyond the talent, I think it was the atmosphere that was so great. It started on the first road trip when K.O. Kealaluhi showed up with his ukulele. He would play and sing and get everyone else to join in. It was a pleasant change of pace, because normally plane trips and bus rides to and from games were quiet as a tomb. Not every kid can get up for a game the same way. That team was special. They won 14 games, including a victory over Kansas State in the Cotton Bowl.

I have a lot of great memories of my time at BYU. Some of my favorite experiences were the times I spent with the students. Whether it was teaching our student athletic trainers or sharing the Gospel with amazing athletes like Ty Detmer, Moe Elewonibi, Garth Fennegan, Brian McDonald, Curtis Brown, Jamal Willis, Eddie Sampson, and Ford Poston, just to name a few.

BYU is a special place because of the influence of the Church of Jesus Christ of Latter-day Saints. It was so nice to be a part of the religious atmosphere at BYU and to be associated with the Church, even in a small way. Romans 1:16 tells us that we should not be ashamed of the Gospel. I learned that lesson at BYU. I also learned the importance of trust.

I loved the family atmosphere at BYU. My family benefited so much by being around the university and all the amazing student-athletes. My wife, Jan, and I have six girls and two boys. All of my children—except for our fifth child, Kara Lee, who passed away in 1982—have attended the Y. Three of my girls competed on athletic teams at BYU.

The student-athletes at BYU are remarkable because of their maturity level. Many of them are married, most have been on missions, and some even have kids. I loved when they would bring their kids by the training room and they would call me Uncle George. To me, it was a sign of respect.

To be a Cougar means that I'm part of a close-knit family—a family of people who believe in similar principles, like the Golden Rule, and keeping the Sabbath Day holy. The university is truly a band of brothers and sisters linked together in love, cooperation, and consideration.

I lived a charmed life. At least that's the way I feel about it. Working at BYU was a dream come true. I have been truly blessed and lucky. I don't think I ever felt like I *had* to go work. I loved being at the Y.

George Curtis came to BYU in 1985 and was the head football trainer for 20 years. Prior to becoming a Cougar, Curtis was the head trainer for the L.A. Express of the USFL. In 1996 Curtis was honored by the National Athletic Trainers Association with the inaugural Athletic Trainer Service Award. In 1999 he was named the Outstanding Athletic Trainer of the Year by the All-American Football Foundation. Curtis was inducted into the BYU Athletic Hall of Fame in 2009.